MILESTONES OF
CIVILIZATION

LINDA BLANDFORD

PETER DAVIDSON

NEW HOLLAND

Dedicated to the memory of Paul Hirst

First published in 2009 by New Holland Publishers (UK) Ltd
London • Cape Town • Sydney • Auckland
www.newhollandpublishers.com

10 9 8 7 6 5 4 3 2 1

Garfield House, 86–88 Edgware Road, London W2 2EA, UK
80 McKenzie Street, Cape Town 8001, South Africa
Unit 1, 66 Gibbes Street, Chatswood, NSW 2067, Australia
218 Lake Road, Northcote, Auckland, New Zealand

ISBN: 978 1 84773 065 7

Senior Editor: Kate Parker
Editorial Direction: Rosemary Wilkinson
Commissioning Editor: Aruna Vasudevan
Editorial Assistant: Nicole Whitton
Design and cover design: David Etherington
Illustrations: Alan Marshall and Debbie Maizels (pages 15 and 18)
Cartography: Lovell Johns Ltd
Production: Melanie Dowland

Reproduction by Pica Digital PTE Ltd, Singapore
Printed and bound by Tien Wah Press, Singapore

Front cover: Lascaux cave painting of a bull and an AK47 – symbols of the duality of
human endeavour.
Back cover: the Pill, metal, the boat and the development of bacteriology – all milestones
of civilization.

Opposite: Athen's 5th-century BCE Parthenon was blown to pieces by the Venetians in
1637, then crumbled beneath neglect, vandalism and pollution; Berlin, the emblem of
Prussian power, was pulverised by air raids in the Second World War. Civilization is
marked by the ability of human beings both to create and to destroy.

Contents

Introduction

'Milestones of Civilization?' people said, 'Where is the chapter on the Greeks? Where is the Renaissance? What about Mozart and Bach?' Edited highlights of the flowerings of Western culture had never been our aim, however.

We began this book by standing in the kitchen and looking around us. We saw the microwave, the fridge, the sink with its taps waiting to deliver running water. Then we became aware of the kitchen itself: a workshop dedicated to food preparation. In the living room, we saw framed pictures on one wall, shelves of books on another and the television. We turned it on to see a news report showing soldiers from our country in another land. We looked out of the window to see a traffic jam of frustrated yet obedient people in cars. In the distance, we saw more people coming out of a supermarket carrying bags of food – plastic bags, some of which now blew across the tarmac road.

We saw around us not the natural world, but a world constructed by human beings. From where we were standing we could find no part of our physical surroundings that had not been engineered by people – including the plants in the garden, the trees in the street and the vegetables in the kitchen. Nor could we understand what anyone was doing without referring to a whole barrage of cultural information.

We knew how to function in this world because we had been born into it, formed by it. Accounting for its existence, however, was a harder task. At some point in the past, people had been born into a largely natural world, without buildings or machines, without

Constructing a physical world in Ancient Egypt. The first farmers brought animals and plants under their control and reshaped the landscape around them to suit their needs. They laid the foundations for the built environment most of us inhabit today.

Constructing a social world in Mayan Mexico. A middle man (standing) presents a more powerful man (sitting) with a group of less powerful people (in bondage), to make use of as he sees fit. Larger communities produced management structures and specialized professions.

even language. Thinking about the lives those people must have led, we could find no necessary reason for their descendents to have developed the world we live in now.

Because we began by wondering how and why the structure of modern daily life had come to be, we conceived our book as a progression of themes rather than as a review of cultural or artistic triumphs. Our chapters would deal with tools, cities, revolutions of different kinds and so on. We wanted chapters that showed how human beings have sought to control their environment by organizing their growing communities in ever more complex ways.

This broad idea of increasing social complexity gave us a working definition for 'civilization', a notoriously tricky word to define. Often it has been linked to the idea of living in cities – *civitas*, the Latin for city, is the origin of the word, after all – but it seems to mean both more and less than this. We say the Maya, for instance, had civilization because they had writing, architecture, a sophisticated style of art, even though they lacked cities as we know them. In contrast, there have been large urban settlements with none of these other features of civilization.

Not wishing to lose ourselves in problems of definition, we stood back and took a more general view of civilization. We thought of it as a world humans have been constructing for far longer than they have been living in cities; a buffer placed between themselves and nature. This buffer has always been both a physical and a conceptual construction, built from wood, brick and steel but also from language and ideas. Increasingly, it, rather than nature, has produced the structures within which people live their lives.

Certain principles of social organization have been fundamental to these structures. Beyond an early stage, civilization has been realized by dividing society into the powerful and the weak, and by specializing the work people do. Inequality and specialization have enabled civilization to develop its various spheres of political decision-making, technological improvement, scientific enquiry, trade and refinement of religious and artistic expression. Whether inequality is necessary to the development of civilization remains unclear.

The fact that civilization has been built by people in different environments has meant that it has manifested itself differently from place to place, while retaining certain underlying features. In this way civilization acquires many individual variations and we can speak of the Minoan, the Greek, the Roman or even Western civilization.

To avoid confusion we have tried to restrict ourselves to considering 'civilization' as one general concept, rather than 'civilizations' in the plural. Where we do refer to a particular civilization it serves as a reminder that attempts to cultivate civilization have come and gone. Decline sets in for any number of reasons. Many a civilization has been laid waste by invasion. Others have been hit by disease, or simply failed to adapt or develop new structures beyond a certain point. Decline may even reflect too much success

Military art often reveals history's larger, underlying narrative. Europe's sense of growing superiority is displayed in the 'higher' positioning of the Spanish conquistadors, while the Indians appear almost as supplicants. Note the priest in white, bringing God's blessing to the mission.

in controlling the environment, suggesting that the logic by which a civilization develops may also contain the seeds of its own destruction. Looking around, we see nothing to suggest that our own particular form of civilization will be the first to resist decline.

If we have been thinking of civilization in terms of the structure of society, then what counts as a 'milestone' must be something that brings about a change in this structure. A 'flowering of culture' could only qualify if it does this. Also, this change cannot simply be society fragmenting and reverting to a previous stage; it has to usher in a new pattern of social organization that pushes civilization forward. A milestone seen from a passing train brings with it the idea of progress.

We attach no moral dimension to progress of this kind. That a move from hunting and gathering to farming brings with it new and more complex forms of social organization is an observation, no more. Whether the consequences of this change are judged to be good or bad is another matter entirely. We have tried to keep our own value judgments in the background, though undoubtedly we have not always succeeded. Try as we might, we are the products of our own time and place.

In choosing the milestones themselves, however, subjective judgments have been unavoidable. The introduction of farming is one of the more obvious milestones, but even this has involved a selective focus. This is because social change rarely happens overnight; a 'milestone of civilization' is more often a chain of events rather than a single event. Choosing to focus on one link in the chain rather than another has to be a personal decision not everyone will agree with. This book was never meant to be an objective, authoritative account of human history. It was intended as a subjective and personal attempt to think about the origins of the world we find ourselves in.

We have divided our book into two parts. The first deals with the emergence of what we commonly take to be standard features of civilization. The heart of this section traces the coming of villages, cities and states, remarkable for their similarity in separate regions. It goes on to look at the spread of civilization beyond any one state or culture in the pre-modern world. Trying to explain the coming of urban living, however, has meant reaching back further to deal with earlier technological and conceptual developments. So the first part of the book begins even before humans like us arrived on the scene.

The second part takes us into the modern world. It looks at how the West, over the last few hundred years, has built on the largely universal foundations of civilization covered in the first part to produce the world we see around us. The West has delivered the nation state, modernity, medicine as we know it and millions of war deaths. It has cast a long shadow over the rest of the world during this short period, even as other possible arrangements now emerge. In the second section of our book, we ask how we got to the state we are in today. How has civilization come to this point – and where were the markers for change?

This book was not written by one person, but by two. We frequently argued with one another over which milestones should be chosen and which aspects of them should be emphasized. Disagreements have been many, often unresolved. The relative importance of war in shaping the world we live in has been a constant sticking point between us. Beyond that has been the more general issue of whether ideas, material circumstances or human instincts have been the greater force driving civilization forward.

We hope you will read our book in the spirit of curiosity and often exasperated debate with which it was written. It is a general book, which skims the waters of history like a fast-moving hydrofoil. If it inspires you to fish more thoughtfully in one place or another later on, it will have done half its job. Ideas are exciting, and if you get fired up enough to disagree with ours, our book will have done the other half of its job.

Trade, transport and construction: three of the elements of civilization.
A Phoenician merchant oversees the loading of his cargo ship with timber,
most likely from the cedar trees of Lebanon. He may have been on his way to
Egypt; Lebanese cedar was used in Egypt to build special funeral barges that
carried the bodies of pharaohs along the Nile to their tombs. From the palace
of the Assyrian king Sargon II (721–705 BCE) at Khorsabad in modern-day Iraq.

Part 1: The Elements of Civilization

The last few thousand years has brought a great gear-change in the human story. Twenty, thirty, forty thousand years ago small groups of people moved from place to place, taking their food from the wild. They had the same physical abilities, the same basic drives and psychological needs, the same mental capacities as us. Like the ancient Egyptians or Chinese, however, we are separated from these people by the fact we live within a state that has reshaped our jobs, our ideas and our relationships almost beyond recognition. This transition is the subject of Part One.

The opening chapters are largely concerned with the twin preconditions for civilization: tools and language. Our starting point is the shape of the human body, which led early humans to make tools and was in turn altered by their use. Later, the honing of toolmaking and other skills went hand in hand with the development of speech. Language, spoken or otherwise, created meaning and enabled people to build an imagined world through which to make sense of the real world around them.

The following few chapters deal with a change of lifestyle from finding food to producing it, which emerged at the end of the last Ice Age. This was a fundamental conceptual move; from adapting themselves to their environment, some humans switched to adapting their environment to themselves. The idea of controlling nature suggested itself to people who settled in one place to fish or take advantage of larger wild harvests, as well as to dog owners. Farmers invented hard work and land ownership, and supported specialized professions with a stored surplus of food.

The next chapters chart the growth of farming villages into cities and states, generalizing from the first Mesopotamian examples. Communities of such a size had never been known and the challenge of management was met by the birth of an administrative hierarchy, with co-operation soon guaranteed by force. A class system followed, providing a luxury market that encouraged trade. As wealth and urban opportunities grew, and as beliefs adjusted to a new environment, ordinary people accepted the social order as much as they were coerced into it.

The final chapters in this section look at intellectual innovations spawned by early state societies, which form part of a package of elements common to civilization wherever it subsequently appeared.

1: The Footprint

The first and most significant milestone human beings passed on the road to 21st-century civilization was to stand up and walk. The ape that stood up embarked on a journey to alter its physical appearance, grow a bigger brain and develop a complex web of technology, language and social relationships.

Above: Mother and daughter. The 3.7-million-year-old footprints of australopithecus afarensis (also known as 'Lucy'), preserved in volcanic ash at Laetoli in northern Tanzania. The big toe is no longer separated from the others as with other primates, and the footprints have been made by the heel striking the ground first, followed by the toe pushing off – the way we walk now.

Palaeoanthropologists trace the evolution of our ancestors through the skulls and bones they have dug up. They classify these remains into an ever-expanding number of so-called 'species', to which they give names. These are not true biological species – that is to say, a group whose members can interbreed. So far, DNA from fossil remains has been too rarely available for this to be judged. Instead, palaeoanthropologists decide that a skull belongs to a particular species on the basis of its shape alone.

Because of the unavoidable vagueness of defining a species by looking at the shape of a skull, each new discovery fuels an on-going debate concerning the classification of these species and their evolutionary relationships to each other. Behind the details of this debate, however, lies an overall story on which there is broad agreement.

Down from the Trees

Primates are one of the many types of mammal that first appeared while dinosaurs still roamed the earth. About 40 million years ago, mammals were dividing into different forms, one of which is thought to have been the common ancestor of modern apes and humans, although any of its remains have yet to be found. This common ancestor walked on all fours but lived in the trees, where reaching up to grab hold of branches and pick fruit led to its front limbs becoming more flexible than those of other mammals.

To stand or to climb? A chimp's foot (left), with its long toes and opposable big toe or thumb, is another hand, built for climbing. A human foot (right) has become a tougher, less flexible pad for walking on. Shorter, aligned toes and an arch give us our characteristic gait.

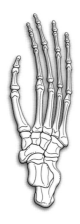

By about 14 million years ago, in several parts of the world, our line of descent had split off from that of the other apes and produced a creature that was beginning to spend more time on its hind legs. As a result of having to bear less weight upon its front limbs, its fingers became more sensitive and able to manipulate sticks and stones.

Our earliest, recognizable ancestors, however, came later, and seem to have been the products of climate change. They lived in the African Rift Valley, which straddles present-day Ethiopia, Kenya and Tanzania. As temperatures dropped and rainfall lessened in sub-Saharan Africa, so the rainforest that sustained these creatures retreated, and they came out into the spreading grassland to look for food.

By around four million years ago, this changed environment had produced in them a posture that was unquestionably human. This more upright posture allowed these early humans to see farther ahead and to walk or run longer distances on open ground, developments that meant they were better able to find food and avoid being eaten themselves.

The Division of Labour

Using only the hind legs for walking on open ground altered the shape of feet, making them less flexible. This ushered in a fundamental change in social relations based on the sharing of food. Now that a baby's feet had lost the ability to cling onto its mother like a second pair of hands, the mother had to carry the baby in her arms. This meant her ability to find food while she had small children was limited to what she could easily find nearby, which was usually not very nutritious.

On the other hand, the male had an increasingly wide food-gathering area over which to roam, together with a free pair of hands with which to carry food back to the female, now more restricted by her motherhood. It seems that a division of labour and the use of a temporary home base began to emerge in response to this imbalance, and it may be that it is from this time that human beings became a largely monogamous animal, in contrast to other apes. In addition, some have suggested that as males found that the food they brought back to the females could be exchanged for sex, this led, through natural selection, to other distinctive human characteristics, such as females remaining sexually receptive throughout the year.

Tools for a Change of Diet

Standing up freed the hands not only to carry food but also to use tools. To begin with, early humans simply picked up sticks or stones suitable for a particular task, such as digging for roots or cracking nuts, and then discarded them, much as chimpanzees do today. But by about 2.5 million years ago, a crucial conceptual step had been taken: tools had begun to be deliberately manufactured.

Manufacture meant planning. Instead of improvising as and when the need arose with a found object to serve some immediate purpose, the need for a

certain tool was conceived in advance. Appropriate raw material was sourced, designed and crafted to produce a tool intended for use in another location at some point in the future.

This first planned tool was made by striking one stone against another in order to chip small pieces off one stone until a sharp edge was formed. It was used to cut plants, to skin meat and to crush bones in order to get at the protein-rich marrow inside. The meat had come either from scavenging the leftovers from kills made by other predators or else from animals small enough for our smaller and weaker ancestors to catch. Either way, these early humans were getting used to more protein in their diet, and this allowed their brains to begin slowly increasing in size.

By around 1.3 million years ago, the hand-held cutting tool had become far more refined due to a new process of manufacture developed by the last

With its four hands, a baby orang-utan can easily hold onto its mother, leaving her arms free so she can get on with her business. A human baby, with feet designed for walking rather than gripping, is much more restricting for its parents to carry.

The knife. Now meat began to appear on the menu. These knives were made by early humans who lived 1.88 million years ago in Tanzania's Olduvai Gorge. Hence, this style of toolmaking is called Oldowan technology – though earlier examples have since been found in Ethiopia.

The hand-axe, the tool that enabled Homo *erectus* to conquer the globe. The classic shape is on the left. Sharp-edged, pointed and comfortable to hold, the hand-axe was the longest-serving tool ever made. Its design remained unchanged for well over a million years.

forerunner of modern humans, Homo erectus. Now it was being made not by hitting one stone against another but by using a piece of wood, which could be controlled much better, to patiently and delicately tap away thin flakes from a stone to produce a sharper, pointed blade with a rounded bottom that would fit comfortably in the palm of the hand. This iconic tool has been called the hand-axe and was the first design classic. It was a tool to treasure as a permanent possession.

The people who used the hand-axe looked much more like modern humans, though they still had flatter heads and heavier features. At around the same height as us, they were considerably taller than their forerunners, with longer legs and by now a completely upright posture, which meant they could run faster. As such, Homo *erectus* was more of a

The Olduvai Gorge in Africa's Rift Valley. In the 1930s, Louis Leakey found the earliest design of manufactured tool here. Two million years ago, Olduvai was a lake drawing animals to its shores – including early humans, who left their tools lying around.

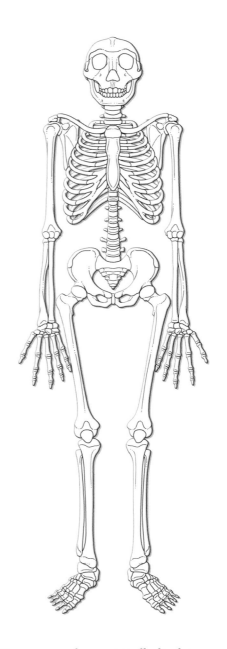

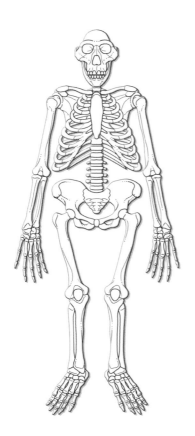

Meat in the diet. 'Lucy' (left) had no stone tools and could not run very fast, so she was mainly vegetarian, giving her a large belly. Catching more meat led to the greater height, narrower waist and larger brain of Homo erectus (right) – much like us but with a heavier face and a brain still only two thirds the size of ours.

hunter, relying less on scavenged meat than earlier humans had. As well as for cutting food, the hand-axe was used for sharpening sticks with which to stab prey. There is evidence to suggest that Homo erectus had figured out ways to outwit and kill larger animals by driving them over a cliff or into a bog. Better hunting techniques meant increasing amounts of meat in the diet, enabling the brain to continue growing in size.

Hunting larger animals requires planning and co-operation with other people to be successful and so Homo erectus characteristically lived in groups of a couple of dozen or so – though some recent studies suggest considerably larger groups in open country. A band of hunters requires a large territory to be able to feed itself, however. Perhaps for this reason, very gradually, some of the Homo erectus population began to move out of Africa into Europe and Asia in a perpetual search for new hunting grounds. This was less a conscious emigration, more the cumulative effect of thousands of years of moving to the suburbs.

Fire

Fire is the tool that distinguishes humans from other animals – more so even than language. Exactly how and when humans learned not simply to flee from fire but to make it to order and manipulate it for their own use remains unclear. Perhaps the habitual chipping away at pieces of flint to make tools led to a spark landing in the right place one day and this began the process. There is some tentative evidence that fire was deliberately made in Africa perhaps even before the development of the hand-axe. There is stronger evidence that fire was made to order 790,000 years ago in present-day Israel. A cave at Zhoukoudian in what is now northern China is also home to suspected deliberate fire-making from 460,000 years ago.

A weak and puny animal such as the human can frighten an animal of any size simply by walking towards it holding a burning stick. The ability to influence other animals was probably the first use to which early humans put their discovery of fire. Fire could protect a human camp and it could also be used to drive animals into a trap. In addition, fire could provide essential warmth for people migrating from warmer to cooler climates. Most likely, the gradual move out of Africa could only have been possible with the help of fire.

There is evidence from charred bones found at the sites of many ancient fires around the world that Homo erectus subsequently found a use for fire that would change human anatomy: cooking. Heating meat softened its fibres making it easier to chew. There was no longer a need for so powerful a jaw and for such large teeth, particularly canines. Back in Africa, a group of people with less heavy faces was finding that its members could survive more easily on this new cooked-food diet, which also made protein easier to digest.

By about 200,000 years ago, these people looked very much like us. The focus of their community was a campfire, which they constantly fed and poked, around which they would one day be telling stories.

The centre of human social life for hundreds of thousands of years. Feared by all other animals, nothing draws a group of humans together like a fire they can warm themselves by, protect themselves with, cook over and gaze into while they talk.

2: The Ritual

Deep in a cave in Wales, the bodies of a number of young Neandertal men have lain undisturbed for 225,000 years. How did these people get there? Could they all have ventured into the dark recesses of the cave and met with unfortunate deaths? It is possible but unlikely; similar discoveries elsewhere make it hard to avoid the conclusion that their bodies were placed there after they had died.

Above: Meaningful behaviour from 100,000 years ago: the antlers of a deer placed on the grave of a teenage boy. They seem to have served a symbolic rather than a practical purpose. From Qafzeh Cave, Israel.

Our Older Cousins

The Neandertals were our closest relatives; an older cousin to modern humans (currently referred to as *Homo sapiens*) rather than an ancestor. They began to appear in Europe around 350,000 years ago and spread into western Asia. From about 100,000 years ago, when we began arriving in the region, they lived alongside us until they died out around 30,000 years ago.

Neandertals had similar-sized brains to ours (actually slightly larger). They developed finer toolmaking techniques than *Homo erectus* and made rudimentary clothing from animal skins. They also seem to have tried to care for the sick and the elderly. It is not thought they used spoken language to any degree but they were nevertheless the first humans to leave evidence of a concern about death.

Recent testing of Neandertal DNA suggests they did not intermarry with modern humans. In many places, however, the two kinds of human lived near each other. How much cultural contact there might have been between them is unclear, though there are similarities in their treatment of the dead.

Why Bury the Dead?

The placing of the dead in a particular site could, of course, have been simply a way of keeping decaying and smelly corpses away from the campsite where food was prepared and all the other activities of the living were carried out. If that were the only motivation, however, simply dumping the body would have been enough.

In contrast, at a number of sites from around 100,000 years ago, Neandertals scraped the flesh off the bones of corpses – not in the way meat is cut from the bone to be eaten but in the way corpses of important people used to be de-fleshed for transportation (the body of the explorer Christopher Columbus is a famous example). In the same manner, bones are still cleaned for reburial after the flesh has decomposed in several parts of the world today.

The earliest actual graves found so far also date from around 100,000 years ago but contain the bodies of modern humans. At Qafzeh Cave in present-day Israel, a woman of around 20 years of age was buried with a 6-year-old child at her feet. A little distance away a 13-year-old boy was buried with a deer antler on his chest.

Neandertal graves become more common from about 70,000 years ago. They are mostly very simple affairs and accompanying objects, such as tools, are rare. At Shanidar Cave in present-day Iraq there is evidence that flowers may have been placed on a grave, though this is still a matter of debate. At another site a child seems to have been buried after decomposition, with some care to lay the bones out in the right order.

From around 30,000 years ago, the graves of modern humans increase in number and become more distinctive; bodies are often heavily sprinkled with red or yellow pigment and accompanied by sometimes hundreds of objects, such as tools, antlers or jewellery made from animal teeth.

What are we to make of this behaviour, behaviour that seems to go beyond the simply practical disposal of a body? Is it religious? Does it show belief in an afterlife? Did it fulfil some kind of function for the community?

Coming to Terms With Death

In parts of West Africa, bonobos or pygmy chimpanzees sometimes show their distress at the death of one of their number by various sorts of curious group behaviour: repeated loud calls, dragging the body away, gathering around it in silence, grooming it, inspecting the scene of death, and so forth. It seems that, like us, they find losing a member of their community sad, frightening and confusing, and need to take part in a ceremony or ritual of some kind to help them mark the event as important before they can move on.

In place of deer antlers, many modern graves are marked by slabs of stone engraved with a series of signs that communicate something to the living. The details have changed but the function and even the underlying form remain the same.

How humans create a rite of passage. Particular artefacts, clothing and gestures – all choreographed to imbue the ending of a human life with significance and ease the minds of the bereaved. In this case a Zulu *Sangoma* or witchdoctor leads the enacted funeral ceremony.

Early human burials, with their gradually evolving sophistication, seem to fit this picture of a group trying to find a way to deal with one of the major transitions in life by going through a performance of some kind.

Some experts have argued that Neandertal burials do not show a sufficiently clear concern with anything other than hygienic disposal of a dead body. Others disagree. Still others argue that Neandertals merely began to imitate modern humans once they arrived on the scene. Drawing conclusions about the thinking of Neandertals remains controversial but the graves of these modern humans suggest quite clearly that burial

was a ritual performance of some kind, largely because of the objects buried with the dead. Since none of these things could have been of any practical use to the dead, they must have served some other purpose for whoever put them there – presumably to help them accept having lost someone.

How, though, would placing objects in a grave have achieved this? A common answer is that they were believed to be of use to the dead in the afterlife. In this way many people, with the benefit of hindsight, take the emergence of ritual behaviour concerning the dead to imply religious belief.

This is a natural enough assumption. Certainly the germ of spiritual belief lies somewhere way back in our evolutionary journey, and there are many natural phenomena, such as sleep, that could have helped to give rise to it. Watching someone sleeping is a strange experience; it is hard to understand where

Body Language

Early burials have left us evidence that, for tens of thousands of years, people have been thinking in terms of symbols and ideas, but language in this sense must have emerged gradually out of the more instinctual ways other animals seem to communicate. The example of the pygmy chimpanzees is perhaps a halfway stage.

All animals use body movements, facial expressions, vocal noises and sometimes colour changes of body parts to express simple impulses, such as aggression, fear or invitation. Humans began to refine the desires they communicated by gradually gaining more control over these instruments of expression.

As we developed the ability to use symbols and ideas it became possible for our body language not only to communicate practical desires but also to portray ideas that required a less immediate response. The ritual became possible; in other words, it became possible to perform.

The first performance was the dance-song; moving the body, stamping feet on the ground, using arm and hand gestures, making facial expressions and making noises. As control over the voice increased, song was able to become a performance of its own. There is a theory that mothers making sounds to comfort their babies helped develop this vocal control.

Colour change was the hardest of our instinctual body responses to control – we remain largely unable to stop our faces turning white with fear or red with anger or embarrassment. In order to bring colour into our conscious vocabulary it had to be artificially applied. Face and body painting developed beyond expressing aggression or invitation to symbolize ideas, such as the protection of the body from pain or disease, belonging to a certain group or having a certain social status.

Adorning the body in other ways extended this vocabulary. First there was cutting or piercing, then tattooing, and finally the wearing of jewellery. Much of this adornment concerned the clarification of a person's identity. Tattooing, for example, could communicate detailed information about a person's lineage – more permanently than make-up.

There is a difference between dance and song – symbolic behaviour where the body is a subject taking action – and jewellery and make-up – symbolic adornment where the body is treated more passively, as an object to decorate. In some cultures this difference has become associated with gender, so that the bodies of women, for example, have become more adorned than the bodies of men.

On the stage, however, these different kinds of expression have always been combined for maximum effect. Whether the stage is a clearing in the centre of a temporary camp or the raised platform of a rock concert, all available kinds of body language will be exploited. The power of any performance is rooted in the body.

Showbusiness. At harvest festival in the Ivory Coast, movement, body paint, jewellery, clothing and hand-held idols all contribute to the performance. The Dance is our original art form.

their personality has gone. Being asleep oneself is an even stranger experience; it seems we leave our bodies, travel to distant places and interact with all sorts of people and animals, some of whom we thought were dead.

However it may have come about, at some point in the past human beings began to express and elaborate the idea that they lived in a world alive with spirits. They did this primarily by creating rituals.

But is it necessary to look for evidence of religious belief in these graves? Many of today's funerals express no religious beliefs at all, yet are extremely ritualistic. Finding evidence of ritual behaviour in itself might be more important than trying to extrapolate what it meant to the people concerned.

A Language Older Than Speech

Ritual is not particular to humans. It is a form of communication common to all animals. To a large extent, however, there is a difference between animal rituals and human rituals. Animal rituals, such as set patterns of courting behaviour, work at the level of

Effective communication of a complex cultural idea. The bended knee, the open ring-case, the happy smile of acceptance, and – of course – the ring itself, placed on a specific finger. A language clear and precise, the forerunner of speech.

instinct; a particular signal triggers a particular response. This is their function.

Human rituals have a function, too, but they can also have a meaning. This is because most human rituals use symbols that stand for ideas, rather than signals that trigger instincts. A burial ceremony, for instance, is a sequence of symbolic actions, each of which stands for an idea, each of which *means* an idea. The connection between the symbol and the idea is the important thing to grasp because that is what creates meaning. People are trying to grasp this connection when they say an object buried in a grave means the person who put it there had a religious idea in mind.

The connection between symbol and idea is the basis for language. A symbolic act means something just like a word does, so a ritual made from a sequence of symbolic acts is rather like a sentence made from a sequence of words. Ritual is one kind of language, communicating thoughts in spoken sentences is another. In order to be understood, both sorts of language must have rules about which symbol stands for which idea, and how these symbols can be put into a sequence.

Because these rules cannot be a matter of individual choice but have to be accepted by a group, they hold the group together. The rules of German, for instance, hold German speakers together; the rules of the Holy Communion ritual hold Christians together. Of course, a ritual can become so ingrained that behaviour becomes automatic and people no longer think about its meaning. When this happens it will function even more strongly as a kind of glue holding society together.

This does not mean, however, that human rituals are set in stone. Some are more established and formal than others, but there is a continual process of the modification of existing rituals and the creation of new ones as social conditions change. Rituals expressing religious ideas make up only a very small part of this process. The significance of the first burials is that they point to the beginning of language in general.

Civilization is underpinned by food and shelter. Upon these basic necessities, however, sits a vast network of ritual – from overtly religious behaviour to christenings, weddings and funerals to dinner parties, Friday nights out and the exchanging of Christmas presents. Culture in itself is based on the ability to read symbols – for example, to understand that a ring on the third finger means 'I am married' in a particular society. This precondition for culture was beginning to form while we lived alongside our Neandertal cousins.

3: Better Tools

100,000 years ago there were several kinds of human living side by side on the planet: humans similar to us mainly in Africa, our Neandertal cousins throughout Europe and western Asia, and Homo *erectus*, still surviving in east and south-east Asia. By the end of the last Ice Age, however, we were alone.

Above: Flint arrowheads (several times life size), showing varying qualities of workmanship. Modern humans produced smaller and finer tools than their predecessors, as a result of an obsession with honing and discussing their skills. The earliest such arrowheads have been found at Bir el Ater in Tunisia and are about 100,000 years old.

The first distinctive product of modern humans was a standard set of tools that were more finely crafted and tailored to specific tasks than those made by earlier humans. The set included hunting weapons of various designs, several kinds of cutting, chopping and scraping tool, increasingly set into wooden handles, and tools for making clothes, shelter and jewellery – as well as spoken language.

Modern humans were not the first to make tools but they introduced a speed of innovation outpacing all that had gone before. At one time Homo erectus produced a brilliant new technology, the hand-axe, but then just kept on churning out the same old product for the next million years. Humans like us have been around for, at most, 195,000 years, yet we have turned that hand-axe into a computer. Talking about it made the difference.

Teacher and Pupil

All living things pass on genetic information, thereby preserving instinctive behaviour through the generations. Humans, though, far more than other animals, supplement this mode of information transfer by passing on cultural information. This means that one of our most basic relationships is that of teacher and pupil.

Cultural information can be passed on in different ways, however. Chimpanzees often use certain tools but when as infants they are taught by their mothers how to crack a nut between two stones, she has to teach by example. The process can take several years. Even among humans, teaching by example alone can be laborious. A tradition of innovation requires a teaching method sufficiently quick to allow people to learn existing skills and ideas, make their own contribution and pass that on in turn. Spoken language fits these requirements.

Although both Neandertals and Homo erectus obviously had ways of communicating clearly enough to allow them to hunt in groups, it is not clear how much speech they had. Studies of Neandertal throat anatomy imply they may well have been able to form words but with difficulties in pronunciation similar to those experienced by young children. On the other

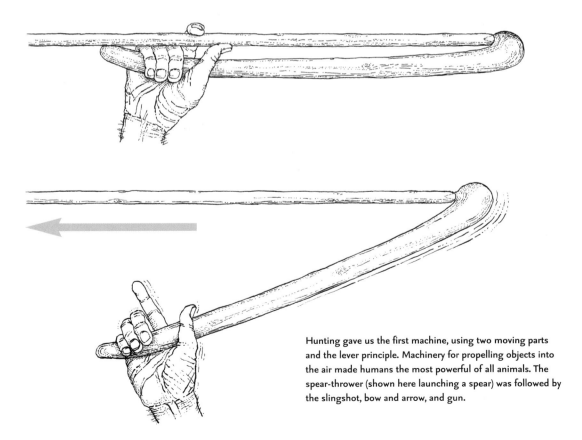

Hunting gave us the first machine, using two moving parts and the lever principle. Machinery for propelling objects into the air made humans the most powerful of all animals. The spear-thrower (shown here launching a spear) was followed by the slingshot, bow and arrow, and gun.

hand, current research into FOXP2, the so-called 'language gene', suggests Neandertals could not have possessed a form of FOXP2 that would allow sufficient control of their tongues and mouths for speech to be possible at all.

Our case is different. We can teach by telling as well as by showing, and this enabled our ancestors to establish a tradition of technological progress. The result was that they outhunted the other humans still living alongside them.

The Arms Industry

The immediate reason for our greater success in the hunt was the development of weapons that could be thrown. When hunting a fast animal such as a gazelle it is not easy to get close. When hunting a large animal such as a mammoth it is not a good idea to get close. Neandertals lost out on both counts. They possessed lethal spears made by mounting a stone point onto a wooden shaft but these spears were too heavy to be thrown. Instead, Neandertals had to try to run up to their prey and use their spears for jabbing.

Modern humans also made two-piece spears in the same way but they passed their skills on to the next generation through speech as well as by example. This both made learning faster and opened up a discussion concerning possible improvements. The result was that they gradually honed their manufacture of spears, experimenting with materials and techniques to produce progressively finer tips that would sit in lighter and better-balanced shafts, until they were turning out spears that could be thrown with accuracy and power enough to kill.

Spears of this quality may have been made in the Sahara as early as 100,000 years ago but certainly from around 40,000 years ago, they seem to have become the norm among modern humans everywhere. In addition, it is possible that the early stages of this process of using verbal communication to refine toolmaking helped to develop the structure of language itself.

Though a few had left earlier, around 60,000 years ago, significant numbers of modern humans migrated out of Africa to people the globe in the same way Homo erectus had previously. Since the capacity for spoken language is universal among modern humans, it must have existed before this exodus took place. But for language to develop into a complex structure it needed ideas to feed on, such as the ideas toolmakers wanted to express to each other in the teaching and discussing of

their craft. The more precise and considered their workmanship became, the more precise and considered their explanations needed to be. They needed a technical vocabulary but they also needed a certain grammar – constructions of the form 'if you do this, then you will achieve that', for instance. In this way, language and toolmaking most likely had an effect on each other's development.

In time this language-assisted innovation process led to the invention of the world's first machine: a tool with two moving parts. By at least 20,000 years ago people in south-west France were no longer throwing spears directly by hand but launching them with a spear-thrower – basically, a lever. The extra power it provided could project a spear well beyond 100 metres (330 feet) at much greater speed than previously possible.

The spear-thrower spread all over the world and is still used in parts of Australia today. In Europe and North Africa the idea of launching a spear rather than throwing it evolved into the bow and arrow. Preoccupation with the mechanics of flight also produced a quite different invention, even more effective over long distances than the spear-thower: the boomerang. It could be thrown accurately up to a distance of 200 metres (650 feet). The earliest boomerang found to date, carved from the tusk of a mammoth, comes from a cave in Poland and is 23,000 years old.

All tools vary in their quality and therefore in the advantage they confer on their owner but the ability to project a missile is always the crucial test. At any one time, whoever can design the long-distance tool that best combines range, power and accuracy will eat the best food – either by out-hunting or by eliminating rivals. Today this means possessing the most advanced guns and surface-to-air missiles; earlier on it meant possessing the most advanced spears. In either case, detailed discussion of all aspects of the design process has made the difference.

Politics and Economics

Success with this Palaeolithic or 'Old Stone Age' tool kit led to social change. Better tools meant more efficient hunting. This allowed the population of modern humans to grow, which brought with it more complicated relations between people. As with innovations in toolmaking, new social structures depended on spoken language being able to express certain ideas.

Big-game hunting took up a lot of space, which meant an area that could be covered in a day would support little more than about 50 people, depending on the environment. Consequently, conflict could easily arise between nearby hunting bands, especially as they moved from one seasonal hunting ground to another. One way to prevent fights over territory was to arrange a marriage: a contract between two members of different bands. This involved negotiation.

As a result of negotiated marriage alliances, larger tribes that were loose groupings of several smaller bands began to form over wider areas. Some of these larger units might contain 500 people or more. People continued to live and hunt in small bands of a few families but behind these immediate relationships they were now aware of a second set of political relationships.

Lessening the threat of conflict between groups through a system of extended family connections meant a new form of co-operation became possible: trade, an insurance policy against hard times, such as a drought might bring. Sub-Saharan peoples were transporting food up to 300 kilometres (180 miles) well over 50,000 years ago – evidence of trade, not migration.

These types of relations involved making arrangements with people – talking about people who were not present or situations that had not yet come about and so forth. Without a spoken language capable of expressing past, present and future tenses as well as many abstract ideas, this would not have been possible. Equally, it may have been this very pressure to find solutions to social problems that pushed language to develop further its expressive power in the first place.

Objects of Beauty

Slicing a tomato with a really sharp knife is, for some, a pleasure akin to driving a luxury car. Such pleasures are the result of painstaking attention to detail in the selection of materials, the drawing up of designs and the refining of manufacturing techniques. Tens of thousands of years ago, people were giving this attention to producing tools of the best quality possible – spears with the optimal combination of cutting power and aerodynamics, for instance.

The more attention the crafting of tools received, the greater difference there came to be between a really top-quality tool and others. The importance of the hunt brought this difference to the fore. The hunter with the best spear had an edge on his fellow hunters, so he was respected and envied by them. High-quality tools became valuable objects that marked a person's status. And then something interesting began to emerge.

The pleasure a hunter took in the way a spearhead flew through the air began to fuse with admiration for the way it looked. A top-quality spearhead had a certain shape and a certain colour, the colour of the best stone for the job. The manufacturing process was largely guided by aiming to perfect these visual characteristics.

The point was reached when form and function were perfectly balanced; the design of the spearhead could not be improved to make it operate any better. However, the process of improving the appearance of the spearhead did not stop. The spearhead continued to grow longer and thinner and ever more finely sharpened until it became an object to be admired more than to be used.

Some of the Ice Age spearheads found in graves in eastern France are so finely worked they may well have broken the first time they were thrown. Much later graves from the Labrador coast of Canada contain tools thin and brittle enough to be ritually snapped at the burial, releasing the spirit of the tool to accompany the dead into the next life. The value of these objects had become determined solely by their shape and colour, not their usefulness as tools.

Alongside this increasing attention to the aesthetic qualities of tools, a jewellery industry was growing. Jewellery had a similar meaning to finely worked tools; it too signalled information about who a certain person was by its shape and colour.

But jewellery was a broader-ranging industry than toolmaking. A purely decorative tool still had to look like a tool but jewellery could look like anything and could make use of almost any material. So jewellery became the main driver of the search for new materials – a search that would one day deliver metal, initially far too soft for tools.

Arrowheads made from gem-quality Vanport flint by the late Stone Age Hopewell culture of the eastern United States (200 BCE–400 CE). The design is practical but the pretty colours do not help the arrow to fly any better.

New Industries

As the last Ice Age built to its climax between 30,000 and 15,000 years ago, many people found themselves living in very harsh environments. In order to survive the cold, they needed warm clothing and shelter that would keep out the draught. This forced them to widen their range of craft skills.

They began to make delicate needles from bone or antler. With these they could sew clothes and make tents from animal hide. But hides had first to be prepared, for which they needed a scraping tool. A bone needle could not easily pierce hide, however, so they also needed an awl to make holes for the needle to pass through. Then they needed something to sew with, so they made thread from animal sinew. They also found they could supplement leather by weaving fabric from mammoth hair. Then they needed something to hold their clothes together, so they carved toggles from bone.

The tool kit. By the height of the last Ice Age, modern humans the world over had armed themselves with a more or less standard set of tools. It contained projectile points for hunting, knife blades that could be set into wooden handles, tools for making clothes, and a drill or engraving tool for jewellery.

1. speartip   2. hide-scraper   3. awl   4–7. arrowheads
8–9. knives   10. drill/engraving tool   11. bone needle

In this way one thing led to another. Tools for making clothing and shelter were different from tools for hunting in that they required prepared materials to work with. The finding, preparing and working of these materials created several further industries alongside the toolmaking industry, all generated from an improved kit of tools, of which the sharpest and most indispensable was the tool of spoken language.

4: Art

People who look like us have been around for perhaps 200,000 years – the development of human anatomy is quite well charted by the fossil record. For most of this time, however, evidence of recognizable human behaviour has been more elusive. Finally, from the time of the last Ice Age, our ancestors begin to speak to us.

Above: A 10,000-year-old autograph book. People wanting to leave their mark outline their hands with spray paint in different colours. From Cueva de las Manos in Patagonia, Argentina. The same technique is found around the world from about 35,000 years ago.

At the beginning of the last Ice Age, around 30,000 years ago, human beings took a quite astonishing step forward. For tens, perhaps even hundreds of thousands of years, people had been using natural lumps of pigment, such as yellow or red iron oxide (rust), white chalk or black charcoal to daub colour on their bodies or to sprinkle it at special sites. They had also drawn or scratched lines and patterns on pieces of rock, bone or eggshell. But now, in small pocket-sized figurines or on the walls of hundreds of caves across Europe, we find the world not only decorated but represented.

It is possible that people had been making pictures and models for a very long time before this date; there are many small, supposed sculptures that are much older. But with all of them it is hard to tell if their suggestive shapes have been carved by hand or by nature. Certainly, the delicacy of many of the paintings and sculptures of the last Ice Age would be much easier to understand if they did not seem to have erupted from nowhere.

A New Set of Skills

There is a variety of techniques to be found in this Ice Age art. Most of the several thousand little figurines are carved out of stone or ivory from mammoth tusks but some are made from a wholly new material that was to have huge implications for the first settled communities once the Ice Age was over: fired clay. Modelling in clay was far less restricting than carving and very occasionally larger clay sculptures were modelled and left unfired in caves. Sometimes larger bas-reliefs were carved in stone and left in situ too.

On the walls of these caves there is a mixture of engravings, charcoal line drawings and full-colour paintings using reds, yellows, blacks and whites. Pigments were sometimes heated to produce different hues – yellow iron oxide would become red when heated. They were then ground, mixed with water and applied in several ways. Brushes were made from animal hair or by chewing the end of a plant stalk, but paint was also sprayed on the cave wall by blowing it through a hollow reed.

An auroch – a larger wild ancestor of today's cow – runs from the hunt on the wall of a cave at Lascaux, south-west France, 17,000 years ago. Several spears pierce the animal; perhaps a form of magic or voodoo designed to bring about the same success for the real-life hunters.

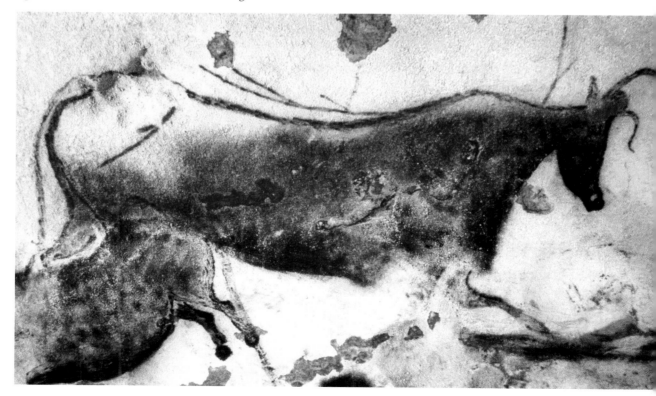

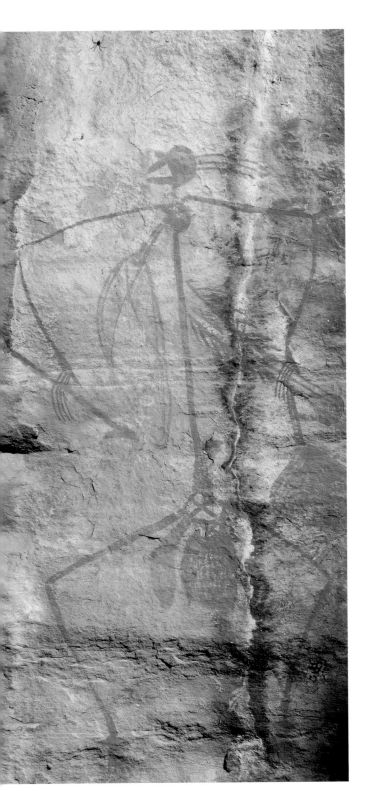

One of the commonest images to be found is a hand outlined by this spray-painting technique, a hand that brings the people of these times eerily close to the present. These hand outlines seem to be truly universal; the rock art in different parts of the world varies greatly in style and subject matter but everywhere, from caves in France and Spain to rock art sites in Africa, Australia and America, there are outlines of human hands.

In Europe, all this work would have been done by lamplight, as no daylight penetrated to the places where most of these paintings were executed. Lamps were stone dishes containing animal fat with a wick made from lichen or moss. Often scaffolding had to be made so that painters could work high up.

A Simplified Copy of the World

These artworks are compelling not only for their techniques of manufacture; they also display ways of thinking fundamental to the development of civilization.

The little carvings of animals and people are much smaller and much less detailed than the real-life animals and people they represent. To translate something seen in the world into a smaller and quite different form and still to be able to recognize what it represents is a very sophisticated ability, without which very little of our culture would be possible. These little figurines opened the way for the doll, the toy and the scale model.

Then there are the paintings; a world made flat. To be able to translate something from three dimensions to two and back again is no less groundbreaking a move than to be able to make sense of a scale model. It is especially interesting that, whereas the animals in these cave paintings are usually drawn with an intimate knowledge of their anatomy and movement, the people can sometimes be simple stick men or women. The later the cave or rock art is, the more this contrast becomes apparent.

Centuries of Western European tradition have given us the habit of regarding naturalistic portrayal of a subject as a great accomplishment but understanding

The universal shorthand for 'man', drawn around 20,000 years ago on the Ubirr Rock in Kakadu National Park, Australia. This is a Mimi spirit holding a spear-thrower in its right hand. Aboriginal people say Mimis taught their ancestors to hunt and paint in the Dreamtime.

what a stick man represents demands a more complex conceptual response than seeing the resemblance between a photograph and the person it represents. To understand any image requires the capacity for abstract thought; a stick man is a form of shorthand that takes this mental translation process to an extreme. Apart from housing the birth of representative painting, these caves are also home to the birth of the diagram, the teaching aid and the pictogram or hieroglyph, with which writing began.

It is a short step from the stick men of France or Australia to a piece of mammoth tusk found at Mezhirich in the Ukraine, contemporary with some of the younger European cave paintings. Carved into the tusk there is a map of the surrounding area. Even today the conceptual ability needed to read a map is beyond many people, as almost any car journey will demonstrate.

Imagined Worlds

Art allowed not only the expression of general ideas but also the depiction of other worlds. A stick man is clearly different from a real man because it is so simplified. It is just a sign for the general idea of 'man'. But when an image is more lifelike the situation changes. A portrait can be painted or sculpted in such a way that it seems to capture something of the personality of the sitter – hence the reason people in certain cultures to this day resist having their photograph taken for fear of losing part of their soul. In this case, the link between the image and what it represents is much stronger than in the case of the stick man or the map.

The cave painters may have drawn stick men and women but they never drew stick animals. One interpretation of the meaning of these cave paintings is that animals were painted in order to encourage real animals to appear in the surrounding countryside so they could be hunted. This relies on a magical link existing between the image and the real thing. Such a link becomes easier to understand the more lifelike the image itself is; the more the painting of the animal seems to capture something of its soul.

What is happening here is that the world of the imagination is coming to life because it is being represented in visual form like the real world around us. This is the beginning of a process of blurring the line between real and imagined worlds. In some of the caves there are hybrid half-human half-animal figures;

The Sound of Music

Music is a mysterious phenomenon because it can have such emotional power while being the least representational of all our languages. The colour red is like blood but what is a note in music like? Even when notes are strung together there is little agreement about what they mean. Yet they have the power to move us.

Before music in general there was song, but beyond song music needed special tools before it could be made. Some of the earliest objects found in caves across Europe are flutes or whistles made from bone and perforated with holes.

The presence of a hole in a blowing instrument means sound was being focused into single notes. The presence of a series of holes means that intervals between these notes were being worked out.

When notes are singled out we can start to hear relationships between them. The first relationship we hear is the octave; for some reason we cannot understand, we can hear that two notes are the same even though we can also hear one is higher than the other. After that we can hear relationships between other notes; some please us, some do not, also for reasons that escape us.

Finding a flute from 30,000 years ago means that people were already taking pleasure in exploring the patterns that give order to the natural world – in this case, patterns of sound. The search for patterns seems to have accompanied, if not preceded, the impulse to make representational art. From around this time we also have counting sticks with notches arranged into groups and on a number of cave walls there are geometrical designs. In fact, the earliest geometrical pattern, etched in the Blombos Cave in South Africa, is 77,000 years old.

One of the natural patterns these people were exploring was the relationship of the mathematics of sound to human emotion. Another pattern was the relationship of the intervals between notes to the measurement of physical materials. They must have worked out where to place the holes of a flute to produce certain notes. At some point later on they would make a tool for music-making that used a vibrating string of animal sinew. Then they would discover that a string half the length of another produced a note an octave higher.

The discovery of a 30,000-year-old flute also shows that whoever played it was counting in sound. They had the twin languages of mathematics and music, and with them the idea of an order in the natural world that humans could try to understand – either through systematic investigation or intuitively, through the playing of music.

images arrived at by combining ideas drawn from the real world to produce a creature of pure imagination.

People have suggested that these hybrid creatures may represent shaman shape-shifters making contact with the spirits of animals, and also that shamans themselves may have painted the caves as part of a ritual to summon these spirits. Whether or not this is true, creating an image of such a hybrid creature makes the idea of it tangible, makes it seem part of the real world. Similarly, many of the little figurines are thought to be idols of spirits; it is much easier to believe a spirit or a god is real if you can see it.

Many other theories have been put forward to explain Palaeolithic art but whatever it means, whatever reasons people had for making it, it represents an imagined world – one which no doubt reflects the real world these people lived in, but indirectly, through the prism of their imagination. At the same time as they were giving visual form to their imagined world, they must have been telling stories about it, too.

Nowadays, with our more powerful recording media, we present images of our world to each other incessantly, only to a small extent through the making of so-called 'art', far more through holiday snaps, advertising posters, soap operas, 24-hour TV news channels and so on. People have been worrying about the distinction between a representation or copy and the real thing at least since the time of Plato, and new technology only makes this line harder to draw.

The most famous shrine of Ice Age art, the caves at Lascaux in France, is too fragile to cope with hundreds of people walking through it every day. So Lascaux II, a replica exact down to every curve of the natural rock and brushstroke of the prehistoric hand, has been built so that tourists can experience the real thing without damaging it.

Right: A creature that exists only in the minds of humans is made real by being given tangible form. This lion-man, found in a cave at Hohlenstein-Stadel, Germany, in 1931, was carved from the tusk of a mammoth around 32,000 years ago.

Below: Art that was not meant to be admired. Far from natural light, many European cave paintings were most likely seen only as they were painted. The act of painting was the important thing, not appreciation of the finished work. This image is from Lascaux II, however, so is seen daily.

5: The Boat

Two thirds of the surface of the planet Earth is not earth at all, but water. To move with any efficiency across this liquid surface our ancestors needed to invent their first form of transport. The boat led to some of the earliest settled communities, and where these communities might be separated by land, the boat brought them together by water. Water transport also led to developments in technology, science and mathematics.

Above: Melting glaciers and rising water levels produced the many inlets and islands of Scandinavia, making it home to seafaring peoples since the last Ice Age. Later rock engravings, such as this one near Tanumshede in south-west Sweden (c. 1800–c. 600 BCE), record their world.

Setting Foot on Virgin Soil

For millions of years humans and their predecessors would have seen branches floating on the water. At some point the step was taken to tie a number of branches together and make a raft. But watercraft tend not to co-operate with the archaeologist. If a boat sinks, it rots away faster than it would on land, certainly in shallow water. In addition, the shoreline of most of the world has receded since the last Ice Age as sea levels have risen, leaving many ancient coastal settlements underwater.

As such, the oldest boat found so far, from 7000 BCE, leaves riddles to answer. If there were no boats before this time how did Australia become populated, for example? People arrived in Australia at least 40,000 years ago, at a time when they could have walked most of the way there through present-day Indonesia. But they would still have had to cross at least 50 miles of open sea with no land in sight. On the Australian side of this channel, rock art believed to be more than 17,000 years old shows a number of people in a boat.

There is also circumstantial evidence that boats were used more than 13,000 years ago by the big-game hunters from the Siberian tundra, who walked across to America during the last Ice Age, when lower sea levels made the Bering Strait dry land. Once there, they found their passage south blocked by a glacier spanning the entire width of the new continent. But places further south were settled before this glacier melted enough to allow travel by land.

So it seems there was a migration down the Pacific coast of the American continent, most likely in small boats made from animal skins stretched over a framework of bone – the materials most available to these hunters – and propelled by a paddle. Light, vulnerable boats of kayak construction are best suited to hunting and fishing on inlets and rivers rather than travel on the open sea, so progress south along the coast would have been gradual.

Settling Down to Fish

Around the same time, people who had been living a similar hunting life in Europe began to build boats as a response to the changing climate. At the height of the last Ice Age, bison, mammoth and reindeer migrated in herds across a treeless tundra stretching from Asia into present day Spain, and the hunters followed these animals. But as the glaciers melted to the north, Europe became warmer and wetter.

Where the North Sea and the English Channel are today there had been dry land sleeping under a blanket of ice. This was now transformed into a marshy fen. Elsewhere forests grew up, cut by rivers and lakes, and the great herds moved off towards Siberia. In their place came red deer and smaller woodland animals that hid in the forest and that could not be caught using the old methods. But there was another, newly abundant source of food swimming in the rising inland waterways: fish.

Across Europe, fishing became a new way of life. Barbed harpoons and delicate fish hooks were carved out of antler or bone, and nets were made. To take better advantage of the rivers, small fishing canoes were made, first from skin as in the Americas, later from bark or hollowed-out tree trunks. These little boats were manoeuvred by paddles or oars. Sometimes two boats would drag a net between them.

This new form of hunting did not require the long-distance migration necessitated by following herds of bison. Instead, it was restricted to where there was water, and involved possessing a boat. Fishing from a boat was more suited to setting out on an expedition and returning home again than being constantly on the move. So communities started to settle in one place for longer periods of time and develop regional differences.

Roads of Water

These Mesolithic or 'Middle Stone Age' fishing communities arose along the edges of the new waterways. As people explored the rivers for fish they came into contact with each other. The boats these people used for fishing provided the first means of transporting more goods than a pair of arms could carry, so a network of trade routes began to connect the continent, both within Europe and eventually around its Atlantic coast as sturdier boats were built. These rivers and coastal routes became the roads of Europe for thousands of years.

In the Mediterranean world of 13,000 years ago, volcanic obsidian for toolmaking was already being imported from the island of Melos in the Aegean to the mainland of present-day Greece. Over the next couple of thousand years, all the main islands of the Mediterranean were settled, ready to link later farming societies by trade. By the early Bronze Age, the Mediterranean was already becoming the hub of commerce from which Phoenicians, Greeks and

Romans would later benefit. The Mediterranean was connected to the peoples of northern Europe first by amber from Denmark and the Baltic, carried south partly by river, partly on foot, and also by tin from Cornwall, shipped by sea.

To the south and east, the Mediterranean linked up to other trade networks. On the Nile as well as in the deltas of the Tigris and Euphrates in modern-day Iraq the first farmers were preceded by fishing people who made their boats from binding together papyrus reeds that grew along the riverbanks. Later, as farming communities appeared upstream, these rivers became arteries of trade in the same way as the rivers of Europe. At the same time, boats were venturing further along the islands of the Gulf.

By 2500 BCE, Sumerian traders were sailing from the mouths of the Tigris and Euphrates out of the Gulf and into the Indian Ocean, bound for the great Harappan cities on the Indus river in present-day Pakistan. By this time, too, Egyptian traders were starting to sail down the Red Sea to a place they called the Land of Punt, somewhere near the Horn of Africa, for perfume, gold and ivory. By the time Egypt and the Mediterranean fell under the control of Rome, these routes had joined up and been pushed further south along the African coast and further east to present-day Indonesia and the coast of China. The Romans imported perfume from East Africa and Arabia, spices from India and beyond, silk from China.

As the Roman empire crumbled and a new dynamic religion spread out from Arabia, the Indian Ocean and the South China Sea became a vast Muslim trading lake. By the 9th century, Arab merchants had established a string of trading ports along the east coast of Africa to which ivory and gold were brought from the interior. Over time these ports grew, producing the fusion of African and Islamic culture that became Swahili.

By the 13th century, city-states such as Mombasa, Zanzibar and Kilwa – the richest of them all thanks to gold from present-day Zimbabwe – were part of a web that reached up to Arabia and Persia, over to India and across to Muslim Malacca, the commercial hub of south-east Asia and gateway to China. To Malacca, Arab dhows brought dyes, pearls, perfume and tapestries from the west and Chinese junks brought porcelain and silk from the north.

While Arab merchants were beginning their colonization of the Indian Ocean, the Vikings were maintaining contact between the Mediterranean and northern Europe through river trade with Constantinople and the Black Sea, trade upon which the cities of Kiev and Novgorod in present-day Ukraine and Russia were founded. To the west, the Vikings traded, plundered and colonized as far as Greenland and the coast of Canada. Here they met descendents of the Ice Age hunters who had walked across the Bering Land Bridge from Siberia thousands of years earlier and used their skin kayaks to paddle not south but east through the islands of arctic Canada.

Science and Technology

As shipping linked societies through trade so it affected and was affected by technological and scientific development. By the time Egypt was building its first pyramids in 2650 BCE, blocks of stone weighing 50 tons were being transported downriver on wooden barges. Egyptian society had developed to the point where there were professional carpenters available who could turn their skills to boatbuilding.

Greek and Roman boats were constructed as though they had been built by cabinet makers. Instead of the planks of the hull being nailed to each other or to a frame, they were all held together by mortice-and-tenon joints, often only 5 centimetres (2 inches) apart, each joint drilled and plugged with a dowel to prevent it from working loose. As much as shipbuilding borrowed technology developed by craftsmen working in other areas, however, the particular challenges of water travel had always been drivers of technological progress in their own right.

Nowhere was this more apparent than in the problem of how to get a boat to move. The earliest boats were pushed and pulled through the water by paddles and oars, but by the time trading vessels were plying between the first Sumerian cities and the island of Bahrain in the Gulf they were using the wind. Humans had harnessed their first source of non-biological power.

To begin with, a sail was a way of trapping wind blowing from behind. On the Nile the wind blows upstream so boats could sail up with the wind, then

A 13th-century dhow sails with the Monsoon winds. Arab merchants enjoy the view while several deckhands adjust the rigging. A dhow's lateen sail could be repositioned to sail into the wind as well as with a following wind, but this was a lot of work so a large crew was needed.

الفرآن ثم ابعد اساطير ملاها وزخارف جلاها وقال اركبوا فيها بسم الله مجراها
ومرساها ثم نفس نفس المعسر من أو عباد الله للمكرمين وقال لك اما انا

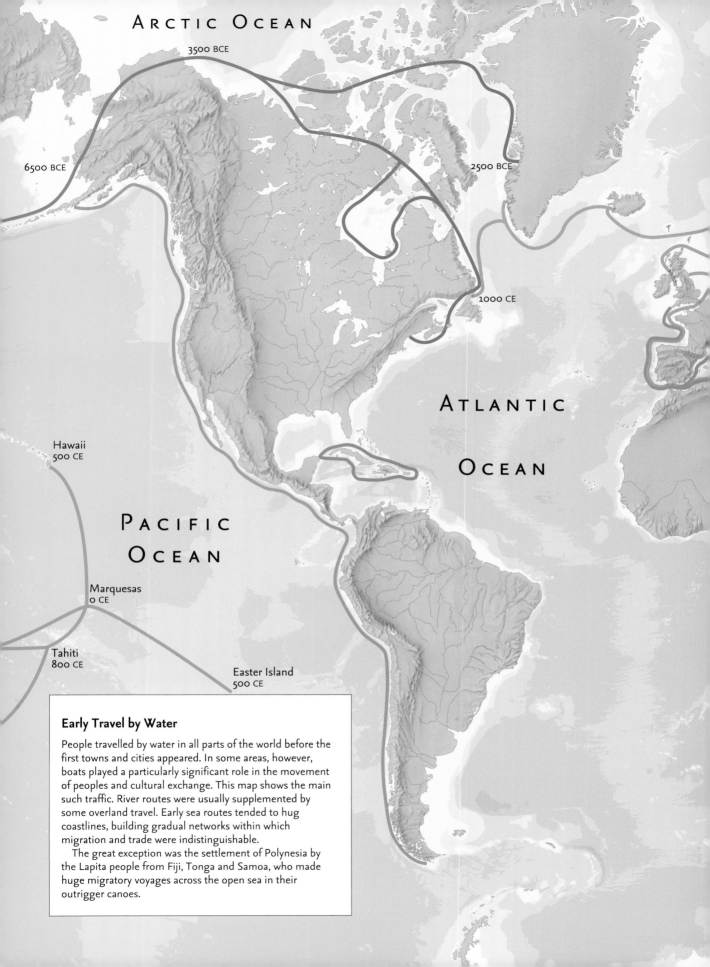

ARCTIC OCEAN

3500 BCE

6500 BCE

2500 BCE

1000 CE

ATLANTIC

OCEAN

Hawaii
500 CE

PACIFIC

OCEAN

Marquesas
0 CE

Tahiti
800 CE

Easter Island
500 CE

Early Travel by Water

People travelled by water in all parts of the world before the first towns and cities appeared. In some areas, however, boats played a particularly significant role in the movement of peoples and cultural exchange. This map shows the main such traffic. River routes were usually supplemented by some overland travel. Early sea routes tended to hug coastlines, building gradual networks within which migration and trade were indistinguishable.

The great exception was the settlement of Polynesia by the Lapita people from Fiji, Tonga and Samoa, who made huge migratory voyages across the open sea in their outrigger canoes.

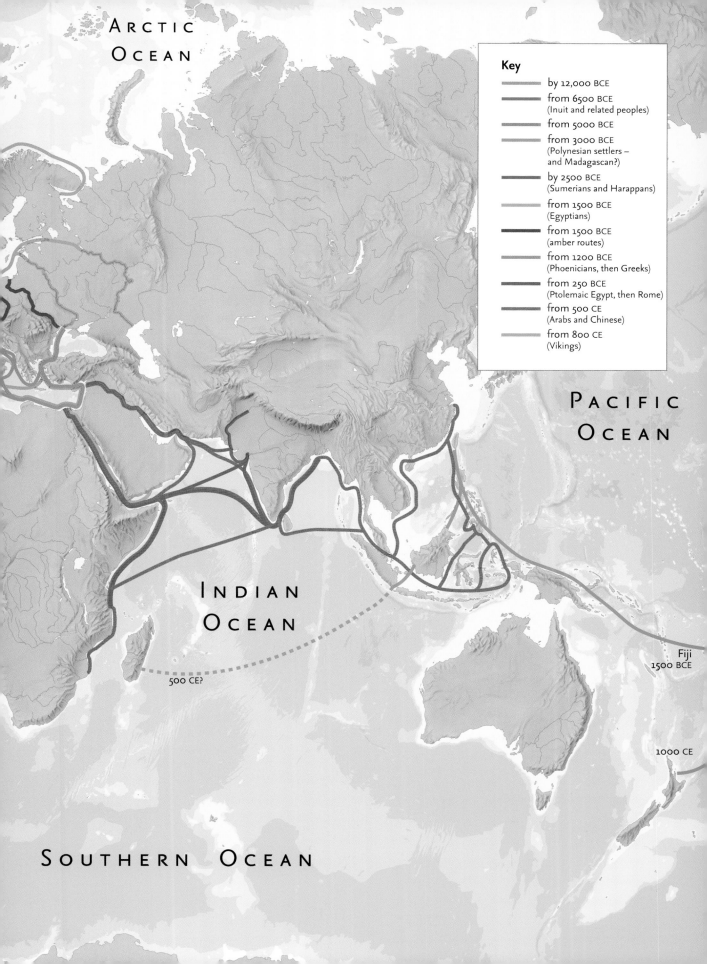

ARCTIC
OCEAN

PACIFIC
OCEAN

INDIAN
OCEAN

SOUTHERN OCEAN

500 CE?

Fiji
1500 BCE

1000 CE

Key

by 12,000 BCE

from 6500 BCE
(Inuit and related peoples)

from 5000 BCE

from 3000 BCE
(Polynesian settlers –
and Madagascan?)

by 2500 BCE
(Sumerians and Harappans)

from 1500 BCE
(Egyptians)

from 1500 BCE
(amber routes)

from 1200 BCE
(Phoenicians, then Greeks)

from 250 BCE
(Ptolemaic Egypt, then Rome)

from 500 CE
(Arabs and Chinese)

from 800 CE
(Vikings)

have their sail lowered and float down with the current. Using the wind in this way remained the fastest way to move a boat until the advent of steam power, but relying on the wind blowing in the right direction is limiting. Certain routes could not be sailed, other routes necessitated waiting months for the wind to change direction.

At some point, people realized that the wind could be used in a different way by angling a sail so that its edge was facing more towards the wind, provided this leading edge was kept straight. If the

On the Nile, fishermen made the first boats from reeds (as on the right), but other types of boat followed. This detail from a 1st century CE Roman mosaic of the Nile also shows a skin-covered dinghy (left), a leisurely sailing barge and a fast, streamlined Roman warship.

correct angle were found, wind flowed past the outside of the sail faster than the inside, creating low pressure outside, high inside. This difference in air pressure made the sail bow outwards, pulling or 'sucking' the boat forward.

The first boats were used for fishing, which led to more settled communities. Here, 16th-century inhabitants of Back Bay, Virginia, have built a weir to trap fish, which they catch with nets and spears in the same way as the very earliest fishermen.

A sail used in this way is an aerofoil, producing lift. This discovery was probably made independently by early sailors in the eastern Mediterranean, the Indian Ocean and the Pacific. Thousands of years later, the same principle would lift aeroplanes off the ground and hydrofoils out of the water.

By this time, navigation at sea would also have played a part in the forming of the modern world. For the first sailors, knowing where they were was largely a matter of keeping in sight of the coast. As open-sea voyages increased during the era of European expansion, however, getting lost became a big problem. A whole scientific industry became driven by the need to find a way for sailors to accurately estimate longitude (the position of their ship east or west). Modern astronomy, precision clockmaking and mathematical advances, such as graphs in particular, were all driven by focusing on the problems of navigating large bodies of water.

The Catamaran

Thousands of years before Columbus, human beings in another part of the globe were already undertaking open-sea voyages inconceivable in the developed world before his time. Sometime after 3000 BCE, a people living on the island of Taiwan moved south to the eastern edge of Indonesia. By 1600–1200 BCE they had settled Fiji, Samoa and Tonga from where they continued their settlement of the Pacific. From the easternmost islands of Polynesia they sailed 2000 miles north-west to Hawaii around 500 CE and even further south-west to reach New Zealand by 1000 CE. Nor were

The template for much modern boat design: a traditional twin-hulled Polynesian canoe. For open-sea voyages, longer canoes fitted with a sail were used.

these epic voyages one-way journeys. Having discovered New Zealand, these seafarers sailed home again to tell of their discovery before returning with more of their people to settle this new country.

The Polynesians achieved all this using canoes hollowed out of a single tree trunk 24 metres (80 feet) or more in length. But whereas early dugouts in Europe had been gradually built up to the point where the dugout itself formed the keel of a larger boat made from planks, Pacific dugouts were lashed together to form catamarans. These boats had great stability and could travel much faster than the large ships that brought Tasman, Cook and other European explorers centuries later. The Polynesians also navigated over the open sea without equipment, relying on the sun, the stars and their reading of the wind and the different patterns it made on the water.

In the 21st century, after thousands of years of boatbuilding innovation across the developed world, the latest state-of-the-art sailing boats used for racing and round-the-world record-breaking attempts are all catamarans of Polynesian design. More and more passenger ferries are also catamarans because of the smooth ride they offer.

6: The Dog and Other Animals

For hundreds of thousands of years human beings hunted wild animals. Then, as the last Ice Age melted away, the idea of controlling them instead was born.

Above: Goodbye to the hunt. A dog trained to round up other animals makes killing them an easier prospect for the human. It also means they can be kept to produce other products, in this case wool.

Recent research has traced the DNA of all domestic dogs to three breeds living in east Asia sometime before 13,000 BCE. From there, the dog spread across all continents, accompanying the Ice Age hunters across the Bering Land Bridge to America, and reverting to the wild in Australia, where it became the dingo. After the dog was domesticated, other animals followed and the relationship between humans and animals became closer and more ambiguous as civilization came to depend on them for work, leisure and food.

The Humble Servant

Human beings and wolves have always been enemies. Wolves were rivals in the hunt and a menace to the campsite, where fires were kept alight to ward them off. They were valued only for their skins.

But wolves and wild dogs hunt in packs. This means the survival of the individual depends on the smooth functioning of the group. Equality could endanger this. Instead, each wolf must know its place in the hierarchy if the pack is to remain an efficient hunting machine. At the top are the alpha male and female to which all the other members must submit. At the bottom is the omega wolf, which all too often goes hungry.

As humans gradually became less nomadic, larger rubbish dumps grew up around their campsites. Wolves and other wild dogs were attracted to these dumps but they were wary of humans and easily scared off. For the lowest in the pack, however, hunger outweighed fear and these animals became more accustomed to being around humans.

Once this stage had been reached, it became apparent to humans that they could benefit from the mentality of an animal programmed to fit into a strict social structure. All the human had to do was take over the role of the dominant pack leader by providing food and laying down rules. The need of a dog to adapt to the behaviour of a leader means it is very good at reading signals such as body language. In other words, it can be trained.

At first, humans trained dogs to guard their campsites and to help in the hunt. The different environments in which they hunted led humans to breed dogs to bring out certain characteristics. Nomadic hunters across the plains of Asia wanted dogs with deep chests, long legs and keen eyes, capable of spotting prey in the distance and running it down silently and swiftly over treeless terrain. So

they bred 'sight hounds' such as the Greyhound, the Saluki and the Afghan hound.

Later on, as the climate changed and Europe became one great forest, speed over open ground became less important than stamina and the ability to track prey over a long period of time. So 'scent hounds' such as the Bloodhound, the Beagle, the Dachshund and others were bred.

Across the still frozen north, sled dogs were bred to provide a form of transport.

From Hunting to Herding

Hunting, however, became more difficult as the last Ice Age came to an end. Across all continents, large animals died out or became more scarce as a result both of climate change and over-hunting. To begin with, hunters tried to stop numbers falling further by killing only male animals, leaving females to bear offspring. But the dog had given humans the idea that animals could be more closely controlled than this.

Around 9000 BCE, hunters across the hillsides of south-west Asia began to turn their attention to animals that could be herded rather than hunted, animals such as the wild mouflon sheep and the wild bezoar goat. The fact that these animals would let humans take charge of their herd meant they could be

Dominance and submission: the reason a dog can be trained. The wolf on the left accepts its inferior status and remains alert to small nuances in body language so it can comply with the wishes of the alpha wolf (right). A human dog-owner takes the role of this alpha wolf.

protected to some extent from other predators, they could be milked and they could be bred.

Now there was a call for dogs to help humans herd these and other animals, so over the centuries breeds such as the German Shepherd and the Border Collie were developed. The Portuguese Water Dog even herded shoals of fish into the nets along the coast of Portugal.

As settled farming communities spread, more animals were tamed. The wild boar became the domestic pig and, by around 6000 BCE, the now extinct auroch, or wild ox, painted by Palaeolithic hunters on the walls of so many caves, had become the cow. In China some time before 5400 BCE the Red Junglefowl of south-east Asia became the chicken.

These farms had pests to control and here cats as well as dogs could assist. The cat helped the very earliest farmers to keep rats and mice away from grain stores and to kill snakes. Later, fiesty little terriers were bred to burrow after foxes, rabbits, badgers and also, like the cat, to control vermin that might spread disease.

All these domestic animals were bred to bring out specific traits but they also shared certain general characteristics that made them easier to manage. They were all smaller than their wild cousins, they all had smaller brains, and if they had horns these were also smaller now that there was no need for males to compete for females. There were other consequences of animal domestication, too.

Herding animals and settling in larger communities gave rise to one of the hallmarks of civilization unknown to the hunter-gatherer: the epidemic disease. Epidemics require large populations in which pathogens can stay alive by moving quickly from one host to another. This condition was first met by dense human and animal populations living alongside each other. Human diseases such as measles, smallpox, tuberculosis, and influenza mutated from diseases affecting herds of animals. Other diseases such as typhus benefited from humans living near their own and animal faeces. These initial conditions were exacerbated as populations became denser and came into closer contact with each other following the

Milking time in Egypt, 2450 BCE. The cow is a large and dangerous animal – and used to be more so – so a farmhand restrains it with a rope. Exactly how and why such a difficult animal was first domesticated remains unclear. From the tomb of Ti, an official of the Old Kingdom.

Blessed by an elephant at the Hindu temple of Kamakshi Amman in Kanchipuram, India. In return for its labour, the Indian elephant has become revered. It has rarely been truly domesticated, however, as it usually returns to the wild to breed.

growth of cities and trade routes, making the spread of infectious disease even easier.

Herding animals also ushered in a confusing relationship between humans and the animals they not only killed, but cared for first. Gone was the honourable contest of the chase in which something was expected of both animal and human. No longer could the hunter distinguish himself by his skill, no longer could the animal be revered for its power and its will to stay alive. There was little skill in killing a penned animal that had grown up to trust its provider and little reason to respect such an animal. There was an element of shame about the whole affair that had not existed before.

People tried to make sense of this through religious ideas that explained human-animal relationships in terms of a natural hierarchy of masters and servants. In addition, as long as only one animal was involved, the killing could be made into a ritual. As cities grew and the scale of slaughter increased, this became more difficult, but at the same time fewer and fewer people had any contact with the process. Despite their differences, the identity of both hunter and herder was directly bound up with their relationship to animals. For the city dweller, however, this was no longer the case, so the ambiguity of the new relationship between human and animal was easier to ignore.

Making Dogs Fight

In the move from hunting to herding, humans felt they had lost an important part of themselves. Ever since, they have sought to recapture something of that essential contest in various kinds of sport. The Roman Colosseum and the Spanish bull ring have housed merely the most obvious examples. The sport of dog-baiting is a more curious phenomenon.

In Norman times, English farmers bred bulldogs to help them bring bulls in for breeding, castration or slaughter. These dogs would protect the farmer by biting the bull's nose if it became troublesome, holding on until it submitted.

But bulldogs had no desire to fight, so they were crossed with terriers to produce more aggressive breeds, such as the Staffordshire Bull Terrier. For hundreds of years, these dogs would be baited into enough of a frenzy to attack each other while people gambled on the outcome. The popularity of this amusement peaked in the time of Shakespeare.

In the 19th century, English and Irish immigrants took these dogs to Boston, Massachusetts, where they were bred to produce today's Pit Bull Terrier. Today dog-baiting is popular in most parts of the world, including Britain and the United States, despite now being outlawed in these countries.

More curious still, several English newspapers of the 19th century contain reports of the so-called 'arbite', where the sport was to place bets on a dog and a man fighting it out. Man's best friend has helped humans to realize their desires in all sorts of ways.

The Advantage

Not all animals can be domesticated. There are tests to pass. An animal must have the right social structure: a pack or a herd where the human can take over the dominant position. A territorial herd is no good. Different herds of antelope, for example, would never tolerate being penned together, nor would herds of deer in the rutting season.

Domesticated animals also need to have a calm and docile enough temperament. Gazelles cannot be shepherded because they panic easily and bolt. Zebras bite and hold on to express conflict within the herd.

There are economic tests to pass, too. Keeping an animal for food is usually only economically viable if it eats vegetables and if it produces offspring at a fast enough rate.

Crucially, a domestic animal needs to breed in captivity. The cheetah is a far better hunter than the

The Domestication of Animals

A glance at the unequal distribution of the earliest domesticated animals – draught animals in particular – gives a clue as to why civilization advanced in certain areas more quickly than in others. On this map, the dog, as the first and most versatile domestic animal, has its own colour and is shown in several regions at the date it arrived from its east Asian origin. Other animals are shown only where they were first domesticated. In some cases, such as the pig or the cow, this happened independently at different times and places. The elephant is included even though it has only recently begun to breed in captivity.

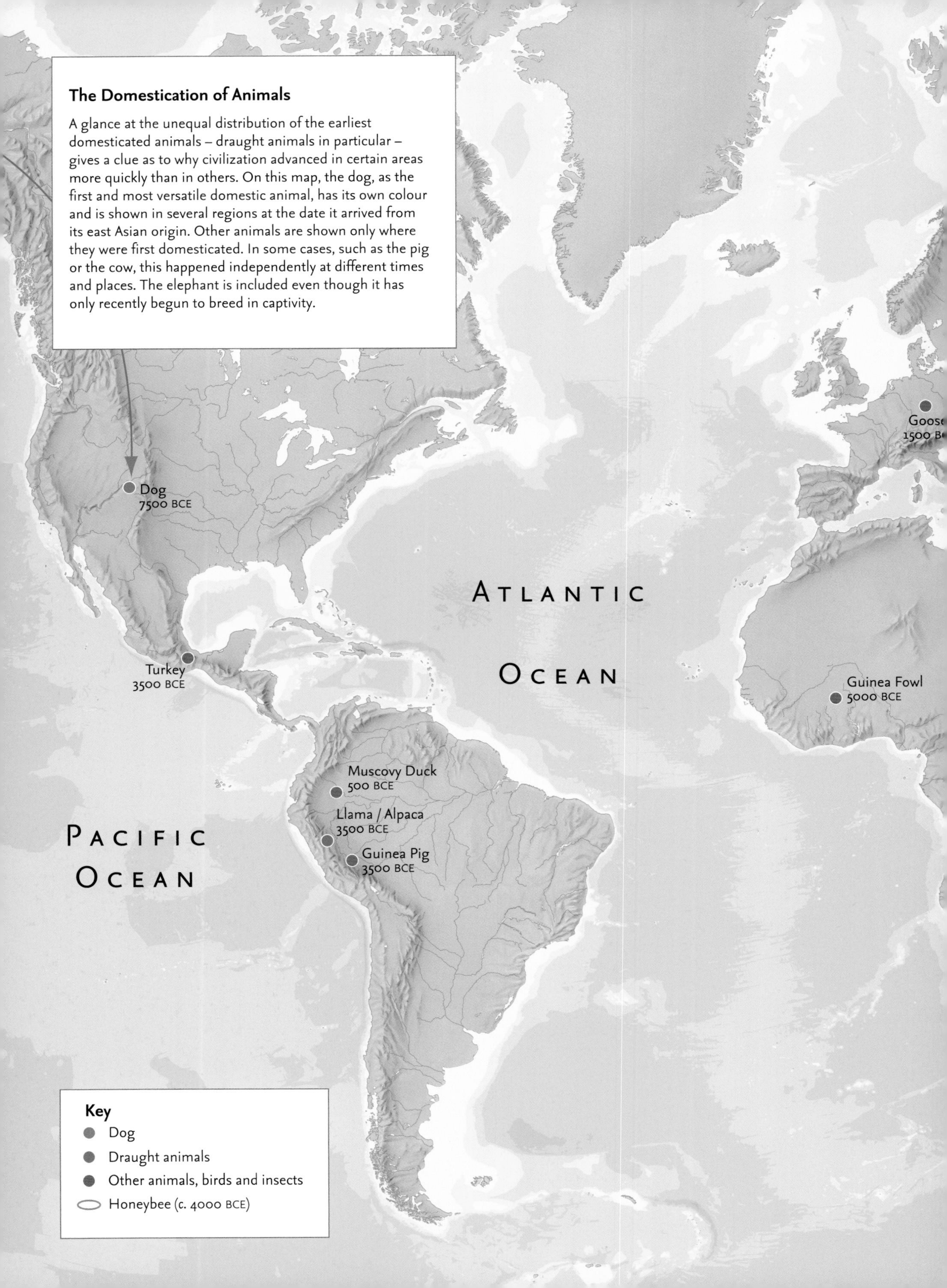

ATLANTIC

OCEAN

PACIFIC

OCEAN

Dog
7500 BCE

Turkey
3500 BCE

Goose
1500 B

Guinea Fowl
5000 BCE

Muscovy Duck
500 BCE

Llama / Alpaca
3500 BCE

Guinea Pig
3500 BCE

Key

- Dog
- Draught animals
- Other animals, birds and insects
- Honeybee (c. 4000 BCE)

ARCTIC
Ocean

Reindeer
1000 BCE

Horse
4000 BCE

Bactrian Camel
2500 BCE

Pig
8000 BCE

Cow
6000 BCE

Dog
10,000 BCE

Sheep
8500 BCE

Goat
8500 BCE

Yak
2500 BCE

Dog
13,000 BCE

Pig
7500 BCE

Dog
0 BCE

Pigeon
3000 BCE

Cat
7500 BCE

Zebu or Humped Cow
6500 BCE

Silkworm
2700 BCE

Donkey
0 BCE

Goose
3000 BCE

Asian Elephant
2000 BCE

Chicken
6000 BCE

Domesticated Duck
1000 BCE

PACIFIC
OCEAN

Dromedary Camel
2500 BCE

Water Buffalo
4000 BCE

Banteng
3000 BCE

ow
00 BCE

INDIAN
OCEAN

Dog (Dingo)
1500 BCE

SOUTHERN OCEAN

The Horse

When the Spanish brought the horse with them to the New World in the early 1500s, they were only reintroducing a native American animal. The ancestor of today's horses evolved there and spread, during the last Ice Age, across the Bering Land Bridge into Asia. At the end of the last Ice Age, the horse was one of the animals that died out in America.

Across Asia and into Europe, wild horses lived on and continued to be hunted. In the steppes north of the Black Sea and the Caspian Sea, people who were probably shepherds began to herd the horse and soon afterwards, around 4000 BCE, to ride it. For this they needed to invent the bridle so they could turn the horse left and right and make it stop.

Suddenly, the land opened up for these people. On horseback they could cover ten times the distance they could before. Thousands of miles of grassland were now open to them for grazing, hunting, trading and stealing. The horse made them into a warlike people because it was so easy for them to ride into a village, kill, burn and steal, and ride off again too quickly to be followed.

During the next 3,000 years or so, these people spread all over Europe and down into present-day Iran and India, taking variations on their original Indo-European language with them, which is why English, Russian and Hindi, for example, are all related to each other.

The horse continued to be central to warfare but fighting while riding bareback was a difficult skill to learn. The cartwheel, which had been developed in Mesopotamia by the Sumerians sometime in the 4th millennium BCE, offered a solution. A horse could pull a chariot, which made things a lot easier. In 1652 BCE, Egypt fell to the Hyksos, a chariot-riding people who ruled the country for 100 years until the Egyptians copied their methods and threw them out. By 1500 BCE, chariot warfare was standard across the developed world.

A mounted rider, however, could fight from higher up than a man on a chariot, and saddles made riding more comfortable. So Alexander the Great put his soldiers on horseback again and cut a swathe from Greece to India with cavalry charges. But he lacked a deadly, central Asian weapon: the stirrup – at first simply an aid to help novices mount.

By 310 CE, northern China was being overrun by nomadic horsemen with stirrups, able to balance on their mounts easily enough to fire arrows accurately and to brace themselves securely enough to swing a sword with real power from their raised position. By 450 CE, Attila the Hun was doing the same in Europe.

Europe's response was to copy the stirrup and add the lance to the combination, an extra-long spear that depended on its user being able to put his weight behind it by digging his feet into his stirrups. When metal armour was added, a kind of tank was created that could keep the invaders at bay. Horse, weapon, armour and skilled lance-wielder did not come cheap, though. Lacking the disposable cash to pay for a standing army, kings gave land and property to mounted soldiers in return for military service. Some argue that in this way the stirrup gave rise to feudalism in Europe.

By the industrial era, warfare had moved on but horses continued to be used in cavalry charges and more than ever before on the farm and for transport. Over the last 100 years, however, horses have finally been able to retire from war, agriculture and transport to find jobs in the leisure industry.

Love and marriage. Alexander the Great is carried to India by Bucephalus, from whom he had been inseparable since the age of 12. When Bucephalus died in battle in 326 BCE, Alexander named a city after him (believed to be Jhelum in present-day Pakistan).

High in the Andes, the llama was the only animal on the American continent that humans could get any work out of – besides the dog. This left American civilization with a crucial handicap waiting to be exposed by the arrival of Europeans.

dog and is able to curb its instincts enough to be safe to keep. As such, frequent attempts have been made to domesticate it. But it will not breed in captivity, so all these attempts have failed.

The result of these requirements is that there are only a handful of large animals eligible for domestication. Almost all of these existed throughout Europe and Asia 10,000 years ago. Food production and distribution, trade and war are fundamental to civilization. By providing a reliable food source, by pulling carts and later ploughs, and by carrying soldiers into battle, these animals played a large part in the advancement of European and Asian civilization.

Elsewhere, the only mammal of any size able to be domesticated was the llama or alpaca of the Andes. This early handicap in moving from hunting animals to taming them for work or food was the first reason a technological divide began to open up between Europe and Asia on the one hand and the peoples of sub-Saharan Africa, the Americas and in particular Australia on the other.

The Special Relationship

The dog, the cat and the horse are all eaten by humans, along with other domestic animals, but this offends many people because these animals have developed closer relationships with us.

The horse gradually superseded the ox as the main draught animal, but more importantly it allowed itself to be ridden. Riding a large, fast animal is dangerous and requires a special degree of trust and communication between rider and mount. The bond between Alexander the Great and his horse Bucephalus is a famous example of this intimacy. Bucephalus was deemed untameable but 12-year-old Alexander, realizing he was spooked by his shadow, was able to calm and ride him. So began perhaps the closest relationship of Alexander's life.

The dog has taken trust and communication still further. The loyalty and sensitivity to its leader's mood that a pack-hunting animal such as the dog instinctively displays looks to a human very much like other emotions such as love and understanding. Domestic dogs have developed these communication skills far beyond the capabilities of their wild cousins – and added to them by barking, which wild dogs do not bother with as adults.

Adult barking is only one of several general traits shared by all domestic dogs. In addition, they have shorter, rounder faces, floppier ears and curlier tails. All of these things are characteristics that only puppies have in the wild. In a sense, every domestic dog is a puppy. Humans wanted to be master to a servant but they willingly became also parent to a child. The therapeutic effect a pet can have on a human is so widely recognized that it is made use of today by health-care providers.

Although the cat is a lone hunter, it too has adapted its behaviour enough to enter into this sort of relationship. In the wild it is only kittens that meow, just as it is only puppies that bark. As adults, both cats and dogs learn body language well enough to dispense with verbal language. But they realize that humans respond best to verbal communication. This, perhaps more than anything, has made it possible for humans to regard them as one of the family.

Once an animal starts talking to a human it is a short step to regarding their personality as human. Most animals have had mythologies and cults built around them but the dog and the cat more than any other. The cat has been seen as a hedonist at least since Egyptian times, when Bastet was worshipped as the pleasure-loving goddess of music and dancing – also protector of pregnant women. There was an enormous cemetery of mummified cats at her city of Bubastis near the mouths of the Nile.

There were also huge dog cemeteries at Hardai, the sacred city of the Egyptian dog or jackal god Anubis, who weighed the souls of the dead and guided them to the afterlife. Given their loyalty, perhaps it is not surprising that moral virtues should be the qualities most mythologized in connection with dogs. In Homer's *Odyssey* it is only his faithful dog who recognizes Odysseus when he arrives home after 20 years. Equally loyal, Yudhishthira, the hero of the *Mahabharata*, refuses to enter heaven without his dog – whereupon the dog turns out all along to have been Dharma, god of justice.

Role reversal. Supposedly, this Labrador guide dog has a master, but when they leave the house it is not easy to decide who is in control of the relationship. At any rate, it seems that originally, both the dog and the cat largely domesticated themselves.

7: The Grindstone

10,000 years ago, across hillsides in south-west Asia, small groups of people were spearheading a revolution to which all subsequent revolutions in human history would be footnotes.

Above: A new way of life. A farmer ploughs the soil ready for sowing near Tanumshede, in south-west Sweden, sometime between 1800 and 600 BCE. Iron ploughs, which became more common towards the end of this period, allowed farming to spread throughout Europe.

A Reason to Settle Down

As the last Ice Age drew to a close, the climate became warmer and wetter. All over the globe plants flourished and produced new varieties. In the so-called Fertile Crescent, an area of hills and river valleys curving up the east coast of the Mediterranean into what is now southern Turkey and down through present-day Iraq, quantities of wild wheat and barley steadily increased. These were small plants with large seeds, well adapted to long, hot summers and short rainy seasons.

Other types of grain grew wild here too, helped by the variety of growing conditions that could be found in this region. In fact, the overwhelming majority of the world's cereals grew wild here, which gave this part of the planet, and subsequently Europe and Asia in general, a significant head start on the rest of the world in civilization building.

The size and shape of a cereal plant makes it easy to harvest and its large seeds make it worth harvesting because these seeds contain protein and carbohydrate. These seeds will also keep if they are kept dry.

So, as the harvests of wild grain increased, especially along the hills of the Levant, the nomadic hunter-gatherers who came to this area began to move camp only twice a year. In the summer, they would build tents on higher ground where they could take advantage of the wild harvests; in the winter they would move down into the valleys and make camp by the shores of lakes, such as the Sea of Galilee. The harvests they reaped supplemented their hunting and fishing and these people were doing all right.

Around 11,000 BCE, the wild harvests had become so abundant that the members of a culture archaeologists call Natufian gave up moving down to the lakeside in winter and began to build permanent huts in the woodland belt of the hills. Here they turned their attention to getting the most out of their harvesting, becoming ever more dependent on cereals as their staple food.

So they developed new tools. To cut the grain they made razor-sharp sickles with volcanic glass (obsidian) from the mountains of present-day Turkey, where there were extinct volcanoes. To carry the grain they wove baskets from locally available reeds. To grind the grain into flour they made grindstones: one smooth stone that could be slid across a larger one on which the grain was placed. It was a heavy tool, a tool for people who were no longer on the move.

Sowing the Seeds of a Revolution

At the same time, men were hunting dwindling numbers of gazelle and beginning to herd the wild goats and sheep that roamed the hills. They cut down trees to make room for their herds to graze – a policy that in time would help to turn large areas into desert. They took part in the harvest, too, but it was the women who had most to do with wheat and barley, especially at the grindstone; grinding was women's work.

So it was the women who began to notice what happened to the grains that fell around the grindstone and germinated in the disturbed soil nearby, and particularly a little further away on the refuse heap where dung, vegetable peelings, bones and ash acted as fertilizer. Of course they knew how plants grew; all hunter-gatherers are practical botanists. But now that they were living in the same place all year, they could observe how easily these spilled grains germinated and how much better they grew in weed-free and fertilized conditions.

Now there were also more mouths to feed because staying in one place meant women were having babies more often. Nomadic hunter-gatherers used several methods, from contraception to infanticide, to make sure they had no more than one child at a time so young it had to be carried. They could not afford to have children more frequently than one every four years. Now this had changed, which meant that the wild harvests, though plentiful, were getting used up more quickly.

Then, after 9000 BCE, the weather turned cooler and drier and harvests suffered. Some people left the hills and went back to their semi-nomadic hunting, fishing and gathering lifestyles. But others found it harder to move on. They had been settled for a long time now. They had bigger families, smaller children, and heavier possessions, such as grindstones. They had put time into making a home; they had lost the habit of living out of a knapsack.

So they began to help the wild harvests along. By about 8500 BCE, people living in the hillsides of the Jordan Valley had begun to sow wheat seeds in soil they had prepared to be soft, fertilized and free from competing plants.

As ye have sown, so shall ye reap. A farmer from the 5th millennium BCE carries the tool of his trade over his shoulder: a sickle for harvesting grain. For thousands of years, however, people reaped wild harvests before they ever sowed grain themselves.

The Cultivation of Plants

Today, thousands of plants are cultivated around the world, many for food or other products. Of these, a small number fuelled the growth of early settled societies in a handful of zones. The importance of the Fertile Crescent (shown in the inset box) is two-fold. Early cultivation of a package of crops in this region led to the first towns. In addition, grain farming was exported from this zone to India, Egypt and Europe. Some crops, such as rice or squash, were cultivated independently at different times and places; others, such as cacao or poppy, far from their natural habitat. Dates, especially for tropical crops, must be provisional.

ATLANTIC OCEAN

PACIFIC OCEAN

Oats 2000 BCE
Poppy 5000 BCE

Maygrass 500 BCE
Sunflower 2500 BCE
Little Barley 500 BCE
Squash 2500 BCE

Cotton 4300 BCE
Cacao 1000 BCE
Maize 4000 BCE
Avocado 7000 BCE
Peppers 4000 BCE
Common Bean 300 BCE
Squash 5500 BCE
Agave 5000 BCE

Pearl Millet 2000 BCE
Sorghu 2000 B
African Yam 7000 BCE
Rice 1500 BCE
Oil Palm 3000 BCE

Tobacco 3000 BCE
Cassava 3500 BCE
Common Bean 2400 BCE
Sweet Potato 3500 BCE
Lima Bean 2000 BCE
Potato 5500 BCE
Peppers 7400 BCE
Coca 3000 BCE
Cotton 3200 BCE
Quinoa 4000 BCE
Peanut 5500 BCE

Key

Staple foods
- Cereals
- Roots and tubers
- Pulses
- Fruit
- Other seeds
- Plants grown mainly for oil
- Plants grown mainly for fibre
- Stimulants
- —— Extent of Fertile Crescent
- – – Extent of Fertile Crescent after 5000 BCE
- ⟶ Wheat, barley and flax reached here from the Fertile Crescent by the date shown.

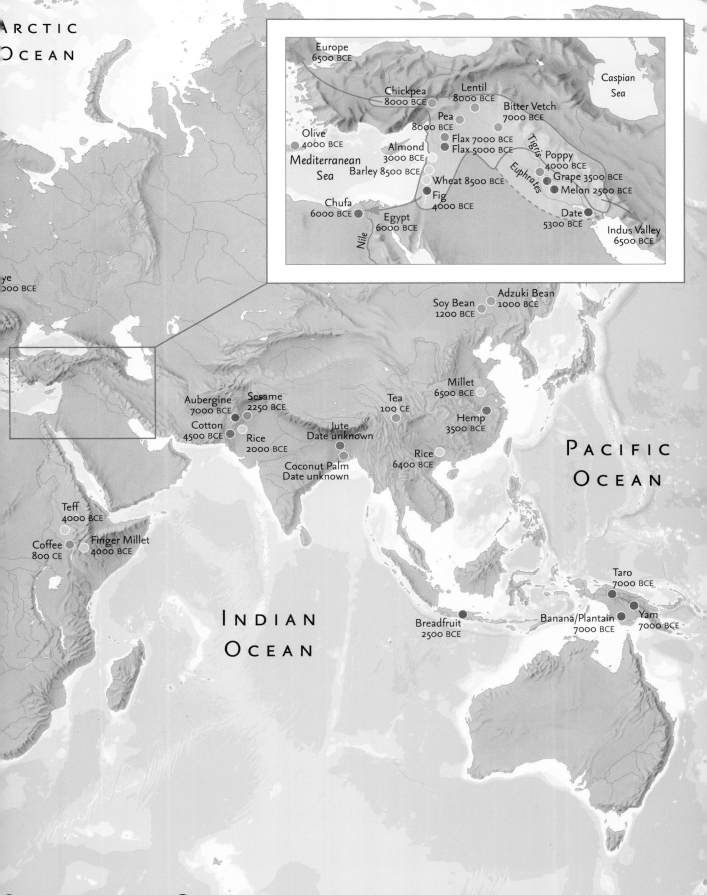

ARCTIC
OCEAN

Europe
6500 BCE

Chickpea
8000 BCE

Lentil
8000 BCE

Bitter Vetch
7000 BCE

Caspian
Sea

Pea
8000 BCE

Flax 7000 BCE
Flax 5000 BCE

Tigris

Poppy
4000 BCE

Olive
4000 BCE

Almond
3000 BCE

Mediterranean
Sea

Barley 8500 BCE

Wheat 8500 BCE

Euphrates

Grape 3500 BCE
Melon 2500 BCE

Chufa
6000 BCE

Fig
4000 BCE

Egypt
6000 BCE

Date
5300 BCE

Nile

Indus Valley
6500 BCE

ye
00 BCE

Soy Bean
1200 BCE

Adzuki Bean
1000 BCE

Millet
6500 BCE

Tea
100 CE

Aubergine
7000 BCE

Sesame
2250 BCE

Hemp
3500 BCE

Cotton
4500 BCE

Jute
Date unknown

Rice
2000 BCE

Rice
6400 BCE

PACIFIC
OCEAN

Coconut Palm
Date unknown

Teff
4000 BCE

Coffee
800 CE

Finger Millet
4000 BCE

Taro
7000 BCE

INDIAN
OCEAN

Breadfruit
2500 BCE

Banana/Plantain
7000 BCE

Yam
7000 BCE

SOUTHERN   OCEAN

The Fruits of Labour

To begin with, the so-called Neolithic, or 'New Stone Age', Revolution did not appear to be bearing much fruit. The first farmers had invented hard work but they were still struggling to put food on the table. The skeletons of these people show a sharp increase in both arthritis and malnourishment in relation to their hunter-gatherer predecessors.

However, they had committed themselves to their pioneering experiment and they stuck it out. By 8000 BCE, yields had become more plentiful because adequate rain was falling once more – in addition to which, the farmers, by cultivating grain, had unintentionally selected certain traits.

The stalks of a wild cereal such as wheat are brittle. This allows the seeds to break off and scatter one by one as they become ripe, giving the plant the best chance of reproducing itself. Some, of course, are

The technology that started it all. The grindstone made wild grain a useful food, thus increasing demand. In addition, it discouraged people from moving due to its weight, and it encouraged seeds to spill and germinate around the campsite.

more brittle than others. The least brittle will hold onto its seeds longest and this plant will have the worst chance of reproducing itself.

The seeds of these plants, however, being all still attached to the stalk, are more likely to be harvested, more likely to fall around the grindstone, more likely to get sown. So, paradoxically, it is this plant that has the best chance of reproducing itself if there are farmers around.

In this way, the farmed wheat gradually became less brittle and more able to hold its seeds in place, allowing the farmer to reap a little more each year. Within a framework of cultivation, a process of natural selection was taking place. One day the farmer would learn to produce new plant varieties deliberately. For the moment it was happening accidentally but the result was the same: the cultivated grain now looked very different from the wild grain and yielded a bigger harvest. When this stage was reached, there began to be an investment to protect.

So there came to be property. The grain the farmer had nurtured was now worth more than the wild grain. But this was only as a result of the farmer's

Agribusiness around 1375 BCE. As the mainstay of the Egyptian economy, grain farming was an industry organized to maximize production. Nevertheless, in the soft river silt of the Nile Valley it was still feasible to plough by hand, as in this scene from the tomb of Unsou, an official of the New Kingdom.

labour, so it was natural to feel the cultivated grain belonged to the farmer. This grain, however, was growing on a particular patch of ground, so farming people began to consider they had rights not only to the crops they tended but also to the land on which the crops grew. After all, they had laboured on this land.

Then they noticed that some areas of land were more fertile than others, more worth labouring on than others, more worth owning. So they moved to these areas, planted crops on them and declared the land their property. This was a new way of thinking about humans and their relationship to the natural world that brought farming people into conflict with hunters and gatherers of wild food. So the farmers began to elbow out their neighbours. It was the beginning of a long tradition.

The Grindstone   59

The Plough

Before humans hit one stone on another, there was the digging stick. It was the first tool of all, used to break up soil and get at edible roots. Millions of years later the first farmers used it in the same way, but to sow seeds instead.

Breaking up hillside soil, however, required force, so the design was modified. A branch with the stump of another branch sticking out at the end could be swung between the legs like a pick-axe while the farmer walked backwards. The hoe had been invented.

Around 6000 BCE, hillside farmers moved down into the river valleys where the soil was lighter. Here it was often enough just to drag the hoe along the ground, leaving a furrow into which seeds could be dropped.

The end of the hoe would jump about, however, when it hit a stone or a harder clod of earth. So a handle was attached at this end on which a second person could press down while the first person pulled the hoe along. The hoe had become the plough.

By about 4000 BCE, this wooden plough was being drawn by an ox instead of a person. It still could only cope with light soil, however, so agriculture could not spread far from river valleys.

As iron became more widely available in the 1st millennium BCE, the plough was redesigned. A narrow blade or coulter broke the soil first and set behind this a wider, flatter ploughshare turned it to one side. The new, stronger material and more efficient design meant all kinds of previously unworkable soil could now be cultivated. It is really from this time that farming finally moved out of a few particular locations to claim large parts of Europe, Asia and eventually the rest of the world.

Flour Power

At the centre of the new farming life lay a new food: bread. At first there were unleavened breads such as pita or chapati. Then, by 4000 BCE, bread leavened with yeast appeared in Egypt. As societies grew, grain production and trade became big business – Egyptian wheat was exported to Greece and Rome. Bread became the fuel that allowed urban communities to exist.

More bread meant more flour. A woman with a family of four could expect to spend three hours at the grindstone each morning. To speed things up, new designs were introduced, such as the rotary quern shown on page 58, but soon a search for new sources of power began. First, oxen or teams of workers were used to turn giant rotary querns. But in Alexandria by the 2nd century BCE, mammal power was giving way to water power.

The watermill, a virtual perpetual-motion machine, brought round-the-clock grinding. From the 3rd century CE, big state-sponsored milling complexes spread throughout the Roman Empire, stretching engineering expertise and enabling military expansion. At Barbegal in Provence, a complex of 16 millstones fed by aqueduct produced 28 tons of flour a day, enough for the nearby port of Arles plus garrisons across southern

Modern monoculture. Mechanized ploughing, sowing and reaping has transformed the landscape of huge areas of the world in order to put bread on the table. It is a transformation that has allowed an ever-expanding population to be supported, but not without cost to the environment.

France. Watermills were so indispensible to big cities that when the Goths cut the water supply to Rome in 537 CE, the population only avoided starving by mounting waterwheels on barges moored on the River Tiber.

Ship-mills of this kind, using strong currents, really took off within the Muslim world, where most farming was concentrated in large river valleys. In the 10th century CE, Baghdad's population of 1.5 million was supported by ship-mills on the fast-flowing River Tigris, each producing 10 tons of flour a day.

A source of constant power having been harnessed, industry developed. In China, waterwheels for husking rice were adapted for papermaking and forging iron by the 1st century CE. This involved activating mechanical hammers, which meant tranferring rotary motion to linear motion by inventing machine parts such as the cam and, later on, the crankshaft.

In Medieval Europe, the windmill became widespread, though water remained the main source of power. Rivers were dammed and waterwheel technology expanded, driving industries from timber to textiles – and, by the 18th century, generating electricity.

The consequences of the Neolithic Revolution are hard to exaggerate. For most of our time on this planet we were hunters of wild animals and gatherers of wild plants, living in small, roughly egalitarian groups. As soon as we began producing our own food, we opened the door to faster population growth, property rights, industrial-scale technology and a raft of economic, social and political developments that followed suit.

Natural selection reversed by unconscious human intervention. Simply by repeated harvesting and sowing, wispy and brittle wild einkorn wheat (left) turned into a more substantial and manageable domestic variety (right), which now depended on humans for propagation.

8: Pottery

We live in a world of stored food. Fridges, freezers, tin cans and vacuum packs allow us to pursue all kinds of jobs that have nothing to do with the constant search for food that dominates the lives of other animals. Pottery, the first material not just worked on but created by humans, opened the door to this world.

Above: Early kitchenware. Ceramic cooking pots of this design were being made in Japan as long as 16,000 years ago. The pot's pointed shape allowed it to sit with its base buried in the embers of a fire, while a stew simmered inside.

Carving and modelling represent different approaches to manufacturing. The carver begins with an object and reduces it, removing material to reveal another object. The modeller begins with material and builds it up to form an object. It is an easier, more versatile process, as long as you have the right material. Clay is ideal; it is smooth, it sticks together and it keeps its shape. The use of clay is limited, however, because it will absorb water even after it has dried. But when clay is dried at a high temperature, its chemical structure is transformed so that it can no longer absorb water. The result is pottery; a permanently hard material that can have been made in all kinds of different shapes.

The earliest pottery was made at least 30,000 years ago by placing clay items directly onto the campfire. At this time people were not living in permanent settled communities, so their pottery consisted of figurines small enough to carry. Later, when their living circumstances had changed to allow heavier items to be made, pottery would lay one of the foundation stones of civilization by freeing some people from the continual cycle of looking for food.

Kitchen and Larder

Shards from the earliest ceramic pot found so far have recently been dated to around 14,000 BCE, and come from Japan. Over the following few thousand years, plant species proliferated throughout Japan as the climate became warmer and wetter. Evergreen, deciduous and coniferous forests spread up the centre of the islands, and with them animals multiplied. Sea levels rose, surrounding Japan with shallow waters teeming with hundreds of varieties of fish and other seafood.

For the various peoples who inhabited the country (called Jomon after the style of pottery they made), wild food became so plentiful they found they could hunt, gather and fish all year without moving camp. The less they moved, the more easily they could live with heavy possessions, such as pots.

The pots they made could hold food and drink. They could also withstand heat, so people could now boil their food as well as roast it. Boiling gave them more things to eat. The oak forest was full of acorns, which were a highly nutritious food – except they contained toxins. Now, however, these toxins could be boiled out. Green vegetables, such as cabbage and lettuce, which previously would have shrivelled up on the campfire, could now be boiled or added to stews.

More seafood became available, too; the most tightly shut shellfish would yield after a few minutes in boiling water.

Boiling produced not only more food, it also produced softer food and soups, food that was easier to eat for people without strong teeth. This meant babies could be weaned earlier and old people could live longer. As a result, populations slowly began to grow and spread until, by 5000 BCE, the whole of Japan was fairly evenly settled by villages, mostly of a dozen or so houses.

But there was an equally important use for pottery that villagers now started to exploit: storage. They dug underground pits about 1.8 metres (6 feet) deep and wide in which pots and baskets of food could be kept cool. Nuts that would keep well over the winter, such as acorns, walnuts and chestnuts, were a particular favourite for the larder.

An abundance of food, staying in one place and making pottery containers gave Jomon communities the ability to store a surplus of food. This allowed them to alter their social relationships in a way that brought them to the threshold of building a civilization.

The Professional

A stored surplus of food gave Jomon people choices. By this time, ceramic pots were making such a difference to people's lives that it made economic sense to give some of the stored food to someone who could specialize in making pots full-time. This person was now free to develop their skill and produce better-quality pots in bigger quantities, while the other villagers could spend more time gathering acorns or boiling the toxins out of them. So the potter came into existence, the first professional craftsperson. There is evidence to suggest that other crafts, such as basket-weaving, may have followed suit.

The increased efficiency that this division of labour produced was never fully realized by Jomon cultures, however. By around 3000 BCE they had moved from making purely functional items to producing elaborately expressive works that were as much sculptures as pots. But they continued to live in villages with seldom more than 50 houses. They never made metal tools, they never wove textiles, they never developed writing.

Why did they not evolve in the way we would expect? There could be a number of reasons. Relative isolation from societies on the mainland and an

abundance of wild food, the lack of which might have pushed them into organizing themselves to work together. Or perhaps it was simply that they were hunter-gatherers, opportunists – not farmers thinking in terms of systematically increasing production. As such there was a limit to the amount of surplus food they could stockpile.

The Town Centre

Elsewhere, the situation was different. In south-west Asia people began to make pots around 6900 BCE, up to 7,000 years after the earliest Jomon pots, and it took several hundred years more for them to produce pots strong enough to cook food in. But these people were not living on an island, they were living at the crossroads of Europe, Asia and Africa, where ideas spread and where there was competition for resources. They were not gathering wild food either; they were cultivating it.

Instead of nuts gathered from the forest, the surplus these people stored was mainly grain they had grown. Other cultivated crops followed – dates, various vegetables and, by 4000 BCE, the olive, from which oil was pressed. People in this region were also herding animals and getting milk from them. Pottery allowed them to store these products conveniently, especially the liquids. In addition, deliberate cultivation meant that more and more of these foodstuffs could be produced. As farmers increased production, they made more pots to store more food to allow more people to do other jobs.

Perhaps even before they built permanent dwellings to live in these people built a communal storeroom for their valuables – their sacred objects and their surplus food. Long after farmers had settled for good nearby, the shepherds and goatherders of the community continued to roam and therefore to rely on the storeroom. The person in charge of the storeroom played an important role, being responsible for safeguarding both produce and religious artefacts. Increasingly, people came here to make votive offerings as well as to deliver surplus produce.

After about 3000 BCE, Jomon potters moved away from churning out containers of simple, functional design in uniform batches. Instead, they became more interested in the expressive, ornamental and ceremonial potential of their craft.

While later Jomon potters were expressing themselves, professionals in Crete were producing bigger storage vessels to support larger communities. Many pithoi in the storerooms of the Palace of Knossos (c. 1700 BCE) were over 1.5 metres (5 feet) tall.

The storeroom became the centre around which the village grew. The space outside the storeroom became the natural place to hold the various religious festivals that punctuated the farming calendar and which drew people from many miles around into the village. These festivals were always accompanied by a market, at which craft products could be exchanged.

Gradually, over the course of many hundreds of years, the potter, the basket-maker, the weaver each began to practice their trade in a workshop instead of in or around the home, and the natural location for these workshops was near the marketplace. So the professional set up a business in premises across from the storeroom in the centre of the village.

The Wheel

The Jomon and all other early potters built their pots up from coils of clay. They rolled the clay into a long sausage and coiled the end of it round to form a circle. They continued coiling round on top of this circle until a second circle had been formed. Then they smoothed these two coils into each other to make a flat wall. On top of this they continued the process, building up the wall of their pot coil by coil.

If you try this yourself you will find you naturally keep turning the pot with one hand as you work on it with the other. To make turning easier, early potters built up their pots inside a bowl and turned the whole bowl. Turning a round-bottomed bowl is quite easy because only a small portion in the centre is in contact with the ground or the table.

Once the pot had been formed, however, it was easier to remove it from a flat surface than from a curved one, so pots began to be built up on discs of wood with a flat top but still with a rounded underside. The underside shrank until it was no more than a central knob allowing easy turning.

But it is easier to work on something if it is anchored in one place. There were two ways this could be done. The rounded or knob-like underside of the worksurface could be lengthened to form a pole that slotted into a base. Alternatively, a hole could be made in the underside and the worksurface mounted on a fixed spike. Either way, turning the disc-shaped pot stand around a fixed axis was the crucial step. The story of the wheel is not the story of a circular object, it is the story of an axle.

This point was probably reached before 4000 BCE in south-west Asia and perhaps independently around 3000 BCE in China. From here, the potter's wheel developed in different ways. A heavy flywheel was added to provide enough centrifugal force for thrown pots to be made. By the early 1st millennium BCE, a potter's wheel had been mounted on its side to become the wood-turning lathe. By the 3rd century BCE, in both China and the West, a potter's wheel with notches around the edge had become the cog wheel, the starting point for watermills, clocks and all kinds of complex machinery.

Already by 3000 BCE, the wheel was being used for transport in Sumer, in today's Iraq – first to make chariots for war, later to make carts. But the wheeled vehicle needs a strong domesticated animal to pull it and an even surface to roll on. The First Emperor of China (221–210 BCE) made axles a standard length so the wheels of all vehicles would run in the same furrows. The wheel was known to the peoples of Mesoamerica by at least 500 BCE but they put wheels only on the toys they made; they could build no chariots or carts because they had no animals to pull them.

Right: The coming of the wheel. Circular objects are all around us but once we try to turn them the need for an axle becomes obvious.

Below: This is one of the earliest Sumerian images of the wheel – already a single wooden disc, which easily warped and split, had become three pieces joined together and surrounded by a rim.

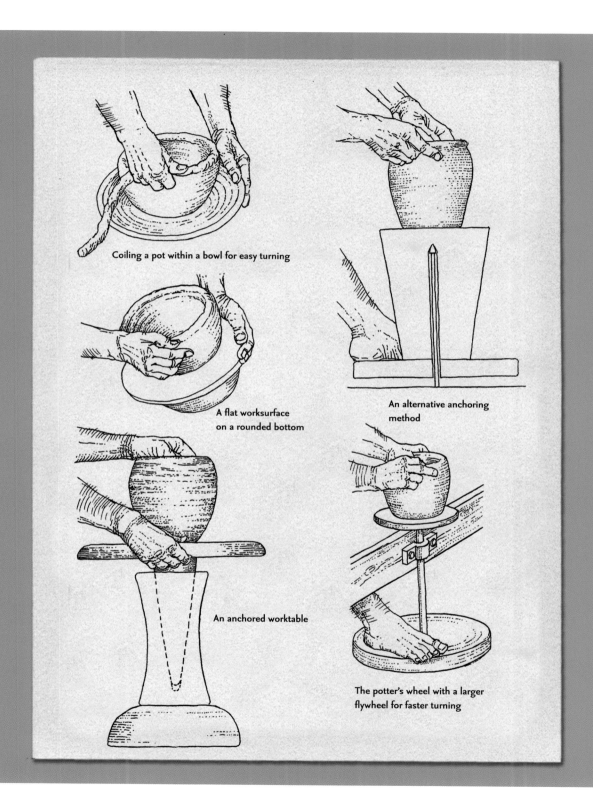

Coiling a pot within a bowl for easy turning

A flat worksurface on a rounded bottom

An alternative anchoring method

An anchored worktable

The potter's wheel with a larger flywheel for faster turning

The Status of Women

The place of women in society was not helped by the emergence of the professional craftsperson, who was almost always a craftsman, not a craftswoman. Most early crafts had been developed by women because they were the ones who spent more time near the home with their children. The men could hardly make things while they were hunting, fishing or herding animals.

Basket-making, weaving and sewing, and making pots were all skills women practised when they found the time. The products they designed and made generally arose out of needs they identified in their roles of gathering and preparing food and keeping order in the home. Baskets in which to carry food back to the home, pots in which to store it, cook it, serve it, mats to lay on the floor; these were all important items and the person who made them was valued for her skills.

Full-time specialization did not fit in well with women's lives, however. Who would look after the children and the home? By contrast, men's lives were more suited to concentrating on a single activity all day. Consequently, as crafts became professional, they passed from women's hands into men's hands, and as they did so women lost the standing they had had in the community as the makers of essential items, such as cooking pots.

The new full-time potter was an important person, more highly regarded than part-time potters had been because now the whole village relied on this person for all its pots. The professional potter, weaver, basket-maker became a pillar of the community – but this person was no longer a woman.

A storage pot from Çatalhöyük, modern-day Turkey. Çatalhöyük was one of the largest early farming towns, with a population of several thousand people during the 7th millennium BCE. The holes may have been for hanging the pot from the rafters, so it was probably used to store something light.

9: The Public Works Programme

With people rushing around and buildings jostling for space, a city can seem a chaotic place. If it really were chaotic, however, it could never survive; every city has to be a highly-structured organism.

Above: The basis of urban living: an efficient sewage system. In 2500 BCE, the drains of Mohenjo-daro in the Indus Valley of present-day Pakistan kept a city of 40,000 people functioning smoothly.

Civilization is bound up with the growth of cities. At its simplest, a city is an organism facing the same basic problems as the body: how to take in nutrients and get rid of waste. Management of water and sewage are the foundations of civic life; without them no settlement can grow beyond a certain size.

However, municipal water and sewage works are large-scale projects requiring planning and the co-ordination of a labour force, hallmarks of a certain type of social structure. In some parts of the world a particular environment pushed people into developing this structure and where this occurred cities followed.

A New Location
Growing plants depends on water. The easiest way to get this water is to wait for it to fall out of the sky. That is why farming began on hillsides across the Fertile Crescent where there was adequate rainfall. By 6000 BCE, however,

people started to move down from the hills into the valley created by the course of the Tigris and Euphrates rivers. The Greeks called this place Mesopotamia – 'the land between the rivers'. Today it is Iraq.

The first people to farm in Mesopotamia settled along the Tigris in the north of the valley where there was still just enough rainfall but around 5300 BCE some of these people moved down to the extreme south of the region near the Gulf where there was hardly any rain at all.

Here the two rivers broke their banks every spring, flooding the whole area and turning it into a

Evidence of planning and co-operation. Cutting terraces for rice cultivation into the hillsides of northern Luzon in the Philippines is a construction project of awesome scale, requiring the mobilization of thousands of labourers. Once cut, terraces have to be constantly maintained.

land of marshes and reed beds. Then, as the waters receded and no rain came, the earth baked dry in the unrelenting heat. In time, this inhospitable place would become known as Sumer, and the people who settled here would build the world's first cities.

Although there was a challenge posed by the lack of rain and the behaviour of the two rivers (especially the violent and unpredictable Tigris), the soil in this region was very fertile. It was mainly silt brought down by the rivers in the spring floods, a new layer being delivered each year. It was light enough to be broken up by the wooden plough – little more than a digging stick – which was used by these people. For the land to be of any use for growing crops, however, the rivers would have to be tamed.

Water Management

Dykes had to be built along the riverbanks to stop the flooding. Then water had to be led in a controlled way to the fields. Several methods of doing this were tried but the most popular was to dig a canal leading from the river, then to dig smaller canals leading off the first canal, then yet smaller canals leading off these, and so on, until the fields were criss-crossed by a lattice-work of irrigation channels bringing water to the crops throughout the season.

This proved to be a very efficient way of farming, producing yields that were twice what they had been further north where rainfall alone had been relied upon. On the other hand, the construction of this kind of combined flood-prevention and irrigation system was a monumental task.

Building the first dykes and digging the first canals demanded all available labour. Moreover, each spring the swollen rivers would eat away at the dykes and deposit silt in the canals so that they had to be dug out again. Maintaining these dykes and canals became an ongoing project – and one that affected the whole community.

For hundreds of years, people lived in small villages and clubbed together informally to meet this task when they had the time or when there was an emergency. Maintenance was a matter for each village to sort out. But gradually some villages grew larger, becoming centres for religious ceremony, trade and other services to a group of surrounding villages. Now local irrigation networks began to merge to form one large, interdependent system.

As this happened, the need for overall management became more apparent. The system had to be constantly monitored for weak spots; too much or too little water in one part of the system could affect a field in quite another area. Programmes of essential works had to be drawn up and prioritized. Teams of labourers had to be collected together, told what to do and, most importantly, fed.

In these early days, the Sumerians operated a simple form of democracy that had evolved out of village life. The heads of the various extended families that made up the village formed a small council that met to decide matters affecting the community. On particularly important issues this council of elders would call a general assembly of all adult villagers (there is conflicting evidence as to whether this included women). The irrigation system now required continual overseeing, so the assembly decided to elect a full-time manager.

The Tax Collector

The natural choice seemed to be the person who already looked after the storeroom where both surplus food and religious objects were kept. These objects – votive figurines, offerings of different kinds – were concerned with the worship of gods important to the fertility of the land. They had begun to form a sort of shrine in the same building where the products of this fertility – the food surplus – was kept. The person in charge of this building was respected as the agent of a religion that specialized in guaranteeing good harvests. He was consulted to decide the best time to plough and the best time to sow. Who else but he should oversee the irrigation network?

The Sumerian title for this new manager was *en*, often translated as 'priest' or simply 'lord', but which carries more the idea of 'charismatic leader and manager of production'. His first problem was how to support his work-gangs. In the past, these work-gangs had been comprised of farmers in the off-season, fed from the food they had produced and stored themselves, and this arrangement continued to operate.

Now, however, the *en* also started to assemble other work-gangs of non-farmers at times when the farmers themselves were not available. These people produced no food but their work benefited everyone by making food production possible. So the *en* decided to set aside a portion of the stored food for these work-gangs.

Since the food surplus was made up from varying amounts of food produced by families reaping bigger or smaller harvests, the most workable way to set aside a portion was to claim the same fixed percentage from each family's harvest – in short, to create a tax system.

Together, council and assembly still formed the highest authority in town but they were not involved in day-to-day management. They had elected an *en* who controlled a public workforce paid for by taxes that he himself had set. Society was now, in effect, run by a centralized administration with one man at the top giving the orders.

Town Planning

With a taxation system in place to pay for maintaining the water works, other construction projects in the public interest became possible. The first of these was the division of the storeroom into two separate buildings: the granary and the temple. Once a single-use religious building had been constructed, other elements of a planned urban landscape followed.

All the earliest civilizations came into being on a similar model. Along the Nile in Egypt, in the Indus Valley of present-day Pakistan, along the Yellow River in northern China, as well as in Mesoamerica and the

The Home

Humans first sheltered as a group – in caves, then in large tent-like huts made from branches. Inside these huts they made a fire within a ring of stones. A hole in the roof let the smoke out. Such structures were built at Terra Amata, southern France 380,000 years ago.

Little changed in house design for hundreds of thousands of years. By 16,000 BCE, people were using mammoth bones, tusks and skins to build pretty much the same communal shelter in the Ukraine. All these huts contained two essential features of any home: shelter from the elements and somewhere to cook. However, they lacked other important features; they were not permanent, they were not private and they had only one room.

By around 10,000 BCE, gatherers of wild grain who had settled in the hills of the Levant were investing more time in building the huts in which they intended to stay. They built

A dwelling from the Skara Brae settlement (3100–2500 BCE) on Orkney, off the coast of Scotland. The interior space of the home has been compartmentalized for different functions – there is even a sideboard – but there is still only one room.

stone walls and sank them into the ground. By the time people in this area were sowing their own grain, they had invented the mud brick. After 8000 BCE, these bricks were being mass-produced in moulds.

Over the next 2,000 years, villages of flat-roofed, mud-brick houses huddled close together were built throughout south-west Asia. Çatalhöyük in present-day Turkey was the largest. The houses of Çatalhöyük were not large communal shelters but small family dwellings. In addition, each house had separate rooms. One room was for storage, one for sleeping and one for cooking. Instead of a fire in the middle of the floor there was a stove set into the wall.

All the buildings in Çatalhöyük were joined together. The front door of each house was in its roof with a ladder leading down into the house itself. By Sumerian and Egyptian times, houses were separated by streets and entered at ground level.

By the time of the Harappan cities, the division of functions inside the home was very similar to that in the homes of developed countries today. Each house contained an inner courtyard, bedrooms and a kitchen. It had its own well, a brick-floored bathroom and a flushing toilet that emptied into the public drains through ceramic pipes.

By 1700 BCE, the king of Minos had hot and cold running water in his bathroom at Knossos on the island of Crete. He also had a modern-style individual bathtub. By Roman times, lead pipes had made plumbing much more common. Wealthy houses now had central-heating systems too.

The house had become more than a communal shelter from the weather with a place to cook simple meals. It had evolved into a permanent dwelling for a single family, split up into rooms in which different activities could be performed. Advances, such as plumbing, refined the kinds of activities the house could offer, making it into a machine for living a domestic life.

There were now two very distinct kinds of life a person could live: a public life and a private life.

river valleys of the Peruvian coast, societies grew up based on centrally organizing labour to construct flood defences and irrigation systems, or sometimes other huge landscaping projects, such as cutting terraces out of a hillside to make fields. A tax system was common to societies in all these areas, and other public building projects followed on from agricultural works, producing cities with striking similarities in parts of the world often completely cut off from each other.

Perhaps the most remarkable examples of early town planning were the Harappan cities of the Indus Valley, the best known being Harappa itself and Mohenjo-daro, each with populations of about 40,000 people. These two cities, about 650 kilometres (400 miles) apart, were built around 2500 BCE. They shared the same basic layout, with the temple and granary at the centre of the city. Harappa had two granaries with several grinding rooms, which were linked to dormitories housing municipal workers who did the grinding. In Mohenjo-daro, there was an assembly hall, a college and public baths – great pains were taken to make the pool watertight.

Both cities were laid out on a grid. The main streets ran north-south and other streets crossed these

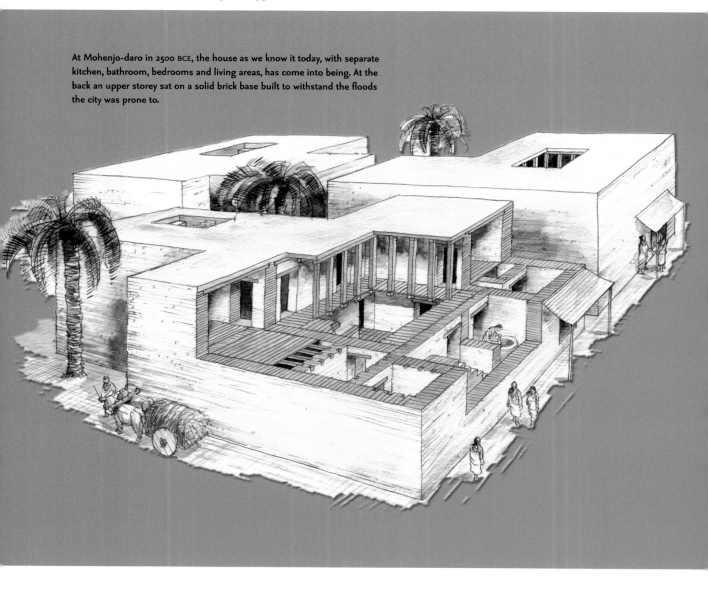

At Mohenjo-daro in 2500 BCE, the house as we know it today, with separate kitchen, bathroom, bedrooms and living areas, has come into being. At the back an upper storey sat on a solid brick base built to withstand the floods the city was prone to.

at right angles. Two- or three-storey brick houses were built according to a standard blueprint. Buildings had plumbing and a system of drains ran all over the city. There were manholes every so often so the drains could be monitored and cleared if necessary by the sanitation department.

By 100 BCE, a similarly planned yet much larger city existed about 40 kilometres (25 miles) north-east of present-day Mexico City. Teotihuacán had a population of between 100,000 and 200,000 people. Like the Harappan cities, it was laid out on a north-south, east-west grid. Several temples, administrative buildings and a workshop complex were located in the centre of the city. There were also canals and reservoirs. The temples, in common with all Mesoamerican temples, are striking for their resemblance to both Sumerian ziggurats and Egyptian pyramids.

Moving to Town

A thousand years before the great Harappan cities of the Indus Valley, the early Sumerian cities of Eridu and Uruk (which may be the origin of the name 'Iraq') were already beginning to experience certain knock-on effects of their taxation policies. As municipal facilities became more sophisticated, the lure of city living was becoming stronger. People from smaller villages were starting to think about leaving home for the bright

Irrigation works and other large-scale projects were realized by similar centralized management structures in various parts of the world. Accordingly, the first public architecture expresses the idea of central authority in equally similar styles wherever it is found. On the left, the Sumerian ziggurat at Ur (c. 2100 BCE), in present-day Iraq. On the right, the Toltec pyramid-temple of Kukulcán at Chichén Itzá (c. 1100 CE), in the Yucatán peninsula of present-day Mexico.

lights, the glamour and the new opportunities life in the big urban centres seemed to offer.

Taxation also created negative reasons to leave the countryside as much as positive incentives to move to town. As the size and grandeur of his building programme steadily increased, the en had to raise taxes in an effort to meet the increase in public spending. Farmers were hit hardest by this because taxes were levied on agricultural produce. Consequently, the more taxes went up, the more farmers tried to find a way out of their situation. Gradually, a drift from country to town began – a drift that, for reasons that will be dealt with in the next chapter, was destined to pick up pace over the coming centuries.

Over thousands of years, the practice of intensive, irrigation agriculture in itself would make country living impossible and spell disaster for the Sumerians. Rain or flooding drives salt in the soil down into the subsoil and bedrock but irrigation in a dry environment has the opposite effect. As water evaporates from the surface, water from lower down is drawn up and with it comes salt, which prevents crops from growing. Increasing levels of salt in the soil was perhaps the main reason Mesopotamia eventually became a desert.

In the Yucatán peninsula of modern-day Mexico, the same process of irrigation-induced salinity affected the Maya around 800 CE and has taken place more recently in Pakistan and the San Joaquin Valley in California. China and Egypt favoured different forms of irrigation, which made use of regular and predictable flooding and their soils were saved as a result. However, the building of the Aswan Dam in 1964 put an end to the age-old flooding of the Nile Valley and as a result salt levels in the soil have started to increase.

The Geometry of Time

Across the world, the first cities were societies of the calendar. From Sumer and Egypt to the Indus Valley, China and America, the same pattern repeated itself: the authority of the 'priest' stemmed from his ability to tell the time and this led directly to the design of public buildings.

Keeping a rough track of time is not difficult. Anyone can see for themselves the moon changing shape over the course of a month. There are also changes in the weather that roughly follow a longer cycle connected to the pattern of stars in the sky. Without electric light, people quickly notice that each sunrise the stars have moved round a little from where they were the previous morning. They come round to their original position in relation to the rising sun roughly 360 days later.

As people began to farm, the movements of the stars became more important to them because they could be used to predict the changing seasons upon which growing crops depended. Greater accuracy in pinpointing where they were in the year became associated with more reliable harvests and was therefore prized, even though being a few days out may not have affected the harvest to any noticeable degree.

The sun itself can be used to determine exactly which day it is but this involves special equipment and careful measurement. The more accurately time is measured, the more specialized a skill it becomes. The person who was elected to manage irrigation and taxation had already established his standing in the community as a guardian of the harvest by his superior timekeeping skill.

This person measured time by the length of the shadow cast on the ground by an upright post. During the course of the day this shadow moved round part of a circle and changed length. At the middle of the day the shadow was at its shortest and divided the world into two halves – east and west. The line of the shadow pointed north-south. Each day at this time the shadow was a different length because the sun had moved along the north-south line. On one day in the year the shadow was at its longest, on another it was at its shortest.

Out of these observations developed geometry. The shadows cast at sunrise on the longest and shortest days lay in different directions from the post. If lines were drawn to mark these shadows they made an angle stretching out from the post. The line that bisected this angle pointed due east-west. On two days of the year the sun rose and set along this line and the lengths of day and night were equal.

The more precise the equipment, the more precisely these measurements could be made. The ground was made smooth so the shadow would not curve. The post was set perpendicular by holding a string with a weight on its end, which made a right angle with the flat ground. Later, the rising position of the sun or stars at certain points in the year was permanently marked by other posts.

Architecture emerged from this culture of precise calendar measurement. The sides of the Great Pyramid of Khufu at Giza face north, east, south and west. The perimeter of its base is 2π its height; the relation of the circumference of a circle to its radius. This gives the sides a perfect 52-degree slope. It is hardly surprising that the streets of the first cities were often laid out on a north-south east-west grid.

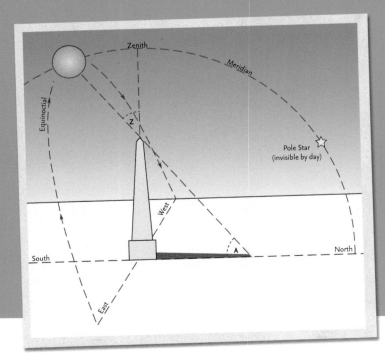

Telling the time at noon on the spring and autumn equinox, when the sun rises due east and sets due west. The plumb-line, the right-angle, the degrees of a circle; buildings of any size could not be built without these measurements.

10: The King

Whenever people come together to form a group they face the problem of how and why to co-operate. While the group is small, family ties can be used to knit people together. As the group becomes a city of thousands, relying on personal connections becomes more difficult and a new kind of social glue is needed. No society has got very far without the threat of centrally planned violence.

Above: The machinery of war, c. 2500 BCE. Above, the war chariot, the tank of its day. Below, the infantry in body armour and helmets. War was another public works project, requiring central mobilization of a large workforce. From the Royal Standard of Ur, Sumer.

A Threat From Outside

The first cities grew up in the south of Mesopotamia in particularly vulnerable circumstances. Crop cultivation was a delicate endeavour requiring the careful management of finite resources. There was a clear limit to how far from the river crops could be grown. To the north and east of this boundary there were hills and then mountains, to the west there was a desert plateau. In both places there were people who watched the blossoming of the valley into a well-tended and high-yielding garden with increasing interest.

Between 3500 and 3000 BCE, successive waves of raiders coming down from the mountains or out of the desert became an occupational hazard for the Sumerian farmers. Small outlying villages were most at risk. The inhabitants of these villages were too few to stand up to the sudden appearance of a raiding party and too isolated to summon help in time. So they left their villages and the population of Sumer became concentrated in and around a dozen or so cities. But the raids continued.

In the cities there were various specialists: potters, weavers, priestly administrators – and also people who

The spoils of war. King Eannatum of the Sumerian city of Lagash (2454–2425 BCE) boosts his personal power by taking prisoners from a battle with a neighbouring city. If they will co-operate, he can put them to work for him. If not, he can kill them.

specialized in violence. These latter each had a gang. They jostled with each other and were in the business of threatening people or offering protection to those who could be useful. In this way they built up their power.

Taking on this threat from outside, however, required all the forces the city could muster to be combined and managed with the same efficiency as the irrigation system. The various violence specialists could see this but they were rivals to each other. So the city assembly elected a lugal or 'war leader' from among these specialists in violence. The lugal was given emergency powers when the threat of raids was high. He had access to the tax revenue, he could make use of the municipal work-gangs as well as the forces of the other violence specialists, and he could take any other measures he considered necessary to the defence of the community without consulting anyone.

The other powerful families in the city were placing themselves at risk in this situation but the lugal's own henchmen made up only a minority of his troops. The rest were conscripts, which meant the balance of power still ultimately rested with the assembly and the aggregate of powerful families. So when the danger was over the lugal stepped down and handed the running of the city back to the en or 'priest-manager' whom the assembly had elected in peacetime.

An extension of this assembly eventually saw off the raiders. All the main Sumerian cities formed a league that met in the city of Nippur to co-ordinate their military response. Such a council of war made Sumer unassailable.

Bad Neighbours

After 3000 BCE, however, a new threat to the security of villagers began to appear, about which the Nippur League could do nothing. With everyone crowded into the main cities and their satellite farming villages, the finite nature of Mesopotamian resources led to arguments. As the fields administered by one city reached the fields administered by another, border disputes arose. Which city was entitled to the tax from this field? Who should control that section of the irrigation network? Too much water was already being drawn off for that city's fields upstream at the expense of this city's fields downstream. So one city sabotaged another's irrigation channels, and this demanded a response.

This time the scale of war was quite different from what it had been in the days of the desert raiders. In

The wall: favourite construction project of military leaders. The distinctive mud walls of Bam, on the old Silk Road in southern Iran, kept intruders out for much of its 2,000-year history but could not withstand an earthquake in December 2003. Today, the city lies in ruins.

2800 BCE, the city of Uruk had a population of around 80,000 people. Like all the other cities, it had a taxation system that could pay to train and arm soldiers with weapons churned out by teams of skilled craftspeople. This was war as an industry. Very quickly, what had started as border and irrigation disputes escalated into the full-scale sacking, looting and burning of cities themselves, and the killing of their inhabitants.

Before long, however, the lugal realized there was a better option open to him than simply to kill his enemies. The kind of society Sumerians had constructed meant he could make use of conquered people, especially people used to Sumerian life. Farmers were taxpayers. Their lives could be spared on condition they paid tax into a new kitty. City-dwellers could be taken as slaves. At first this applied only to women, who could be used for domestic chores or for sex, but soon men were being taken too and used on public works programmes. The first such project was the building of a high defensive wall around each city.

The Takeover

The protection the lugal afforded his city benefited everyone but most of the spoils of war became his alone – so much so that in the Sumerian language the very word for 'owner' was itself 'lugal'. The prisoners he took became his personal property. He had spared their lives, now he fed and clothed them, gave them a bed and put them to work. Many of them found jobs in the army that had captured them.

The loot and land taken by the lugal was important for buying loyalty. His gang of henchmen grew larger, mostly with captured prisoners of war. They formed the all-important core of his army, eating at his table and supporting themselves with land he had given them in return for military service. Crucially, this growing core was loyal to him personally.

The wars between the Sumerian cities became endemic to a far greater extent than in the days of the desert raiders. In those days the warfare had been ended by cities co-operating to form a larger force. Now the cities were fighting each other, and they were too evenly matched for any one city to gain the upper hand for long. So the lugal's job effectively became a permanent position.

Regardless of the balance of power between the cities, within his own city continual war made the lugal

far more powerful than his fellow violence specialists. Here, he had something close to a monopoly on the use of force. As long as he prevented the city from being sacked, he enjoyed popular support, too.

The question of his relationship to the rest of government now arose. He took over the role of the *en* who managed taxes, irrigation and public works, and oversaw agricultural production, central to which was maintaining good relations with the gods to ensure a decent harvest. In some cities a separate *lugal* had never been elected in the first place, the *en* himself assuming this role in time of war. In either case, the roles of peacetime priest-manager and wartime military leader now fused together to produce a king.

The Police

The key contribution the new king made to government was to keep order. Taxes became easier to collect now that the tax collector was armed, and disputes could be settled in a new and decisive manner.

Before the village became a city, life had been based on family connections. A person's security lay in the physical strength of their extended family because there was no higher power. This created bonds that were so tight that individual identity and family identity were hard to distinguish – all property was family property, for example.

Out of this family identity, a code of honour developed that went some way to maintaining an uneasy peace. A person knew that stealing from someone would force the victim's family to retaliate in order to protect its honour. If it failed to do so it would lose face and other families would see it was weak. Awareness of the cycle of revenge that would be sparked off discouraged a person from stealing in the first place.

The council of elders emerged from this family-based society. As heads of the various family groups, they had the best chance of resolving a dispute if one arose. If they could not reach agreement they would call a more general assembly. In either case, however, the judgment relied on the same code of honour for

Habitual war pushed a society to define its identity against others. War came late to Egypt, but by the time of Ramesses III (1190–1158 BCE), palace walls were sporting friezes of captured enemies. From the left: Syrian, Hittite and Nubian captives, on leashes.

its enforcement: the pressure that if the judgment was not complied with, families would be forced to resort to violence.

As villages grew into cities, families became dispersed and unable to maintain the same balance of collective pressure between them. But the importance of personal connections remained. The only way to guard against being cheated was to establish a bond of trust with someone through dealing with that person a number of times. A reputation for trustworthiness could then spread by word of mouth.

At the same time, inequalities of wealth and power became greater, so if a person was cheated there was little they could do about it unless they had a protector. Violence specialists offering protection flourished. This meant that judgments of disputes passed by the council or assembly carried less weight than they had previously. In effect, enforcing a judgment was left up to the wronged party. This was worse than useless in diffusing resentment and discouraging persistent feuding.

Now, however, one person had managed to concentrate more power in their hands than the rest of the city put together: the king. The new king used this power to enforce judgments regardless of whom they went against. This allowed him to assert his authority against the strong, to win broad support from the more numerous weak and to keep order.

The king had not brought in rule of law; there was nothing to guide judgments other than custom, and the king could override a judgment at any time and for any reason. But he had established a single police presence. Society began to change from one based on family ties or the protection of powerful friends to one held together by the power of a central civic authority.

A civic identity in this sense came earlier to Sumer than to many other societies, where cities continued to be battlegrounds for clan rivalries. Outside the city walls, however, these rivalries persisted in Sumer, too. The kings had established order by force within their own cities but no one of them was powerful enough to do so over a larger area. This meant no one could lay down their arms because there was no higher power to guarantee any agreement they might make to stop fighting. Inter-city relations continued to be based on personal dealings between kings, involving honour, reputation, alliances and war.

11: Metal

Civilization has been made out of metal. Wherever there is metal there are industries mining, smelting, trading and fashioning it into anything from earrings to bridges, rockets and silicon chips. Nowadays, metal is part of everyone's life, but for most of its history it was the preserve of the rich.

Above: The mesmerizing lustre of gold. A head-dress from the Moche culture of northern Peru (c. 100–700 CE), representing a sea-god with the face of a cat and the tentacles of an octopus. Only for those who could afford it.

Gold was the first metal. For thousands of years before it was ever mined small pieces were found lying on the ground. By at least 4500 BCE, it was being made into jewellery around the shores of the Black Sea. The fact it never tarnished gave it an other-worldly quality, and its softness made it easy to shape. By 1000 BCE, the Etruscans of northern Italy were using it for dental bridge work, mostly cosmetic.

After gold came six other metals discovered by the ancient world: copper, silver, lead, tin, iron and mercury or 'liquid silver', a substance so mysterious and fascinating it was worshipped by the Egyptians. These different metals all shared a common quality: they were valuable – so much so that some of them came to symbolize value itself.

A Market for Luxury Goods

The cities of ancient Sumer were able to come into existence due to a stored surplus of food that allowed some people to be freed from farming. A tax system redistributed this surplus to provide services that benefited the community as a whole.

The people in charge of the tax system, however – first the storeroom and temple manager, later the king – benefited from it more than others. Power was concentrated in the hands of these people and their lives became quite different to those of other people. The king increased this distinction by seizing land by force and declaring it his own private property. Taxes from this land went into his own pocket rather than the public purse.

The king had a wife, children to inherit his title, and other relatives. They also benefited from the public purse being in his hands. They benefited too from the land, loot and prisoners he seized in war because he gave some of this away, and his family and other relatives received the most. They formed a 'noble' class of people who were freed not just from farming but from work altogether, by taxes or rent paid directly to them by the farmers of land they now owned.

These nobles were in the market for luxury goods with which to display their status. Metal was the natural choice for these goods; it was scarce, expensive and quite unlike any other material.

Accessories to be seen dead in. The earliest evidence of a well-established metalworking tradition comes from a number of graves at Varna, on the Black Sea coast of Bulgaria, dating to around 4500 BCE. They contain over 6 kilograms (13 pounds) of 23.5 carat gold objects, as well as many copper artefacts.

Too valuable for actual use. A Sumerian gold dagger from the Royal Tombs of Ur (2450 BCE), complete with its lapis lazuli handle and staggeringly intricate gold filigree scabbard. In the present turmoil it has gone missing from the National Museum in Baghdad.

The metal in question was mostly either gold, silver or copper from what is now Turkey and Armenia. The only raw material in Mesopotamia was clay; wood, stone and metal all had to be imported down the Euphrates from the mountains. Copper became the most important part of this river trade, so much so that the Sumerian word for copper, *urudu*, became the name for the Euphrates river itself.

Business

Metal had to be paid for and by 2500 BCE this had become a problem. Now there were very few people living outside the city walls. The peasant farmers of Sumer had endured a thousand years of rising taxes and, moreover, increasingly frequent war, with their fields, their flimsy huts and their families taking the brunt of the damage. In response, they had been leaving their land for centuries, as a result of which revenues from taxes and rents had fallen to a point where even the nobles were feeling the pinch.

In addition, the ex-farmers had formed a pool of casual labourers in the city who might find work one day and not the next. They were generally worse off than the slaves. Slaves at least belonged somewhere and knew where their next meal was coming from. Unemployment was more precarious. It was a new and unsettling phenomenon both for the unemployed themselves and for everyone else who saw them hanging around the streets in groups.

So the nobles, no longer able to rely on tax or rental income, went into business and created employment. Previously, they had skimmed off a percentage of surplus produce but they had remained at the mercy of the peasant farmer because they had not actively controlled production. Now they brought everything in-house, turning their households into private companies, paying 'wages' in the form of board and lodging and directing operations themselves.

Farmers who had fled the land were put up in the city and sent out to the fields in teams to do their work. It became obvious that the company could also handle other types of production previously carried out by self-employed people, so workshops were set up and craftspeople were taken on. Craft products became an increasingly important commodity to trade for raw materials from upriver. Managers to handle this trade as well as to oversee other company business were also employed.

A new economic and social unit had been created. Belonging to the company provided ordinary people with the security previously known only by slaves and municipal workers. For the nobles, it brought a new way of thinking about surplus produce: instead of tax or rent it could be profit. Profit represented all the surplus of a production process that could be controlled, not a percentage of one that could not. Profit meant there could be a motive for increasing production. The motive was a desire for luxury goods made from metal.

Exchanging Presents

After 2500 BCE, with production under their control and a motive to create profit, the noble class became far more wealthy. This wealth drove mines and smelting works upriver at the start of the supply chain, stimulated river trade and gave company metalworkers increased opportunities to refine their skills.

Gold, silver and copper were all soft metals but now tin was added to copper to produce bronze, a harder alloy. Although knives and even axes had been made from copper, bronze was really the first metal hard enough to be seriously useful for toolmaking. But it was still expensive – especially after 2000 BCE when local reserves of tin were exhausted and the nearest source was Cornwall.

Cups and bowls made from gold, silver and copper demonstrate wealth and don't come for free. Presenting gifts in Persepolis, the impressive ceremonial city of the Persian Empire, founded by Darius I (522–486 BCE), in present-day Iran.

So metal continued to be a luxury product. A bronze sword might be a deadly weapon but it was for noble use only. Everything made from metal was first and foremost a status symbol; cups and bowls made from metal instead of pottery, metal jewellery instead of necklaces made from seeds or shells, metal musical instruments. All this was treasure.

Treasure became the main reason for kings to storm each other's cities and burn them to the ground; there was treasure to carry off – and metalworkers, who were always sought out and taken prisoner. Raw material for treasure provided increased reason to fight over trade routes, so these had to be more heavily guarded.

However, the main attraction of treasure was that it could be not only stolen but given away. Naturally, what could lead to war could become a bargaining chip in war's other face: diplomacy. War and diplomacy were the only ways kings could relate to each other. In the absence of a higher power to regulate their conduct, everything came down to concepts of honour, shows of respect, veiled threats and outbreaks of violence.

Into this arena came treasure. What act could be more perfect than to make a potential enemy a gift of gold, silver or bronze? A gift shows respect and a desire to please. A gift of great value also displays power on the part of the giver. Most important, such a gift requires something in return.

Exchanging gifts of treasure became the central move in an uneasy game of alliance-building. It was a game that had an elaborate set of rules governing what size of gift was appropriate in each particular case. Too mean a gift would be dangerously discourteous, too ostentatious a gift could be an equally dangerous taunt – a card to be played only by a king confident of his power.

Homer's *Iliad*, set much later in the Greek world of 1200 BCE, opens a window onto this kind of aristocratic Bronze Age society, which endured for thousands of years. Agamemnon risked defeat at the gates of Troy by slighting Achilles' honour through faulty etiquette concerning gifts, and only saved the situation with more gifts.

Money

Treasure could only become such an important bargaining chip in the ancient world because metal had already come to symbolize value. The fashioning of metal into artefacts added an element of tact to the

Iron

Iron, like the other ancient metals, began life as a luxury for the upper class. In its pure state it comes to earth every so often in a meteor. As such, it is very rare. Small amounts of meteoric iron were made into expensive ornaments in both Sumer and Egypt from their early days.

On the other hand, iron trapped in other minerals (iron ore) is one of the most common materials on Earth. But iron is difficult to smelt or extract from its ore because it is very hard, so it will only melt at very high temperatures. At first no one could make a fire hot enough to melt iron. Instead, around 2000 BCE, a method of producing wrought iron was developed in Armenia. Iron could not be melted but it could be heated enough to become soft. It was then reheated and hammered to remove impurities. Nevertheless, the process was so time-consuming that this iron was initially up to five times the price of gold.

But iron, being much harder than bronze, is more useful for ploughing, building and, crucially, fighting. Over the next thousand years, techniques for extracting iron ore were pursued independently in many parts of the world. Whoever possessed iron possessed an overwhelming advantage.

Perhaps as early as 1500 BCE, iron was smelted in West Africa and this allowed the Bantu to dominate the continent south of the Sahara. Shortly after the sack of Troy, around 1200 BCE, iron-wielding tribes of Dorians swarmed down through the Balkans and into the Greek mainland, putting an end to the Bronze Age culture of the Iliad and the Odyssey, and preparing the ground for what would one day become classical Greece. In what is now Pakistan, Aryan tribes arriving from further north with iron swords spelled the end of the Bronze Age Harappan civilization of the Indus Valley, before moving into the Ganges plain, bringing with them the seeds of Hinduism.

In the south of India, a separate iron-working tradition grew up, attaining a degree of sophistication unmatched till the modern era – steel (an alloy of iron and carbon) was in production by 300 BCE. Whether in Africa, Europe or India, however, extracting iron was still a difficult process and therefore not cheap.

The exclusivity of metal was finally overcome by the Chinese. Around 500 BCE, iron-workers in the Wu state around the mouth of the River Yangtze discovered how to build a fire hot enough to melt iron and produce a liquid. This not only made iron quicker and easier to extract, it also meant it could be poured into a mould.

Cast-iron made mass production possible. The Chinese already had large-scale foundries casting bronze vases but these vessels were only used in ceremonies connected with traditional Chinese ancestor worship. As in all other parts of the world, metal production supplied only a niche market.

After China was unified in 221 BCE, however, it became the largest and most powerful state in the world and sought to centralize industrial production for the benefit of the whole economy. The way lay open to a nationalized iron and steel industry, turning out standardized tools for agriculture and standardized parts for engineering projects, a template that would eventually be reproduced around the world.

Metal for everyone. No longer a luxury for the rich, iron and steel have built the modern city with its towering architecture and network of transport systems – as well as the cranes that do the building.

Centuries ago, the islanders of Yap in Micronesia decided on stone money. Their coins can be 3.7 metres (12 feet) tall and are carried or rolled by two or more people using a pole pushed through the central hole. They are still legal tender, although loose change can be a problem.

exchange of gifts but their cost was the real issue. Where an exchange of goods had no diplomatic function, however, craftsmanship was unnecessary.

The more trade expanded, the more there was a need for an intermediate commodity to stand between the exchange of two goods. The problem with straight barter is that the goods both parties want may not be available at the same time. If a person offers plums for apples, they will have to wait for the apples because they ripen later than plums. So, in exchange for the plums, a third commodity is needed that can be kept and exchanged for the apples later on, when they become ripe.

This third commodity, in addition to keeping well, must be portable. Therefore it must be scarce, otherwise a person will have to carry a lot of it around just to exchange for one apple. In addition, it must be measurable and hard to fake, otherwise people will not know from one day to the next how much to exchange for an apple. Metal had all of these qualities but in order for it to become an efficient medium of exchange, it needed to be measured.

By 1450 BCE, balance scales with sensitive pointers had been developed in Egypt on which quantities of gold, silver or copper could be weighed. Accurate scales by themselves were not enough, however, because weighing metal did not measure its purity.

What was needed was the touchstone. Metals of different purities have different colours. Rubbing a soft metal like gold or silver across a stone surface would leave a scraping of metal stuck to the stone. The colour of this scraping could be compared with a range of standard examples to determine its purity.

Weighing, using a touchstone, and then comparing examples all took time, however. To speed up the process, states began to make lumps of metal they had already measured for weight and purity, and which they guaranteed to be accurate. The measurement and the name of the guarantor were stamped onto the metal with a hammer and punch. The first batches of these stamped metal blobs were issued by the state of Lydia, in the west of present-day Turkey, sometime around 600 BCE, and were made of electrum, a natural alloy of gold and silver found locally.

Now money no longer needed to be measured; it could be counted instead. Getting paid the right amount from a customer, a merchant or an employer became a simple matter to check, not dependent on a long-nurtured relationship of trust. Business became possible on a bigger, wider and faster scale.

The Power of a Symbol

Metal drove civilization by becoming one of our many languages; a system of symbolic representation. A feature of all languages is that the symbol can detach from the thing it represents and take on a meaning in itself. Money is perhaps the clearest example of this. Instead of creating wealth, all a person needs to do to change their lives forever is find a big enough lump of the right metal.

So it is that at certain times through the centuries droves of people left civilization as they knew it to search for gold, the vast majority destined to die in poverty and isolation. They associated gold, because it stood for money and because money in turn stood for wealth, with power and freedom. But gold seems also to have had a more mystical fascination for these people, many of whom lost their minds in the search for it.

Nowhere was the spell of metal more bewitching than in the 16th-century quest to find El Dorado, the 'Golden Man', the legendary king of a people living somewhere in the mountains of Colombia who, it was said, covered his body in gold dust each year as part of a religious rite.

12: The Ideology of the State

An organized society can deliver wealth, security and comfort to its people, but it never distributes these benefits equally. A successful government, however, will receive the consent it needs in spite of this shortcoming.

Above: Loyalty beyond the grave. An army of thousands waits in obedient formation to accompany Qin Shihuangdi, the First Emperor of China (221–210 BCE), to the next world. Each terracotta soldier is a life-size individual with a recognizable face.

People often go along with what seems to be against their best interests. In the Royal Tombs of the Sumerian city of Ur, dating from about 2500 BCE, dozens of people were found buried together with the corpses of the rich and powerful. These people, mostly women wearing expensive jewellery and sometimes holding musical instruments, lay in orderly arrangements accompanied by small bowls that may have contained poison. They showed no obvious sign of struggle or distress.

It is entirely possible, of course, that these people did not go to their deaths willingly but simply knew there was no escape and therefore resigned themselves to their fate. But then the question shifts to those in power: why did they think it was necessary to force these people to put on their best clothes and take their own lives for the sake of someone already dead? What function could this serve for anyone?

Forces and Personalities

Early states were characterized by a gradual shift from magical to religious beliefs, and this was a trend that lent itself to an increasingly stratified society.

Magic is concerned with cause and effect. In this respect it is like science, although it has different theories about how cause and effect work. For example, one of magic's theories is the idea that one action will cause something similar to happen because similar things are in fact the same. This means that sticking pins into a doll will hurt the person the doll represents, or painting bison on a cave wall will make real bison appear. This is not science's theory of how cause and effect work, but it implies, as science does, that people can learn to control natural forces.

Religion is different because, in essence, it is based on a psychological view of the world. The basic idea is that any natural event might be at some level the action of a personality, in the same way that placing one foot in front of another is not simply an event but an action taken by a person. What people experience inside themselves when they do things is mirrored in the outside world, which is alive with personality. At the simplest level, the range of natural forces suggests a variety of personalities, one moving the water, another moving the wind and so on.

This idea of personalities inhabiting nature changes how people try to affect their environment. They can no longer try to control cause and effect directly, as with magic or science. Instead, the best they

can hope for is to indirectly influence events by working at personal relationships. They are reduced to asking the personalities behind natural forces what they want or what they intend to do, or to trying to persuade them to co-operate by doing things to please them.

From Magic to a Community God

In practice, magic and religion have always co-existed to some extent. When people began to farm, certain aspects of nature assumed an increased importance to them. The annual cycle of sowing and harvesting crops became the centre of their lives. They were more vulnerable now to water, drainage, pests and anything that affected how plants grew. In response, they performed various yearly plays that blended magical and religious ideas to try to ensure their crops would grow well.

There would be, for example, a play about a marriage between two natural forces important to a crop on which the community depended. Their union

Natural forces personified. An enigmatic figure from Babylon (c. 2000 BCE), quite likely the Sumerian goddess Innana, or Ishtar as the Babylonians knew her. As, amongst other things, goddess of love, sex and procreation, she starred in erotic plays and brought forth the new crops.

in the play would produce children and this meant their union in nature would produce a good harvest. The power of the play to have an effect on nature was a purely magical idea.

On the other hand, the natural forces in these plays were represented by actors, each pretending to be the personality or spirit behind a particular force – a purely religious idea. Seeing a spirit assume human form, albeit temporarily, helped to accentuate the distinction between a natural force and the spirit that controlled it; it helped to clarify the religious idea of a world alive with spirits by portraying them as having bodies.

A permanent body of its own, fashioned from wood or clay or some other material, made such a being into a tangible god. Now that it stood clearly apart from the forces of nature, there was nothing to prevent it controlling more than one force, so its power began to increase.

Persephone, Greek queen of the underworld, was a part-time monarch in tune with the cycle of the seasons. During the winter months, she reigned below ground while plants and seeds lay dormant in the soil. In the spring, she appeared above ground and crops began to grow again. 5th century BCE.

The more clearly defined the gods behind natural forces became, the less it seemed possible for humans to control nature by magic. Between humans and the forces of nature stood a range of gods; any magic necessary would be worked by them. It became increasingly clear that humans would have to cultivate a good relationship with these gods.

Different environments supported different crops – in Sumer, Uruk grew dates, Nippur further north grew wheat and barley. The gods who controlled the forces important to a particular community's crops could protect that community from bad harvests. Gradually, these forces came under the control of one god in particular, who came to be thought of more generally as a protector of the community.

This god would be all the more likely to use its powers to protect the community if the community tried to please it. A god with a body must live somewhere, just like a human being, and this meant the community could build a house in which their protector god could live – a nice house to which food and presents could be delivered, looked after by a priest.

A Career in Politics

In time, as it became a city, the community acquired a protector-king as well as a protector-god, and they came to resemble each other. God and king had the two biggest houses in the city. Both the temple of the god and the palace of the king were great landowning households, with hierarchies of staff running them as private businesses and receiving visitors with pomp and ceremony. As the wealth and grandeur of temple and palace increased, so god and king were regarded with ever greater reverence.

A god's power commanded more respect than a king's, however, because it was part of the natural order of things. If an ordinary king could present himself not as a person who had seized power, but as an appointed representative of the local god, he stood to greatly increase his authority.

Power without authority is a precarious tightrope to walk, so this was one of the first matters new kings tried to address. As their wealth became more conspicuous it became only more important. The ruler of the Sumerian city of Lagash changed the name of his wife's private company from e-mi to e-Bau, after the goddess Bau, wife of the protector god of Lagash. After this renaming of the company, the workforce increased.

As each king became identified with his city's god, so the various Sumerian gods came to relate to each other not according to a theological pattern, but by mirroring the delicate power balance and shifting alliances that existed between the kings. In the early 2nd millennium BCE, the Sumerian cities were finally united under a single leader ruling from the city of Babylon. Once this was achieved, Marduk, Babylon's local god, became head of the pantheon of Sumerian gods.

As a god's political function became more important than its original agricultural function, so there was some rewriting of dramatic material. Babylon's big new-year festival had been a festival of sowing, in which its god had gone out to the fields together with the seed. Now this journey became Marduk venturing forth to do battle with his enemy.

A Protector in Need of Protection

The logical extension of the ever-closer relationship between god and king was that they should fuse into one. For a long time this idea had been heavily suggested in the acting out of the annual sacred marriage play because the people who took the roles of the god and goddess of fertility were the king and queen. Given the magical power of the play, it was unclear whether king and queen merely represented god and goddess, or whether for that short time they actually became them – much in the way there have been centuries of debate about the bread and wine in the Christian Holy Communion ceremony.

It is important to recognize that the identification of king and god was not simply political manoeuvring on the king's part, but an idea in the minds of ordinary people that grew more plausible as their king became more powerful. The first Mesopotamian king to be formally declared a god was King Naram-Suen sometime before 2255 BCE, but this was not his idea. He had fought off a year of attacks by the allied forces of nine cities, defeated them all and gained control of the whole of Sumer, which seemed a superhuman feat to the people of his city. After consulting all the major gods on the matter, they made him their new city god by building

Keeping a watchful eye over his constituents. Marduk, Babylon's protector god, set into the tiled walls of the Ishtar Gate, one of the eight entrances to the city, built by Nebuchadnezzar II around 575 BCE. Marduk used to be a rain god before he went into politics.

a temple to him, making explicit the fusion of two ideas that had been converging for many centuries.

In Egypt, the pharaoh had demonstrated his power to rule a whole country since 3100 BCE and had long been divine. But when a king becomes a god and truly attains superhuman powers the situation for the people becomes delicate.

A king who can protect his people not just by fighting off invaders, but by controlling nature, is a dangerous proposition. His mood and the movements of his body have the potential to affect hugely powerful forces. If something upsets him, if something he eats disagrees with him or if he has an accident while taking a walk, anything might happen. He is more vulnerable in this regard than a god in a temple who never goes anywhere. The people have been handed a double-edged sword; it may be comforting to have an all-powerful god-king, but he will need constant protection.

Investing in the Future

The idea of an afterlife takes the need to protect a god-king for the sake of the community to another level. If the king can exert an influence from beyond the grave, ways have to be found to make sure this influence is a positive one.

The closest most of us come to experiencing an afterlife while still alive is when we fall asleep and dream. In dreams strange things may happen but the world is essentially very similar to the one we inhabit when awake – it has people, places, objects and so on, though they may morph into one another.

Perhaps for this reason, the afterlife for most early societies was a physical one. The dead would need their body so their spirit would have somewhere to live in the next world. This body would need food for the journey across. Once on the other side, it would need clothes and so on. Taking measures to protect a god-king in the afterlife meant trying to ensure he would continue to live in the style to which he had become accustomed while alive.

For some societies, such as Ur in 2500 BCE or Shang China a thousand years later, this meant being accompanied by real servants as well as other

There is always a contract between ruler and ruled, written or unwritten, but building a cult of leadership may help to override this constraint. Hitler and his publicity machine had brief success with this in a blatant fashion, but more subtle examples are all around us.

possessions. These people would have had no escape, but drawing conclusions about the frame of mind in which they met their deaths is not a simple matter.

In ancient Egypt, models of servants who would come to life once on the other side could stand in for the real thing. But the body of the dead person still had to be kept safe, which entailed the construction of huge, hopefully impregnable tombs. The people who broke themselves dragging 50-ton blocks of stone across the sand and up ramps for the pyramids were not foreign slaves being driven by the lash.

Whatever the specific beliefs about fertility cults, god-kings and the afterlife, what is happening here is that the power of the state is being linked to concepts about the natural world, and this is a dynamic union. The idea of a king who either represents or actually is a god has always been the most common and successful way of making this link, but not the only one.

All rulers look for a way to legitimize their power beyond their ability to provide security and economic efficiency because they know these may fluctuate. If they can make people accept them as part of the natural order of things they will overcome this problem. Today politicians are as aware of this as ever when they use phrases such as 'We are the natural party of government', as though there is somehow a natural order to be found in civilization.

Left: King and god become one, bestowing on the state the highest form of legitimacy possible. At Abu Simbel on the Nile (c. 1260 BCE), a giant Ramesses II sits outside his temple alongside his father, the state sun-god Amun-Re. The pharaoh is much larger than the god.

13: Writing

People write things down because they know they will forget them. The need to keep track of debts is how writing began. From these modest beginnings, however, a tool was honed of such power that it would open up the past and change the very way people think.

Above: Accountancy: the first literate profession. A Sumerian clay tablet from the mid 3rd millennium BCE records numbers of sheep and goats. The circles and crescents made with the blunt end of the writing stylus are the numbers.

As people form larger groups, their relationships become more complex. In order to deal with this complexity, they need new tools. If they can find them, new social structures will emerge, enabling the group to continue growing. Writing is just such a tool, produced as towns and cities appeared, in turn enabling whole countries to be governed. Beyond this, writing brought new ways of thinking.

How to Draw Ideas

Writing is marks made on some surface to record ideas. A 30,000-year-old wolf bone has been found in the Czech Republic, marked with 55 notches arranged in groups of five. These notches, however, are all the same. Repetition and grouping of the same idea we tend to call 'counting' rather than 'writing'. What we call 'writing' involves signs for many different ideas.

There are equally early examples of such signs. Highly stylized pictures of men and women on the walls of caves communicate the different ideas 'man' or 'woman'. By themselves, however, individual signs are not writing. Writing communicates language, which means signs have to be put into a sequence.

As farming communities grew so did trade and property transactions. There came to be a lot to remember. The tax collector in particular needed to keep track of who had paid and who still owed.

To this end, clay tokens were made to represent different commodities and put into a kind of piggy bank. Three tokens of a certain shape meant three jars of oil were either owed or had been paid. Later on, the piggy bank was dispensed with and the information was recorded by pressing the tokens into a tablet of clay to leave impressions signifying three jars of oil. By 3300 BCE, Sumerians were drawing a picture of a single jar of oil onto the tablet and pressing three dots into the clay beside it. The phrase 'three jars of oil' had been written.

However, a writing system using pictures for things we can see, plus some numbers, makes it hard to communicate even quite simple thoughts. This is because most thoughts are not about things that can be seen. Each word in the sentence you are reading now represents an idea, but only two of them are ideas of physical objects I can draw: 'you' and 'I'. In order to communicate accurately and efficiently, a system of picture writing would need pictures for all of these ideas, not just two. But how can you draw a picture of something that cannot be seen?

How to Draw Sounds

This problem led to a shift in thinking around 2600 BCE. The Sumerian langauge had a large number of homophones or words with the same sound but different meanings. The spoken word ti meant 'arrow' but also 'life', in the same way that the English word 'seal' has more than one meaning. It is easy to draw a seal balancing a ball on its nose, but not so easy to draw someone sealing their fate. Likewise, Sumerians found it easy to draw an arrow, less easy to draw life.

However, because they used the same sound to represent these two different ideas in their spoken language, they realized they could use the same sign in their written language too. The picture represented the idea of 'arrow' but only the sound of 'life'. Because our

The sign for the Sumerian syllable ti, which could mean either 'arrow' or 'life'. This was originally a drawing of an arrow, but the logistics of writing on clay led to characters becoming stylized into a cuneiform or 'wedge-shaped' writing system.

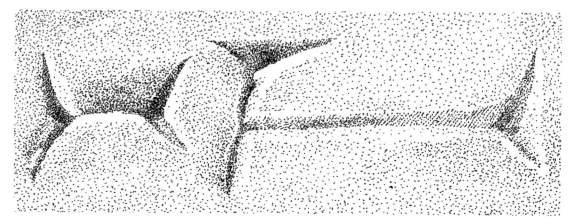

A new type of person: the pen-pusher. While manual workers harvest grapes in the vineyard, an early office worker goes down to the wine cellar to do a stocktake. From the tomb of Userhet (c. 1400 BCE), a royal scribe of the 18th Dynasty employed to keep records of grain production.

present-day alphabetic writing system is itself a set of signs for sounds rather than ideas, it is hard for us to appreciate what a groundbreaking step this was. Before this time, sounds and pictures were two different ways to represent ideas; now pictures were beginning to represent sounds alone, leaving the sounds to represent ideas.

In addition to words that had more than one meaning, a longer word could now be written if there were signs for its syllables. For example, the sound 'seal' has two meanings, but it also forms part of the word 'sealant'. This word can be represented by combining a drawing of a seal and a drawing of an ant. This is how early sound writing developed alongside idea writing.

The Bureaucratic State

Writing created bureaucracy. To begin with, this meant managing accounts to keep track of taxation and trade. But using signs for sounds expanded the kinds of thoughts writing could express. Now there could be contracts, religious texts and records of the exploits of kings, as well as two kinds of document that would have great political consequences: letters and written laws.

Letters were the first form of communication technology capable of transmitting information accurately and confidentially over long distances. In war-torn Mesopotamia, this gave kings the chance not only to sack and burn, but also to maintain control beyond the confines of their own cities and satellite villages. The Babylonian state ruled by Hammurapi from 1763 BCE was the first to unite successfully all the cities of Sumer under one government. Many official letters remain showing how Hammurapi kept abreast of developments up to 320 kilometres (200 miles) away using this new communication system.

Hammurapi also wrote laws to help manage this larger state, but these laws were the thin end of a wedge placed between a ruler and his power. A law expressed rights and responsibilities and the permanence of a written law stood in contrast to the mortality of any one ruler. There was nothing to stop a ruler writing new laws, but as more laws were written, more of a legal tradition built up for each new ruler to inherit. Ever so gradually, power and authority began to shift from the ruler to the state itself. The only way to stop this would be to start burning the law books.

For Hammurapi, this was not necessary, mainly because so few people could read. Literacy at this time was a very exclusive skill, which helped to preserve the status quo. There were thousands of signs for ideas and sounds to be learned – often a confusion of different signs for the same word. Learning to read and write involved many years of memorizing these signs by writing endless lists of words. It produced a small literate class of civil servants who possessed a seemingly mystical ability. Writing systems developed by the Egyptians, Chinese and Maya, among others, also contained large numbers of signs and consequently also produced a small, educated elite serving a centralized bureaucracy.

In most of these societies, the signs themselves added to the awe with which writing was generally regarded. In Mesopotamia, writing had become a series of abstract marks because it was hard to draw pictures on clay, but in Egypt there was papyrus to paint on so writing remained a series of pictures. When a word is a picture it can attain a mysterious iconic power. This is why companies design a logo that consumers feel compelled to display on their clothing. Hieroglyphic Egyptian was an entire language of logos.

Until a writing system with fewer signs and no pictures could be invented, the full implications of a literate society would not be realized.

Signs for the Atoms of Speech

If I draw a seal, how do you know if this represents an animal, or a sound that can just as well be part of other words, such as 'sealant' or 'ceiling'? Around the time of Hammurapi's rule in Babylon, Egyptian writing was using an additional series of abstract signs to show when a picture should be read as a sound instead of an idea. Because a large number of Egyptian syllables began with a hard consonant sound like k or t, these new signs became identified with the consonants themselves, which formed only the first part of the whole syllable. This was the beginning of the alphabet.

The Egyptians sometimes used these signs in isolation to spell foreign words or words for which

The power of the symbol. Aztec hieroglyphs for the 20 days in the months of the solar calendar (c. 1400-1500 CE), each an icon in its own right. Signs like these express the character of what they represent, which makes them resistant to change.

Printing

Pinpointing exactly when a milestone of civilization was passed is not easy.

Printing is as old as writing itself. Before 'three jars of oil' had been written, stamps with designs carved on them were being pressed into clay to signify ownership. As signs for written language developed, so did printing.

The earliest printed document dates from 1700 BCE and was found in the palace of Phaistos on the island of Crete. It is hand-printed with stamps for 45 different characters in a language that has not yet been deciphered.

Printing by hand, however, is barely faster than writing. Clay is also not an ideal material for recording and disseminating texts of any length. Consequently, 1,500 years after the Phaistos disc, multiple copies of books were being produced in Alexandria by teams of scribes writing on papyrus, not printing into clay.

At a similar time in China, paper was invented. Over the centuries the Chinese experimented with printing on paper using woodblocks. The earliest book printed by this method is the *Diamond Sutra* of 868 CE. Each page of the book was carved onto a block of wood, which meant it was very quick to run off multiple copies.

However, carving a new woodblock for each page of a book took a long time. Around 1045, the Chinese overcame this problem by reinventing moveable type. Pottery stamps for each separate character were made, much like the printer of the Phaistos disc must have used. But now these stamps were arranged in a frame that held them in place so they could be printed all at once. Later on, metal stamps were used.

This advance did not bring mass production to the Chinese printing industry, however, because Chinese has

Suitable for a small print-run only. The Phaistos disc, Crete 1700 BCE – printed, but stamp by stamp and into clay. This method of printing did little to extend mass literacy.

thousands of characters. Thousands of stamps therefore had to be made and constantly rearranged.

It was only when Latin began to be joined as a written language by other, more widely understood languages, that printing had much of a reason to develop in Europe, but here it could take advantage of alphabets containing fewer than 30 letters. Now printing could become a major catalyst for change, but only because a number of other conditions were already in place.

One of the numerous consequences of Renaissance printing was the invention of spectacles for people who had difficulty focusing on text. The manufacture of spectacle lenses led to the telescope and the microscope. Without the telescope, the speed of light would not have been determined. Picking out the decisive link in the chain of technological innovation that connects this discovery to the appearance of writing can obscure the fact that all technology relies on other technology.

Quicker by hand? Typesetters working on a Chinese newspaper in San Francisco, 1929, choose from 12,000 separate pieces of type.

they had no pictures, but they never realized the potential of what they were onto. Like other literate cultures, they already had a sophisticated writing system of great antiquity woven into the way they thought about the world, which they had no obvious reason to change.

On the east coast of the Mediterranean, however, various Semitic peoples were experimenting with writing for the first time. They had no prior tradition of literacy to stand in the way of building on what the Egyptians had started. Now they began to pursue a concept as original as the move from drawing ideas to drawing sounds.

What we hear when people speak is syllables. They are the natural unit of song and speech that babies imitate. Trying to break speech down into smaller sounds is a strange and difficult thing to attempt. In English we hear 'cat' as one unit of sound, not 'c-a-t' as three separate units. The strangeness and difficulty of the task these people set themselves is perhaps the reason it was never independently attempted by anyone else.

By around 1200 BCE, one of these peoples, the Phoenicians, were using a collection of 22 signs that looked nothing like pictures to represent the consonants in their language. They did not bother with vowels, so their spelling was similar to text messaging on mobile phones. With just 22 signs to learn, reading and writing now lay within the grasp of whole new sections of the population.

The new Greeks of around 800 BCE borrowed these signs. A previous writing system had been lost in Greece when their illiterate Dorian ancestors had invaded the country from the north several centuries earlier. Greek had fewer consonants than Phoenician, however, so the signs the Greeks did not need for their consonants they used for their vowels instead. The Greek alphabet was the first tool that could record every sound of a spoken language.

Then and Now, This and That

History begins with writing. People did of course have language before writing, and passed stories and other information down the generations, but an oral tradition works in a different way to a literate tradition. A story passed on orally becomes revised or embellished with each telling, however slightly. It is continually being made to fit in with the ideas and attitudes of the present generation.

When a story is written down, however, it becomes fixed. A later generation can compare its own world with the world expressed in this document to a degree impossible for an oral culture. In this sense, a difference between the past and the present was created by writing.

The greater opportunity to compare past and present that written texts provided extended to analysis in general. Spoken language is linear; it flows through the ear like a river, drawing attention always to the last thing said. Written language is spatial; it presents itself to the eye like a picture, all of which receives equal attention. Thoughts expressed as words on a page can be looked at repeatedly, indefinitely, making it easier to spot relationships between them. They lend themselves to being ordered into relevant paragraphs and checked for consistency. The most extreme example of this 'classification of thinking' is formal logic, which began with Aristotle laying out on paper the structure of a valid argument.

All academic and scientific enquiry depends on writing, without which peer review – the checking of one person's findings by the rest of the academic or scientific community – would hardly be possible. Even the division of research into different fields is characteristic of a literate culture.

A more formal style of critical awareness affected political consciousness too. Before writing there were rebellions, but they were merely attempts to rid society of a particular leader. After writing, a picture of the political system itself started to come into focus. People began to stand back from their society and look at its structure as though it had been laid out on paper, which, increasingly, it had. Much deeper social, economic and political change became conceivable and greater engagement in the political process became possible for those who could read.

The Individual

From the birth of writing in Mesopotamia, literate people began to find themselves losing touch with culture as a whole. To begin with, they formed a class of people apart. Then the tendency to classify inherent in literacy began to compartmentalize government into different branches and encourage greater specialization throughout society.

Alienation from a unified culture increased as texts accumulated in libraries. The earliest large and well-organized library was established in Nineveh around 650

BCE by the Assyrian king Ashurbanipal, supposedly the first king who could read. Libraries opened a window onto cultures from other times and places. As people read about these cultures they were introduced to alternative lifestyles, other possible ways of doing things that placed them at one remove from their own culture.

This gradual process of detachment brought an individual into focus. The more a person saw their society from a distance, the more they saw themselves as an individual, not a participator in a communal identity. Reading silently to oneself, which only became widespread after the development of printing in Renaissance Europe, pushed people further into this private world. Writing, even more than reading, accentuates an individual identity because as a person writes they see their words growing into a self-portrait.

People have been worried about the consequences of literacy for thousands of years. Plato thought books could never provide real understanding because a text cannot be questioned or asked for clarification. The Romantic movement of the 19th century, with its rejection of science and rationalism, was largely nostalgia for a lost oral culture and all that went with it – unselfconscious belonging, living in the present and so forth.

But Plato and the Romantics were all writers, and literacy fed their ideas. Our bodies and brains have not changed for tens of thousands of years. This means there were Einsteins and Shakespeares walking around at the time of the Ice Age cave paintings. But they, like us, were only able to realize their potential within the confines of the technology available to them. Most likely, they developed only a fraction of the ideas they could have developed in a literate age.

Greek, the first language to be written phonetically. This tablet is The Code of Gortyn, an early legal document from Crete (c. 450 BCE). It reads left to right, then right to left. Words are not separated and lower case letters did not arrive until the Middle Ages.

14: The Universal Questions

The building of the early state was a cause for pride. Prosperous, well-ordered and stimulating urban culture stood in stark contrast to drab poverty beyond the city walls. Developed society had all the answers. But there came a time when conditions changed and people began to think otherwise.

Above: Voyage of discovery. Buddhist monks make a daily commute across the Mekong River in Laos, echoing the spiritual journey they have set out on in their lives.

After about 1000 BCE, a new intellectual spirit began to emerge throughout the civilizations of the ancient world, a spirit of enquiry less culturally bound than before. People were no longer satisfied with traditional answers to the big questions of life. These answers seemed arbitrary. Instead they wanted answers that measured up to a standard of reason that was universal – even if those answers were sometimes a new rational justification for old customs.

Around 500 BCE, there was a particular flowering of this impulse to reduce and rationalize, which was remarkably similar across societies from Greece to the Pacific. These societies had little contact with each other, but they shared certain features. They were literate cultures undergoing change. Old social structures were breaking down, new ones were struggling to emerge and endemic war was widespread. For many people there was growing uncertainty about where they belonged, as their traditions no longer seemed relevant to their changed circumstances. It was a climate that encouraged questions to be asked.

How Many Gods are There?

In both Mesopotamia and ancient Egypt there had long been tendencies to reduce a variety of gods with various powers to a single god with a general power of protection. Each city had its own general protector god. There was also a custom, especially in Mesopotamia, of choosing a personal god.

A person could choose any of the various gods to be what we might term their own 'guardian angel'. If they had bad luck, this was a sign they had displeased their personal god in the same way that if the harvest failed or the city was invaded it was a sign the people had displeased their city god.

It seems that sometime around 1800 BCE, the personal god of a man called Abraham, who lived in the Sumerian city of Ur, told him to leave his family and city and journey west to settle near the Mediterranean coast. The name of Abraham's personal god was Yahweh or Jehovah. Subsequently, Yahweh became the personal god of all Abraham's descendants, a relationship clarified in a set of laws received by Moses around 1200 BCE.

The people of Abraham and Moses had simplified a pantheon of nature gods to one general god. However, this god was for them only. They still recognized that other people had other gods, they just did not approve of them. At this time, therefore, the Yahweh religion was not truly monotheistic.

Another early attempt to reform religion was made in 1367 BCE by the Egyptian pharaoh Amenhotep IV. He built a new capital city at El-Amarna, halfway between the old capitals of Memphis and Thebes. Here he made worship of the sun-god Aton the state religion, renamed himself Akhenaton, or 'useful to Aton', and tried to banish all the other Egyptian gods.

It is unclear, however, if he saw his newly elevated god as truly universal or as a god for the state of Egypt alone. He probably had at least some political motives. Either way, his actions made him deeply unpopular and when he died the traditional pantheon of gods was reinstated.

The first properly thought through monotheism seems to have emerged sometime around 1000 BCE near the border of present-day Iran and Afghanistan. A pastoral, horse-riding people from further north had settled across present-day Iran and Afghanistan and into the Indus Valley hundreds of years earlier. Now a new wave of similar Aryan tribes came down into the middle of this area, causing tensions. Two cultures emerged, one moving south and east to India, the other moving west into present-day Iran. The group that moved into Iran rejected the old gods.

For a prophet called Zarathustra, or Zoroaster in Greek, there was only one god, whom he called Ahura Mazda. This god, however, was not a personal or state god, but a universal god; the one true god for all people. Zarathustra was able to make this claim because he identified Ahura Mazda not with specific natural forces nor with the protection of specific peoples, but with a universal idea: truth.

A logical concept such as this implies its opposite; where there is truth there must be the possibility for falsehood. These twin concepts of truth and falsehood became associated with the similar complimentary pair of good and evil. So Ahura Mazda, universal god of truth and goodness, gave rise to a universal demon of falsehood and evil, together with the idea of an ongoing human choice between right and wrong. These and other Zoroastrian ideas influenced several other religions of south-west Asia, not least Judaism and, later, Christianity and Islam.

The flame of truth that lights up the world. Zoroastrian temples keep an eternal fire burning to symbolize Ahura Mazda, the light of truth. Many Zoroastrians left Persia for India in the 10th century CE and today a worldwide faith of 200,000 people centres on the Parsi community of Mumbai.

Zarathustra attempted to answer a universal question about what lies behind both nature and human experience – about what makes the world tick. His answer had a logical form. It reduced all forces or mechanisms to an essential principle not linked to the traditions of any one culture. This was a new kind of rationalized religion; it was theology. In time, Zoroastrianism became the state religion of the Persian Empire. Inevitably, a complex of other spirits built up around Ahura Mazda, but there were now theologians to rationalize these spirits as aspects of the one true god.

How Can We Escape Pain?

From the time of Zarathustra, the pastoral culture of the Aryan tribes that had settled Afghanistan and the Indus Valley began to spread down into the plain of the Ganges. Their religion centred on a ritual of animal sacrifice and of inducing visions with a sacred drink made from a plant called *soma* – most likely a hallucinogen. In the Ganges plain they encountered villagers who had their own local gods. A complex religion began to emerge out of this meeting of cultures. A class system also emerged with the priests or *brahmans* in charge of the Vedic ritual at the top.

This society was run by local kings or *rajas*, who fought with each other to extend their territory. As smaller communities became absorbed into larger kingdoms, a sense of rootlessness increased among the people. At the same time, towns were growing, in which the continual sacrifice of cows or horses was impractical and seemed irrelevant. The vision-inducing sacred drink had also been lost because the *soma* plant only grew in the mountains.

These circumstances produced an introspective, analytical turn of mind. By the 6th century BCE, the meaning of the Vedic ritual had been explored in the *Upanishads*, an enquiry into the nature of the cosmos and the self. A set of yogic techniques was also developed, which might achieve the out-of-body experience previously delivered by the *soma* drink.

As well as this, there were increasing numbers of people who questioned established religion and society altogether. These people gave up their possessions and became wandering seekers after personal enlightenment. Their focus was an enquiry into the self, similar to that of the *Upanishads*, but shorn of any attachment to custom. An ethic of pacifism was also a common theme. Northern India

Jains, led by Mahavira, an older contemporary of the Buddha, renounced conventional customs to the point of giving up wearing clothes. Here, the tendrils of nature reclaim the Jaina sage Gommateshvara. Sravana Belgola, southern India (c. 983 CE).

around 500 BCE was home to a number of movements led by philosophical teachers of this kind.

The most radical of these teachers was Gautama Buddha. The rigour of his analysis was what made him radical. He thought religious or metaphysical speculation was beyond the scope of reason and therefore pointless. Instead, he undertook a careful examination of human nature on the basis that this was a study that could produce genuine knowledge. His psychological investigations led him to conclude, unlike other teachers, that the very idea of the self was an illusion subject to the same continual change that marked the world in general.

The Buddha put forward a work programme that might help people accept inevitable change. There was an ethical aspect to this programme, which rejected the class system, and also a set of techniques for training the mind, based on his analysis of human nature. If his programme was followed, freedom from personal suffering – the only real freedom – might be achieved.

For the Buddha and others, custom and reason sat in opposition to each other. The questions they asked were of universal scope and required answers they could only find by thinking outside their culture. This led them to the idea that salvation or enlightenment was not something to be received, but something to be worked at through the acquisition of knowledge. For the Buddha and others like him, knowledge was freedom.

How Should We Live?

China in the 5th and 6th centuries BCE had lost a stability previously provided by Zhou kings in the north. Their authority had broken down and with it a feudal system of mutual obligations, which had kept order. Power had shifted to nobles who fought with each other to extend their territories. War was constant and borders were fluid.

One response to this situation was to turn away from social and political life altogether and search for some permanence in a relationship not with society but with nature. This relationship was characterized by

a concept known as the *tao*. According to Lao-tzu, the supposed founder of Taoism, the *tao* could not be defined in words, but it seems to have included both the idea of an essential principle at work in the world and the idea of a method of tuning in to this principle. Mastering a situation by yielding to it rather than confronting it was a key notion, expressed in metaphors such as water flowing around a pebble in a stream or a willow bending with the wind.

A reluctance to define the *tao*, together with a preference for intuition over knowledge, made Lao-tzu's teachings seem mystical and obscure to many. However, the detachment central to Taoism as well as its interest in nature allowed a tradition of experimental enquiry into the natural world to emerge – medicine and alchemy received particular attention. In this sense, Taoism planted the seed of a scientific method.

K'ung fu-tzu, or Confucius in Latin, a younger contemporary of Lao-tzu, responded to political instability in a different way. Where Taosim was

Confucius surrounded by his pupils. All of the new questioners were educators who attracted a school to form around them. These schools continued to develop their ideas after their deaths – rarely into forms they themselves would have recognized.

detached from social problems, Confucius was committed to them. For Taoists, the feudal system had been an artificial code of duties replacing a natural harmony of human relations. It was inevitable that such an artificial imposition should break down, leaving only chaos in its wake. Confucius, on the other hand, looked back to the era of feudal stability as a golden age he wished to see restored. He saw in feudalism a mirror of traditional Chinese ancestor worship; they both involved a relationship based on the care of a superior for a loyal and respectful inferior.

Confucius, however, was not content to accept this relationship just because it was or had once been customary. He rationalized it into a system of ethics that should apply to all relationships within society. As such, social relations had to measure up to a reasoned philosophy, not to tradition.

Like the Buddha, Confucius sought to separate the worlds of reason and faith. Worship of ancestral spirits provided part of the model for his system of ethics, but as to the reality of these spirits he kept silent. They might well exist, but human enquiry could not decide the matter one way or another.

What is the Essential Nature of Things?

Greece at this time had a rich mythology involving a pantheon of all-too human gods. The conflict between this tradition and the new spirit of enquiry was bluntly put by Xenophanes, a contemporary of Confucius and the Buddha. 'If an ox could paint a picture, his god would look like an ox,' he said.

Xenophanes lived on the coast of present-day Turkey. In the 6th century BCE, Greece was a string of city-states experimenting with various forms of government in a search for political stability, and with a wary eye to a new and growing Persian empire to the east. These city-states were strung out across the Greek mainland, the islands of the Aegean and the Ionian coast of what is now Turkey, which was home to the richest and most cosmopolitan city-states, thanks in part to the recent introduction of money in this region.

Miletus was the largest of the Ionian cities and home to practical men such as Thales, astronomer, civil engineer and inventor. Thales began a new style of enquiry into how the world came to be. Greece had myths to answer this question, but Thales ignored them. For him, the world had been formed from a natural substance – water – and no accompanying story involving gods was relevant.

Anaximander, also from Miletus, put forward a complex account of the creation of the world, involving heat and cold forming a kind of egg from which earth,

The symbol of free speech. The Theatre of Dionysus on the southern slope of the Acropolis, where the issues that mattered to Athenians of the 5th century BCE were explored. Tragedies by Aeschylus, Sophocles and Euripides, and satires by Aristophanes were all premiered here.

water, air and so on separated out. It was very like a mythological account, but with mention only of physical processes – as though myth had been reduced to essential principles.

Other accounts followed and gradually the focus of these musings shifted from how the world came to be to what, essentially, it was made of. Within a hundred years of Thales, a Greek from the mainland called Democritus claimed the world was made from minute elemental particles he named 'atoms'.

By this time – the middle of the 5th century BCE – the Persians had expanded westwards and the headquarters of Greek enquiry had moved to Athens. Here the focus shifted from the natural world to human behaviour. How could a person live a good and fulfilling life? Sophists, such as Protagoras, were comparing their own society with others and concluding that values were no more than expressions of a particular culture. For Protagoras there was nothing to be done but accept this and learn the rules.

In contrast, Socrates pushed to find universal principles underlying all values by asking questions such as 'What is courage?' or 'What is justice?' He wanted to find the atom from which moral universes were built, and he thought he had found it in reason. For Socrates, people should learn how to act not by absorbing the culture around them, but by turning inward and listening to what reason told them. This was the way to a fulfilling life. Only reason could yield knowledge and, like the Buddha, Socrates thought knowledge was freedom.

For about 50 years, Athens produced something of a democratic society with these sorts of ideas – at least for part of its population. This entailed not just a certain form of elected government, but more importantly a culture of free speech, of open discussion of all kinds of questions – personal, social, moral, political, and religious. A new form of theatre was central to this. Protagoras and Socrates were free to take each other to task surrounded by a small coterie of intellectuals, but a larger audience could be reached by the twice-yearly theatre festivals. Athenian tragedy and comedy created drama that explored issues – drama as we know it today.

Eventually, the pursuit of essential principles became something of a cult in itself for Greek thinkers no longer engaged in practical tasks. For Socrates' pupil Plato, the real world was somewhere else and was composed of geometrical forms, of which the objects in this illusory world were merely imperfect copies. Knowledge of these archetypal forms was the only true knowledge. The reasons for this and other ideas are developed with beautiful and compelling clarity in his *Republic*, which deeply influenced Christianity.

A Global Community of Ideas

All of these people lived within a particular culture and many of them continued to observe the customs with which they were brought up. But they all asked questions of a universal nature, which their customs could not adequately answer unless they measured up to a universal standard of logical consistency. These people, though most of them never met or communicated with each other, created a global community of ideas.

To begin with, these ideas were accessible only to educated, literate people. They served to internationalize a divide between intellectual and popular culture that had opened up with the appearance of writing. If they had met, Confucius and Xenophanes would most likely have found more to talk about than either would with a peasant from his own society. In time, however, the appeal of many of these intellectual ideas widened as they were embellished and given colour by the addition of less austere popular beliefs. The growth of the great monotheistic religions, all of which became encrusted with a mass of popular stories and superstitions, is a case in point.

These religions, however, all retained their logical core: a claim to represent the one universal truth. Earlier, there had been many gods but no religious wars because no one had claimed an exclusive status for their god. Now there could be not only wars between religions, but also wars within religions, as teams of logically trained theologians sharpened their doctrines. Religious intolerance had been born.

Both within and outside religion, the idea of self-improvement had also been born. This was not self-improvement for job prospects or social advancement. It was the idea that personal salvation was something that could be studied and actively worked towards. It stood against an older, passive idea of fate.

A certain detachment lay behind much of the change in thinking that emerged around 500 BCE. Naturally, earlier people reasoned their way through all kinds of issues, but most of this reasoning seems to have been applied to specific practical problems. There is little evidence before this time of a more general interest in asking questions of universal scope, such as exists today within the natural and social sciences as well as in religion and the arts.

15: The Zero

Counting is one of the most basic human abilities. Deciding where to start from, however, came very late. Zero – nothing – as a quantity did not occur to people until they started to write numbers down. Even then, it only emerged after thousands of years, as a way of keeping numerals apart.

Above: The scientific community discuss their findings in 16th-century Istanbul. Centuries earlier, Arab astronomers had fused Greek geometry with Hindu arithmetic in order to draw up a new Islamic calendar, giving birth to a hybrid culture of learning and enquiry.

When it finally came, the zero brought with it a number system that made written arithmetic possible. Merchants were the first to benefit from this system, and through them it spread. Subsequently, mathematics and science were transformed, not just by ease of calculation but also by a new way of thinking about counting, central to which was a concept of balance.

Counting

Counting began with fingers, which is why most cultures counted to five or ten before 'moving up a level'. The Maya counted to 20 because they used their toes as well. Ten, however, was the most common base.

Moving up a level required two people. When a person had used up all their fingers a second person stuck one of theirs out and the first person began again. This way two people could count up to 100. When the second person had used up all their fingers

a third person stuck a finger out and the process began again. Three people could count up to 1000.

The early farming peoples of the great river valleys in various parts of the world adapted this system so that only one person was needed. A person made grooves in the sand and put pebbles in the first groove. When they had put ten pebbles in this groove they moved up a level by putting one in the next groove and clearing the pebbles from the first groove. The size of a number was indicated by a pebble's position. Later, counting boards were made to this design from wood or stone. Later still, the abacus replaced pebbles and grooves with beads that slid along rods.

With the abacus, a merchant or a tax collector could add up and subtract jars of oil or other commodities. But records of these sums had to be kept, so a way of writing numbers down was needed. To begin with, a number was represented by the same number of marks, but this was very cumbersome. To save time, the Sumerians and the Babylonians who inherited their culture imitated the way the abacus displayed numbers. They used symbols for only a few numbers and wrote them next to each other in imaginary columns as though they were beads on the abacus. The size of a number was indicated by a symbol in a particular position.

A map of the world as it was known to Ptolemy of Alexandria around 150 CE. The map is curved because the world was known to be spherical. Its circumference had been measured to within 80 kilometres (50 miles) by Eratosthenes around 200 BCE. Measuring the world required big numbers.

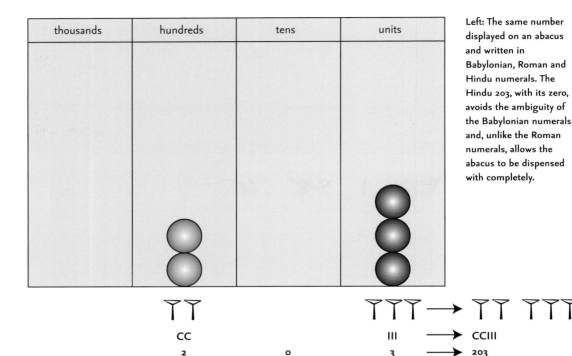

thousands	hundreds	tens	units

CC   III ⟶ CCIII

2   o   3 ⟶ 203

Left: The same number displayed on an abacus and written in Babylonian, Roman and Hindu numerals. The Hindu 203, with its zero, avoids the ambiguity of the Babylonian numerals and, unlike the Roman numerals, allows the abacus to be dispensed with completely.

There was some ambiguity in this system, however, because it was not always clear which column a symbol was meant to be in. Using our numerals as an example, 23 might mean 23 or 230 or 203 – or 2300 for that matter. Later Babylonians sometimes made a couple of diagonal marks to make clear where there was an empty column, but usually they did not. Other cultures – Egyptian, Chinese, Phoenician, Greek, Roman – used a different symbol for numbers belonging to different columns of the abacus so there could be no confusion. In the Roman numerals with which we are more familiar, XXIII (23) cannot be confused with CCXXX (230) or CCIII (203) – or MMCCC (2300).

Measuring

While some people were counting, other people were measuring. There was measuring of angles to find out what day it was and later on what time it was. There was measuring of the length and width of a field for tax purposes. Then there came measuring of angles and lengths for construction work.

Counting and measuring are very different. Counting jars of oil is an exact business involving whole numbers. Measuring can only be as exact as the instruments used, and seldom involves nice round numbers.

The classical Greeks were not too bothered by this. They found they could largely dispense with numbers for measuring by expressing the quantities they needed to know in terms of each other. They drew pictures of lines and angles and made calculations based on studying the logic of their relationships. In this way they avoided the messiness of measurements.

Once the centre of Greek culture moved to Alexandria in the 3rd century BCE, however, this changed. Alexander the Great had been to India and the Greek world had opened up. Alexandrian mathematicians were making maps laid out on a grid of latitude and longitude, for which they needed to know the size of the Earth. They were measuring the distance of the Sun from the Earth. They were calculating the range of artillery – huge catapults at that time. They were making machines with wheels, for which they required more precise values for π. They needed geometry, but a geometry that used numbers.

Right: As the new number system caught on in Europe, calculating races became fashionable, pitting traditional abacus-wielding against the new Hindu-Arabic arithmetic. In this fantasy contest, Boethius races Pythagoras, who looks worried. From the Margarita Philosophica, 1503.

The abacus was too limited for the calculations the Alexandrians wanted to make, which required both multiplication and division. The numbers they were dealing with were both too large and too small for the abacus. So they tried to do without the abacus and make calculations with their written numerals instead. But now they found their numerals would not co-operate. They would record the results of a calculation made on the abacus, but they would not behave like the abacus when used for making the calculation itself. So Alexandrian mathematics reached a glass ceiling.

The Language of Numbers

The solution to the problems of the Alexandrian mathematicians lay in India. By the 5th century CE, if not earlier, Hindus had taken the step the Babylonians had never quite managed. They used symbols for the first nine numbers and placed them in imaginary columns, but to avoid confusion they consistently used an extra symbol to represent an empty column. This was *sunya*, the zero, originally more like a decimal point. It held the other numerals in their positions and made a more powerful number system possible.

The Greek and Roman systems, although unambiguous, had resulted in numerals that had no visual connection with the abacus and therefore were hard to manipulate. The Roman number XXXI, for example, used four symbols to represent two rows of the abacus; the bigger number C used one symbol to represent three rows. The Hindu system reproduced on paper exactly what the abacus displayed.

As it happens, at a similar time the Maya were also consistently using a symbol for an empty column in their number system, but like most other cultures they used their written numerals only for recording. The crucial move made by the Hindus was to throw away the abacus now that they had effectively made a drawing of it. In its place, they began to use their numerals to calculate with, as the Alexandrians had tried to do.

Now there was no limit to the size of numbers that could be worked with because, in effect, the columns of the abacus were free to stretch off into infinity in both directions. More zeros in one direction meant bigger numbers, more zeros in another meant smaller numbers – or rather, divisions of a whole number. Hindu mathematicians began to understand how to manipulate parts of a number as easily as whole numbers.

As they played with their numerals, the Hindus began to see new relationships between numbers. They learned methods for multiplying and dividing that

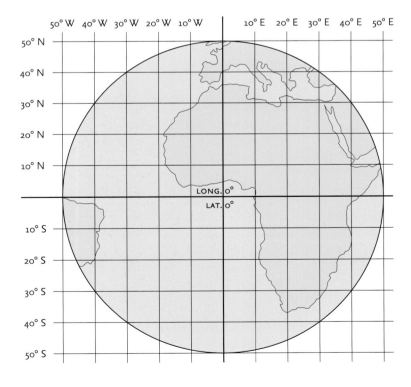

What are graphs but lines of latitude and longitude spread flat? Where the Greenwich meridian meets the equator is zero, horizontally and vertically. Take the map away and the course of a ship sailing across the ocean becomes a line on a graph.

implied general laws of arithmetic. Certain numbers had certain properties – almost personalities. *Sunya* or zero, the symbol for an empty column, affected calculations so it came to be thought of as a quantity in itself. The fact that *sunyata* or 'emptiness' was a familiar and important concept in meditation, associated with the idea of potential, may have encouraged this development.

In 628 CE, in his *The Opening of the Universe*, the mathematician and astronomer Brahmagupta (598–688 CE) laid out the basic laws for using *sunya*, laws that underpin all of our arithmetic:

$$\chi \times 0 = 0$$
$$\chi + 0 = \chi$$
$$\chi - 0 = \chi$$

Brahmagupta also formulated laws for using positive and negative numbers with *sunya*, couched in terms of fortunes and debts. For instance:

A fortune subtracted from sunya is a debt $(0 - \chi = -\chi)$
A debt subtracted from sunya is a fortune $(0 - -\chi = \chi)$

A language of numbers had first evolved so people could keep accounts of their business dealings. The Hindu number system had been created in the image of the abacus, which had been designed for accounting. Now the use of *sunya* was suggesting a new image drawn from the business world: the balance scales of the merchant. Positive amounts on one side and negative amounts on the other pivoted around a central zero. This concept of zero as a point of balance would come to shape the outlook of the modern world.

The Geometry of Numbers

As Brahmagupta was writing in northern India, great changes were taking place further west. Rome had crumbled into a Christian empire of sorts, which led to the closing of the Alexandrian schools. Greek and Jewish exiles from Alexandria had taken their science east to Persia, the inheritor of Babylonia. But now the Persian Empire was falling to Arabs, fired by a new Islamic faith. Unlike Christianity, however, Islam was a religion of merchants who soon began to embrace rather than repress the cultural diversity they encountered.

By 800 CE, Baghdad, about 80 kilometres (50 miles) upriver from Babylon, was becoming a centre of international learning, encouraged by Haroun al-Rashid, the Caliph of the *Tales of* 1001 *Nights*. Chinese

papermakers had arrived in the 750s and Hindu numerals around the same time. Jewish and Arabic scholars were translating Greek and Indian texts. Hindu astronomers were lending their number system to the making of a new calendar. Al-Rashid's son and successor al-Ma'mun set up observatories, the first major library since Alexandria and an academy called the House of Wisdom.

The most famous of the scholars working at the House of Wisdom was Muhammad ibn Musa al-Khwarizmi (c. 780–c. 850 CE). From the last part of his name comes the word 'algorithm', as a result of a book he wrote giving rules for calculating with the Hindu numerals, which popularized their use throughout the Muslim world, from central Asia to Spain.

His main treatise, on solving equations, gave us the word 'algebra'. In this work, al-Khwarizmi took Hindu arithmetic and Greek geometry and put them together. Geometry can be used to check sums. The sum 4 x 3 = 12 can be checked by placing four rows of three boxes together to form a rectangle and counting the boxes it contains. This means it can be used to find an unknown number, such as χ where 4 x χ = 12, by showing how it must relate to other quantities. Geometry brought new power to the Hindu enquiry into number relationships.

Diophantus of Alexandria (c. 207–c. 291 CE) had made inroads into a generalized arithmetic of this sort, but he had been held back by his number system. Greek numerals were not only hard to calculate with, they had also used up the alphabet, which made distinguishing between numbers and general or unknown quantities a problem. Hindu numerals overcame both of these obstacles. In Baghdad, algebra – the grammar of mathematics and physics – was able to take off.

Thinking about numbers as shapes brought the Arabs up against a puzzle, however. Al-Khwarizmi used an arithmetic technique for solving quadratic equations. He then checked this technique by drawing it out as geometry. A quadratic equation is a sentence in number language containing a squared number we want to find. Al-Khwarizmi's example was $\chi^2 + 10\chi = 39$. He drew χ^2 as a square with sides χ units long and found the length of χ by drawing other squares and rectangles around it. This showed that χ was 3.

However, many problems in life have more than one possible solution. Al-Khwarizmi's arithmetic technique gave two answers to quadratic equations. In this case, it claimed that χ could be 3 but that it could

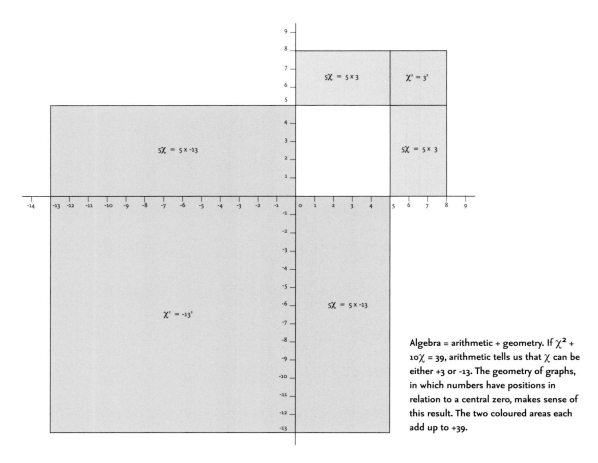

$5\chi = 5 \times 3$

$\chi^2 = 3^2$

$5\chi = 5 \times -13$

$5\chi = 5 \times 3$

$\chi^2 = -13^2$

$5\chi = 5 \times -13$

Algebra = arithmetic + geometry. If $\chi^2 + 10\chi = 39$, arithmetic tells us that χ can be either +3 or -13. The geometry of graphs, in which numbers have positions in relation to a central zero, makes sense of this result. The two coloured areas each add up to +39.

equally well be -13. But what could this mean? A square with sides 3 units long could be drawn, but how could a square with sides -13 units long exist?

The Point of Balance

There was a clue in Brahmagupta's concept of zero as the mid-point on a scale, but for a long time this idea benefited trade rather than mathematics. At the simplest level, it allowed a merchant to see how their business stood by keeping a profit-and-loss account. They could list their income on one side, their outgoings on the other, and add up the totals. If the result was zero they had broken even, if it was a positive number they were in the black, if it was a negative number they were in the red.

By around 1000 CE, trade brought the zero to China, as earlier it had brought it to the Arab world. By contrast, Europeans had less business sense. In 1202, Leonardo Fibonacci (c. 1170–c. 1250 CE) wrote his Liber Abaci. Fibonacci was an Italian brought up in Algiers, where his father organized trade with Italy. He learnt arithmetic from Arab merchants and wrote

a book showing how to calculate with their numerals. A few Italian accountants saw the use of it, but it took centuries to catch on.

This was partly due to a general suspicion of the Muslim world; much of the increased cultural contact from the 12th century onwards was the result of successive European crusades to rescue the Christian Holy Land from the infidel. But there was also a religiously inspired suspicion of the concept of zero itself. Where Indians had been philosophically receptive to the idea of emptiness, Christians saw a void where God was absent. Bringing this void into the world by making zero into a number in its own right had associations with summoning up an anti-Christ.

Eventually, however, an age of overseas exploration would bring pressure for a new geometry plotted on a map, which could show movement through space and time. For this to be possible, there would have to be a starting point, a point of reference from which movement could be made in one direction or another. In René Descartes' (1596–1650) geometry, zero would become the centre of a graph in which all numbers had a position above or below zero and left or right of it. The point of balance on a linear scale between credit and debit would become the point of balance in a scale of spatial relationships. In this context, al-Khwarizmi's square of -13 would find its meaning as a square that stretched 13 units down from the zero and 13 units to the left of it.

The balancing property of zero would become clearer still due to the fact that graphs use lines or curves to express movement. Often the limit of this movement would be the crucial issue, the point where two forces balance each other out, whether they be the gravitational pulls of planets, the forces of machine parts or the fluctuations of the stockmarket. This limit would be expressed by the curve flattening out until its gradient was zero. Zero would become the point of rest in a world of constant motion.

The Door to an Age of Calculation

Alexandria was home to a technological culture absorbed in calculation and mechanical engineering. This culture had discovered most of the elements of an engine, including steam power, but it never took the decisive step into the machine age. Cheap labour was too abundant to create much of a market for machines for one thing, in addition to which there was no cheap and reliable source of iron or steel. But Alexandria's engineers were also crippled by an unco-operative number system.

Pistons that run smoothly within their cylinders require precision machining in accordance with exact calculations. Numerals that will divide easily down to tiny fractions of a whole number are required. Such numerals are also needed in order to calculate how much force a piston will release.

Our world is saturated with ways in which zero makes calculation easy. Engineering is only one example. Tables of statistics, whether showing the times of trains or the results of surveys, are everywhere. We are familiar with number relationships such as interest-rate percentages and betting odds. We understand at a glance graphs showing changing sales figures and rates of unemployment. Reading off a balance scale, whether on a bank statement or on a thermometer, is second nature to us.

The modern world is a world seen through a matrix of calculation. A few hundred years ago, Europe stood at the threshold of this world, holding a new number language produced by a dialogue between cultures.

Zero and One

Zero was always a second-class citizen in the republic of numbers. In its Indian childhood it was merely a point, like our decimal point, kept apart from other numbers in mathematical discussions. Later on it was given a proper shape, but then had to endure centuries of discrimination in Europe; at best it was seen as a numerical imposter.

Certainly zero was not like other numbers. Where other numbers said 'Yes, there are three biscuits' or 'Yes, there are six eggs', zero said 'No, there are none. No biscuits, eggs or anything else.' As the number that always said no, it stood against all the other numbers put together. One day all numbers would become reduced to this binary opposition.

Civilization needs someone or something to do menial work. In Sumerian mythology, the gods created human beings to do their work for them. The Sumerians themselves got slaves to do it. The Alexandrians, to some extent the Romans and particularly the Arabs were interested in machines, though they had more success with water clocks and what we might call 'executive toys' than heavy machinery. Nevertheless, they were interested in automatic processes.

Mechanizing brute force, in any case, is only half the task of producing a robot. A true mechanical slave should be able to take orders just like a human slave. When the Arab interest in clocks and automata percolated through to Christian Europe from the 12th century, it expressed itself in mechanical public clocks that could be programmed to chime a tune on the hour using a series of hammers and bells.

This was a matter of creating a string of commands that told each hammer either to strike or not to strike a bell at each point in the tune. In the Low Countries by the 14th century these commands were being fed to the hammers by a revolving drum perforated with rows of holes. If a wooden peg were inserted into a certain hole it would trigger a certain hammer to strike as the drum turned; if there were no peg in the hole the hammer would not strike. By re-arranging the pegs the hammers could be programmed to play different tunes.

Later, in France, this idea was adapted for weaving, one of the earliest human crafts. Weaving is the process of creating a grid of material by repeated movements. It is an even more highly structured process than music making and therefore ideally suited to simple binary commands. If a pattern is to be woven, certain threads must be raised above the shuttle and others not. Before each movement of the shuttle there is a series of yes/no decisions to be made.

By the early 18th century, these decisions were represented by a series of holes punched in cards fed to the loom. A particular thread would be raised or not depending on whether a hole had been punched in a specific part of the card.

Eventually, punched cards would be replaced by a numerical way of representing commands. Nowadays, the same kind of yes/no orders are given to computers by reducing the language of numbers to a series of zeros and ones.

In Delacroix's painting, Liberty Leading the People, Marianne, a character
invented as a symbol of reason and liberty, leads the French people. With the
emergence of mass politics, old forms of community were destroyed and
nationalism had to be created through just such appeals to the emotions.

Part 2: Into the Modern World

In the first part of this book, we looked at the foundations of civilization, which amounted to human beings' efforts to insulate themselves from their natural environment. It involved buildings and the search for safe spaces, weapons for protection, faith systems to explain and assuage the ultimate fears of life and death.

In time, it involved forming complex societies, none of which were inevitable. Human history has turned out to be unpredictable and largely accidental. Civilization was and is an ongoing series of experiments. It has changed in unexpected ways; it has moved on and progressed, sometimes for the better, but all too often with brutal and destructive consequences.

What have been the drivers of this change? How did they translate into actual events and facts? In this section, we try to identify some of the ideas that over time inaugurated a vital jump in human collective power. We do so by looking at a particular era, perhaps the one we can best understand, even as its legacy remains uncertain: the last several hundred years, the period that saw the emergence of Western hegemony.

Some great events, which seemed to have no resonance beyond themselves at the time, now reveal large structural changes buried beneath the surface – the Black Death was such an event. Other events exploded into the world and their impact was immediately clear: the French Revolution is an obvious example but not necessarily for the reasons one would expect.

This is not a history of several hundred years in one geographical space in the world. It is an attempt to unravel what happened to civilization when it took one very narrow path – the path to modernity. It may or may not turn out to be a dead end.

16: The Great Pestilence

Disease and health are a measure of how well societies can organize themselves. How quickly can they recover from the ravages of a major epidemic? What we are about to look at is not only the biological event that was called 'The Great Pestilence', but also the way it suggests the cultural and political emergence of the European territorial sovereign state, which has become the global norm.

Above: Rumours of 'plague spreaders' rose steadily from the 14th century, giving rise to the witch-hunts, mass trials and burnings of the 15th century. The generalized stress accompanying epidemics and social change was central to such outbreaks of mass hysteria.

The pestilence spread around the known world in five years and killed about 75 million people. It probably started in China in 1334, where perhaps two thirds of the population died. It occasioned the 'invention' of biological warfare, when Tartars retreating from their siege of Kaffa by the Black Sea threw plague-infested bodies over the walls. The Italian merchants sheltering inside the citadel managed to escape and to sail back to the Mediterranean, but the plague went with them and soon raged through Europe, where it killed perhaps 20 million people, a quarter of the population.

The milestone this chapter discusses is not only the biological event that was called 'The Great Pestilence', but also the crucial political milestone an epidemic can become. In the case of the plague, the pandemic changed the whole course of Western civilization.

Even now there is a debate about what sort of plague this was. Arguments rage about black rats, brown rats, dead rats and infected fleas from the latter migrating on to humans. That it spread so furiously and so rapidly was its defining feature. Scientists still dig up graves to analyze teeth and bones seven centuries old in search of the exact nature of a disease known as 'The Black Death'.

So if we are not sure what it was, why is it a milestone? Because a pandemic both reveals and exacerbates whatever weakness there is in a society. Only a fierce political will can hold people together in the face of fear and despair when death strikes so unpredictably. Ibn Khaldun (1332–1406), the famous judge and university lecturer, described the aftermath in Egypt (half the population died in Cairo, then the world's second biggest city with a population of a quarter of a million people) this way: 'Cities and buildings were bared, roads and signposts were abandoned, villages and palaces were deserted; tribes and dynasties were expunged. It was as if the voice of existence in the world had called out for oblivion, and the world had responded to the call.'

Wherever it struck, the plague hit both towns and countryside hard. Because nearly half of the people then lived below subsistence level, they had little resistance. When it arrived, the Black Death thinned out the supply of working poor tied to the land, which shook the political order of the time. The crisis set off peasant revolts through Europe that were put down viciously, but it also made possible new freedoms. With so much farmland left untended, wages rose for those peasants who survived. Not only could they sell their labour at a higher price, they could move away. Wages rose at the same time as the value of land crashed and was bought up by new men. What was left of a centuries' old, rigid, feudal order organized around the invincible rights of the nobility began to disappear.

The Growth of State Power

It was in the growing cities, however, that we see the changes most telling for the future development of the state. The fight against plague – which became the model for disease control – was never separate from a general drive for more control over society. All over Europe, the plague afforded the opportunity for central authority to extend its power where it had resolve – and this in a time of unrest when the poor were already an object of concern to political elites and rulers. Plague controls became a test of political will and authority.

In Milan, the ruling Viscontis were able to impose draconian measures, such as sealing up houses infected with plague so that all their occupants died. To carry out this and other similarly harsh measures, they created a formal and permanent health board. The death rate in Milan, as a result, was only 15 per cent, but the course of action that contained it marked a division between rule as improvisation and rule as routine. In Florence, on the other hand, where merchants were powerful enough to block any legislation that would seriously threaten trade, no less than 60 per cent of the population died.

Venice – a city state run by oligarchs and one of the most highly urbanized areas in the world – provided another example of where a disease tightened and formalized political power. The ruling powers there set up lazarettos or pest houses to isolate the sick, imposed a 40-day quarantine on ships, and interned outsiders. There was a whole raft of public-health ordinances – the emptying of chamber pots was banned, for example – and appointed health officers were given the right to execute anyone who broke these ordinances. None of this could have been imposed without a highly determined centre of power. The pest houses were hated as much as symbols of plague controls as of the plague itself.

The struggle to contain the disease also represents the opening of what became a fierce war between secular and Church power, and the way secular reasoning was beginning to challenge religious dictat. In Venice, for instance, gatherings were forbidden in an attempt to stop the spread of contagion and the government was able to enforce a ban of Church processions in direct defiance of the Pope. If the Christian prelates interpreted the plague

As this woodcut illustrates, the rich were as helpless as the poor when plague arrived. Age-old farming communities, characterized by fixed social hierarchies and a rigid pattern of mutual obligations, broke down as lords and vassals alike perished.

as divine punishment for sin, the ruling powers chose to embrace human action as the way to control it: prayer and penance had their place, but also isolation and quarantine.

The Seeds of the Renaissance and Reformation

The plague brought about a change in the way people were ruled and a new assertion of secular political authority over the over-arching power of the Catholic Church – the only continent-wide institution at that time. It opened the window onto the coming battle between faith and reason itself. A new tough realism entered the arts, and European culture became morbid and pessimistic in outlook, no doubt a result of witnessing such devastation. Sculpture and paintings started to put an emphasis on emotion and individualism. Doctors who had been helpless before the spread of the plague started to take more interest in the way the body actually worked. Here were the seeds of the Renaissance: the response to the 'Black Death' heralded the intellectual social and economic transformation, with its curiosity about and commitment to the accomplishments of man.

In 1630, when waves of plague still swept over Europe, Nicholas Poussin (1594–1665) – a French painter, resident at the time in Rome – painted The Plague of Ashdod. On the surface, it is a large Biblical canvas in the classical style. It shows the Philistines after they captured the Ark of Covenant. A painting has its own internal vocabulary; it is the product of its own culture and context. When Poussin's Philistines bring the Ark to Ashdod, they bring the plague with them, and we can 'read' on this canvas the ways in which Europe had been changed since that first epidemic.

The faces of Poussin's figures are contorted in pain, disgust and revulsion as disease, something 'unclean', strikes the Israelites on their contact with foreigners. This was in a time when Europe was awash with savage

The Journey West

As deadly as the Black Death was, it may be that the worst ever health disaster occurred fewer than 200 years later, when Old World diseases sailed to and decimated the New World of the Americas. Lured by legends of gold and glitter, the Spanish set out to conquer dynamic empires that covered huge territories. Myth would have it that Hernán Cortés (1485–1547), with his tiny band of 300 men, was able to capture Montezuma's mighty Aztec Mexico because of the superiority of European weapons. But guns alone would not have kept him safe on the long, slow climb to the high Andes, surrounded and outnumbered at every turn. Nor was it divine intervention and God's blessing on their conquest, as the Spaniards later asserted when in missionary mode.

Cortés could easily have been cut down as other explorers were in Hawaii (Captain Cook) or Ethiopia (Cristovão da Gama). He avoided that fate in part because the huge Amerindian empires were already over-extended, fighting civil wars, and were themselves the oppressive conquerors of resentful tributaries. Mostly they crumbled before the onslaught of the diseases that the foreigners brought with them.

Montezuma himself died of smallpox before Cortés succeeded in his siege of the Aztec capital of Tenochtitlan (present-day Mexico City). He took a city three times the size of Seville, with a population of 300,000 people. Half the people of Tenochtitlan had died of smallpox by the time Cortés and his band of 300 men finally entered it, backed by Montezuma's disaffected tributaries.

The diseases the Spaniards brought with them did most of the fighting for them. The viruses and bacteria travelled up and down the Americas so quickly, that it is still not possible to trace their paths. It has been estimated that within 75 years, 90 per cent of America's population of 100 million was wiped out by diseases to which they had no immunity. Diseases such as smallpox – which sailed with Cortés – moved across the land faster than the invaders. As epidemics spread, the will to resist died, along with the collapse of all social structures and support. To meet the shortage of labour in the silver mines, the Spanish started importing slaves from Africa as early as 1530. With them came malaria, yellow fever – and other disastrous epidemics.

In this way, germs have been the catalysts of history. Silver soon flooded across the Atlantic to fill the treasury of the Spanish kings – 16,000 tons of silver alone within a century – only to be dissipated in wars. In turn, the wars funded by the Americas brought about more epidemics, not least that of syphilis, which raged through Europe carried by Spanish and French soldiers. It was known as 'the Columbian disease', on the assumption it had sailed back with Christopher Columbus. A bitter and ironic codicil.

religious wars as the Protestant Reformation and Catholic Counter-Reformation fought to break one another's power. In the painting, helpless priests are caught in gestures of fearful dismay among the dead and dying – what Poussin captures is that trust in the unquestioned authority of the priestly caste had been broken and was not about to be repaired.

Persecution of the Jews

There is also the sense of contamination: that it is outsiders who represent mayhem. The imposition of quarantine and the strengthening of borders had brought with them the sense of outsiders as harbingers of danger, even evil. Sometimes, though, the outsiders, who were blamed and demonized, were within; it is no coincidence that the Black Death sparked persecution of the outsider – first and foremost the Jews, who were accused of poisoning wells. There were massacres in Mainz, Frankfurt and Strasbourg. In Basel, Jews were penned into a wooden building and burned alive.

Jews were not the only such victims. Accusations of sorcery and witchcraft flared across the continent. When a stressed society perceives disease as the work of its enemies and reinvents them as scapegoats, it is an expression of its own inner anxiety. It reflects strains and conflicts inherent in its social and political systems. Out of such conflict, came radical change.

During the Middle Ages, Europe had been dominated by a decentralized warrior nobility and the universal Catholic Church. In the devastation of the Black Death, sovereign authority proved to be more dynamic and effective than either – and the pandemic gave rulers the opportunity to seize and exercise ever greater power.

Poussin's *Plague of Ashdod*. A bare-breasted woman lies dead having slain her baby with her milk – a reminder of the stigmatization of women at this time, deemed by Catholic Inquisition authorities to be 'an inescapable punishment, a necessary evil'.

17: The Military Revolution

In 1450, there were probably around 200 independent states, principalities and city states in Europe. Four hundred years later, there were 25. War generated, created and shaped the survivors. Wars were won as much by invisible power and preparation at home as the ability to adjust to new weaponry in the field.

Above: The casting of bronze cannon changed European warfare. Not only were they expensive, setting off a major arms race, but a train of highly-mobile bronze cannon firing iron shot seared through the fragile walls of cities and fortresses. This woodcut, c. 1550, shows Maximilian I of Habsburg (1459–1519) consulting with craftsmen at his foundry.

There is nothing new in violence. The ordinary European man in the 13th century was ten times more likely to be the victim of homicide than his counterpart today. On the other hand, war was more a matter of small-scale, if savage, domestic housekeeping. Nobles commanded their own followers and in many places had the legal right to wage private wars. Professional entrepreneurs hired out to the highest bidder their armed bands of mercenaries, an investment they tried not to put at risk more than necessary. Power was largely local, wielded by the man on horseback or the local priest. The average countryman could go a lifetime without seeing an officer of the prince or king. A ruler's ability to go to war depended entirely on the support of his powerful nobles – who were, of course, also his rivals.

Sometime around the beginning of the 16th century, a military revolution changed fundamentally the way states were organized and war was waged, and created many of the basic features of modern warfare and military organization as we know them today. Inevitably, this had an impact on the formation of the modern territorial state. Technological changes have a habit of acquiring a force of their own; sooner or later, society starts to adjust and reform around them.

War and the State

War is expensive; the ruler who can establish routines, treasuries, courts, central administrations – almost as a by-product of the need to raise money – increases the power of the crown in the process. War needs civil servants to organize it and monitor supplies. Information and intelligence become key. As the state apparatus grows to meet the demands of war, bigger and better planned wars become possible in order to beat off external threats and seize territory. No ruler at this time set out with the intention of designing the modern national state but, nevertheless, this is what came to pass.

Whether the state made war or war made the state, is something of a chicken-and-egg question. Both are true: the new, larger, more powerful state made war, and larger, more destructive wars made the state. Either way, the legacy of this revolution peers at us today if only through the smoke of the 275 new wars in the world and 150 million battle deaths during the dark last century.

Where did this military revolution start? The opening salvo was fired in 1453 when the Turks used cannon to destroy the hitherto impregnable walls of Constantinople. Then, in 1494, the French King Charles VIII led his army into Italy. He took with him a large siege train of modern, highly mobile bronze cannon, which fired iron shot. The fragile, often badly maintained walls of the Italian cities and fortresses were battered to bits. Within a year, the French army had mowed through the city-states of Italy and entered Naples – an unprecedented feat. Some milestones are only clear with hindsight; the radical nature of this first military revolution was clear to contemporaries immediately. The turning point was the arrival in Europe of gunpowder.

Gunpowder

Gunpowder itself was not new. It was first invented by Chinese alchemists, who, ironically, were seeking the elixir of life. It may date to as early as 800 CE, but its use was particularly developed during the Sung dynasty (960–1280), an era that saw in China the introduction of restaurants, fine silks, paper money, the bank note and the movable-type printing presses that ran off Confucian texts for entry exams into the civil service.

Myth has it that the Chinese only used gunpowder for fireworks. In fact, they developed not only fire lances or flame throwers, but cannon too. By the 13th century, a Chinese Bureau of Munitions was running seven factories, which together could put out 7,000 rockets and 21,000 bombs per day. It was probably the military use of gunpowder that enabled China to resist invasion by the Mongols for so long.

The Tartar armies swept out of and across the Asian plains in the 13th century to invade Japan and Persia, and got as far as Moscow, Kiev, Poland and Hungary, bringing gunpowder with them. The timing was crucial – the use and development of gunpowder in Europe was intricately linked to the flowering of humanism in the Renaissance. Men's growing intellectual curiosity and confidence was to create both great art, and better, bigger, more accurate instruments of war. Leonardo da Vinci's notebooks of this period contain sketches for a machine gun, a primitive tank, and steam-powered cannon. Michelangelo repeatedly submitted drawings of fortifications he thought could withstand bombardment by the new artillery.

In the Battle of Lepanto, the 'Holy League', led by Venice, crushed the superior Turkish force, capturing 137 ships and sinking 50. The Turks lost 20,000 men in battle. In Veronese's painting, The Battle of Lepanto, Venice kneels in heaven for Our Lady's blessing.

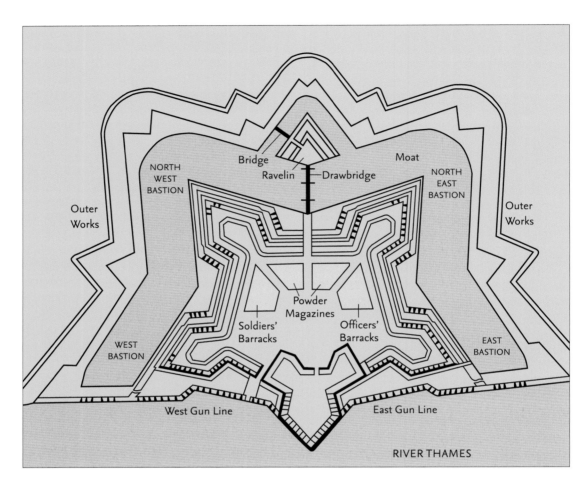

As newer, more powerful weapons and larger armies went into the field, ever-greater defences had to be devised against them. Mathematicians and engineers acquired a new importance in calculating the defensive strength of, for example, a new style of fortress: the *trace italienne*.

Siege Warfare

Improved technology explains only part of the revolution – the response to it is what moved innovation along. The *trace italienne*, originating with Italian architects as its name suggests, was one response to the new offensive weapons. It was an entirely new style of fortress, based on curtain walls that were covered against artillery fire by a series of earthen ramparts and ditches. There were arrowhead bastions at their corners, setting up interlocking fields of fire to cover blind spots. As long as defenders could feed themselves and hold out, these new fortresses could resist the new artillery.

Imitation was another powerful force. By the 1530s, France employed over a hundred Italian engineers to work on its northern defences. Within decades, more than a dozen of these monster fortresses lined that country's border with the Netherlands, defended by more than 1000 pieces of artillery. At the same time, other Italians were working on the Netherlands' defences. Just fortifying the centre of Antwerp with nine bastions cost a million florins – an enormous sum at the time. And, as better, bigger fortifications were built, so larger, newer, more accurate offensive weapons – more mobile, with more hitting power – were developed with which to lay siege to them. The cycle continued.

If the new fortresses were costly to defend, so were they to besiege. It meant numbers counted – there had to be enough soldiers to encircle a town or castle completely, in order to shut off all escape routes. It involved the digging of fortified trenches facing towards the city or fortress, but also outwards to defend the troops in case a relieving army arrived. It signalled the end of the tradition of campaigning only in the summer months and meant being prepared to hold a siege through winter. This in turn required better supply lines, more food, and more animals to draw the carts that brought up guns and ammunition. By the end of the 16th century, it was reckoned that 60 horses were needed to pull one gun and the carts hauling its ammunition. Slowly but surely, in what had hitherto been fairly ramshackle states, more efficient government had to evolve with bureaucracies in place to raise money for, and keep track of, all this activity.

This was the age that saw the emergence of early capitalists – merchants, entrepreneurs, financiers – people who specialized in the accumulation, purchase and sale of capital. Capital was liquid and easily moved, however, as King Phillip II of Spain discovered when his unpaid soldiers sacked Antwerp in 1527 and his source of loans decamped to the safety of Amsterdam. Between 1500 and 1650, the Spanish monarchy's military bill increased by 300 per cent in real terms. Suddenly, kings wanting to go to war were as dependent on bankers as feudal princes had been on their vassal lords.

The Musket

For the ordinary, individual soldier, the development of early firearms and artillery barely changed the nature of war. It had always been messy; it just got messier. The early arquebus and musket were unreliable and inaccurate. The arquebusier in the thick of battle would not only have been blinded by smoke, but he was also carrying a supply of black powder and at the same time holding a lit match. Guns broke bones and, when gangrene set in, often meant the loss of a leg or arm.

The Lion and the Fox: the Emergence of Political Science

'One can generally say this about men: that they are ungrateful, fickle, simulators and deceivers, avoiders of danger, greedy for gain; and while you work for their good they are completely yours, offering you their blood, their property, their lives … when danger is far away: but when it comes nearer to you they turn away.'
NICCOLO MACHIAVELLI (1469-1527)

When the cannon of Mehmed II blasted through the walls of Constantinople, it was the catalyst for a new, ferocious form of military conflict and the emergence of the larger, more powerful state. As princes with disparate inherited realms became monarchs of nations, politics started to be thought about as an autonomous sphere, separate from divine law, the Church and the clergy, who had been the bureaucrats of medieval Europe.

The constant threat of military competition called for thinking that was hard-edged, realistic, secular, looking at political action as subject to a genuinely different morality from that of the Gospels, lifted clear of exalted purpose. Civil peace, order and security were goals sufficient in themselves. The early herald of this new political science was Niccolo Machiavelli of Florence.

By the time he published The Prince in 1513, Machiavelli had seen Charles VIII of France's siege train sweep through Italy, the Florentine republic overthrown and restored, the seizing of power by the Medicis and their downfall. In this battlefield of sovereign power rivalry, Machiavelli claimed that stability called for a ruler who was both the cunning, unscrupulous and coldly calculating fox, and the lion who could take on wolves. The philosopher Bertrand Russell called

The Prince a 'handbook for gangsters'. The historian Friedrich Meinecke said that Machiavelli 'planted a dagger into the politic of the West'. Why? Perhaps because he was the first thinker who allowed that either men could seek salvation in this world or in the next but that the two were not compatible. The world of events was cut loose from divine order.

Contrary to his notorious image, Machiavelli was not without a moral ideal. The welfare of the state was for him the highest form of social existence, for which no sacrifice was too great. The ruler must adopt any methods available to preserve a society's power and glory. When necessary, he had to be pitiless, in order to safeguard a strong, vigorous state governed for the benefit of its citizens. The exercise of brutality and fear would sometimes be the only way to achieve political stability.

If such policies were indispensable, so be it: whoever wills the end, wills the means. Better a few timely executions than constant murder and plundering. Machiavelli neither glorified nor celebrated political ruthlessness as such; he accepted it as necessary. His was not morality for the private individual but it was morality nevertheless – a new morality for a ruler charged with the responsibility for the security of the state.

A century later, another thinker who had survived the raging of vicious religious wars continued the idea that any supreme, autocratic ruler exercising absolute power is preferable to social chaos. Thomas Hobbes (1588–1679) wrote Leviathan in 1651. For him, man's innate nature was such that by reason alone, he would hand over absolute power to any ruler, however unjust, as a barrier to social mayhem. The only alternative was, as Hobbes puts it in one of the most famous phrases in political philosophy, 'the life of man, solitary, poor, nasty, brutish and short'. The debate still resonates.

'Blessed be those happy ages that were strangers to the dreadful fury of these devilish instruments of artillery, whose inventor I am satisfied is now in hell.' Don Quixote's creator, the writer Miguel de Cervantes (1547–1616), understood well what he was cursing – he lost his left hand at the Battle of Lepanto in 1571.

Once the musket replaced the arquebus, any poor, uneducated peasant could be taught to load and fire it. The trick was to break down the peasant's task into a few simple moves, and then to discipline and drill him to march and fire on order. Printing made basic

Printing presses churned out manuals that broke down weapons' training into simple, repetitive movements; peasants could be turned into musket-bearing soldiers within days. The supremacy of the highly-trained, proud Swiss pike-man was broken. Soldiers became expendable.

training manuals available throughout Europe so that a small group of experienced soldiers could quickly train up large improvised armies. Prince Maurice of Nassau (1567–1625) in the Netherlands commissioned just such a training manual from the engraver, Jacob de Gheyn (c. 1565–1629). Look at that artist's woodcut of a skilled Swiss mercenary pike-man ornately decorated, standing with pride, and then at the knowing look of the officer, training men who were cheap, expendable, unskilled and above all, easily replaced.

War meant organization, and the employment of officials to deepen the penetration of government into society to raise taxes. Information about his subjects became important to a ruler. Surveillance, or rather spying, became as much a domestic matter as external. There was a warning too: guns got smarter but they could also be dangerous if they fell into the hands of rebels.

Banking on War

'What Your Majesty needs is money, more money, money all the time.' So Marshal Tribulzio advised King Louis XII, shortly before his invasion of Italy in 1499. European rulers were then spending over 40 per cent of their budgets on their military adventures. War meant glory to the throne. If the escalating cost of the military revolution was a prime factor in state formation, it was also the driving force of financial innovation.

For medieval monarchs, the country's budget was the same as their own purse – and vice versa. To finance the shortfalls of their wars, they mostly relied on personal loans from wealthy banking families. Siennese and Florentine bankers made loans to the kings of England; south German bankers lent to the Habsburgs; Swiss and Italian bankers to the French. The Spanish king borrowed from the marranos (or converted Jews) of Portugal who had been thrown out of his own country. There were drawbacks, of course, for the lenders. The French king, Charles VII (1403–61) was not the first to ruin his bankers by defaulting on his loans. Spain defaulted on loans no less than 14 times between 1557 and 1696. France defaulted 11 times in much the same period. It was all part of doing business. Credit soon revived, but was far more expensive to tap.

Even as war became more expensive, demanding the organization of an on-going state bureaucracy, financing it long remained an arrangement between individuals. Horatio Pallavicino moved to London as collector of Papal taxes under the Catholic Queen Mary. When Elizabeth came to the throne, he converted to Protestantism, pocketed the Papal taxes and laid the foundation to his huge fortune, which he lent to the new queen after becoming her financial agent. Elizabeth died deeply in debt to his family.

The idea of a 'public debt' – as opposed to the ruler's own purse – originated with the city-states of Italy in the 12th century. The Venetian Republic, for example, serviced and redeemed its debt by earmarking the revenues from its state salt monopoly. Other city-states raised loans by issuing life annuities or urban bonds, for which the investor lent his capital in return for a guaranteed income. Gradually, the bonds were made transferable, so they could be sold if investors wanted to get their money out before they matured. In 1587, Venice established the first real public bank, the Banco della Piazza di Rialto, which reformed the republic's currency and payments system. It took in deposits, made transfers between accounts possible and accepted bills of exchange payable to its clients.

Slowly, European monarchs learned to imitate these techniques. One of the most important, copied from Italy, was the establishment of the public bank – which both managed the state's debt and acted as an early form of clearing house, crucial for the development of commerce and trade.

A common way around the shortfall between income and the expenditure of war was the unfortunate practice of debasing the coinage; at this time a coin was still supposed to match face value with the value of the metal it contained. In the 1540s, for example, Henry VIII issued, in secret, debased coins that had a face value of twice the price of the metal they contained. Such practices were so widespread that, by the 17th century, there was monetary chaos in Europe. In Amsterdam alone in 1610, there were about a thousand different gold and silver coins in circulation, which pushed up the cost of doing any form of business.

It was because of the importance of funding war while safeguarding trade that the Dutch and English tried to establish systems of fixed exchange rates for their currencies, and the newly formed Bank of England took an interest in and later responsibility for stabilizing the country's currency. War, as Herodotus had said two thousand years earlier, is the father of all things.

Fugger the Rich, a 16th-century banker. Realising that sovereigns were high risk, he took as collateral for loans to the Habsburgs monopoly on silver, gold and copper mines and, in real terms, made fortunes greater than any modern corporation.

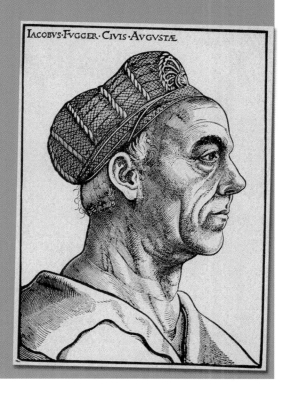

IACOBVS·FVGGER·CIVIS·AVGVSTÆ

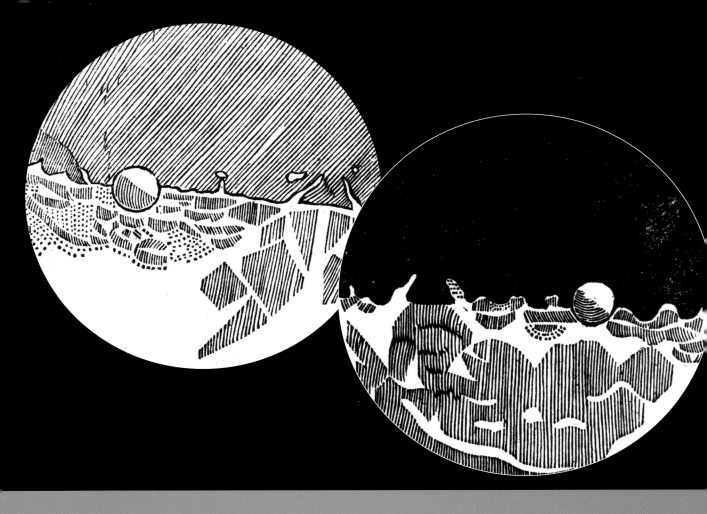

18: The Scientific Revolution

At first, it was neither exactly science nor was it a revolution, since it took the best part of the 16th and 17th centuries. Even so, it is known as 'The Scientific Revolution' and marks a time of fundamentally important changes in knowledge about natural reality, and the way that knowledge was to be investigated and reliably established. This was a crucial milestone in the building of 'the empire of the West'.

Above: Galileo's drawings, from his book The Starry Messenger, revealed the moon to be rough and uneven, not unchanging for all time. By training the newly-invented telescope on the sky, Galileo's discoveries began to challenge beliefs about Earth's privileged place in God's cosmos.

By the end of the 17th century, there had been a radical transformation in the way educated Europe thought about and looked at the world. Almost by accident, new ideas and inventions shook the medieval view of a divinely ordered, earth-centred universe dancing to God's harmonies. In its place came a more brutal, man-centred, functional view of nature, which could be manipulated and made useful.

A Climate of Change

It is hard to pinpoint why this dramatic shift happened and even harder to spotlight why man's sense of his own mastery evolved where it did. At the end of the 15th century, Europe still seemed to be a beleaguered corner of a world in which China had until now generated most of its impressive inventions, Islam had displayed an all-conquering energy and the mighty Ottoman Empire extended over a million square miles. Yet such was the changing tide towards the West that by 1674, the Emperor of China turned over the imperial observatory to European astronomers to run and, nine years later, the great Ottoman army was driven back from Vienna. It was as if the geographical exploration that Europe was simultaneously engaged in was a sign of a deeper shift from a passive to an active mood.

European exploration in the New World helped to undermine traditional, Biblical explanations for the origins and history of the world. If the Flood was a genuine and global event, how could so many species of animals have fitted into Noah's Ark? Were all humans from Europe to Africa to the Americas descended directly from Adam and Eve? If so, how had their offspring reached the furthermost corners of the globe, and how could the differences in the races of mankind be accounted for? If ancient philosophy decreed that the stars, planets, Moon and Sun in God's eternal heaven revolved around the static Earth in constant and perfect circles – how was it that men's own eyes found inconsistencies in the skies?

The Scientific Revolution has to be set in the context of the growing and fast-changing Europe of early capitalism, where trade depended on knowledge, information and an adventuring spirit, and the exploration of the Americas poured silver and gold into the European economy. Slowly, power was shifting to the Atlantic seaboard. It was an era of growing technical ascendancy in warfare and weapons, the development of wind and water power, the compass and magnetism, paper-making, spectacle-making and sheer business acumen married to common sense and industry.

Printing and Literacy

The invention of the printing press in 1454 stirred intellectual activity only indirectly at first. The early bestsellers were almanacs, health tracts, medieval encyclopedias or travellers' tales, which were often largely imaginary. Publishers were businessmen who had to turn a profit. The printing press in itself could not generate new ideas but it created a whole new reading public, and more readers led to the creation

The statue of Copernicus in his birthplace of Torun, Poland. Pre-Copernican astronomy decreed that the Sun revolved around the Earth – in conjecturing about a heliocentric world, this lowly prelate undermined thousands of years of teaching, not least that of the Church.

of more and different kinds of books. By 1500, millions of books were circulating in Italy alone. A literate population (not necessarily formally educated) emerged, which was open to looking at the real world in a fresh way. Leonardo da Vinci (1452–1519), for example, who was not particularly well educated, absorbed ideas and the language in which they were expressed from his reading of published books. Printing reshaped the boundaries of literate culture and created a market for the new, reformed body of knowledge.

All of these developments fostered – and were fostered by – a confidence that how men could manipulate the world God had created was hardly less wonderful than the world itself. This confidence was unintentionally bolstered by Martin Luther's religious revolution, which defied the rule of the Catholic Church in Rome and placed the individual directly before God without the intermediary of priests. The Protestant Reformation shook the whole notion of authority and order, and set off savage wars of religion. This religious schism was part of a general crisis, which occurred at the same time as Europe discovered, translated and printed a raft of previously lost Greek texts. Instead of accepting blindly the wisdom of the ancients, men were inspired by them to investigate for themselves the world they described and the questions they raised.

Standing on the Shoulders of Giants

As unfashionable as the 'great men' version of history is now, the rise of the new science threw up some intellectual giants. When there is one firmly established truth about the world, it takes imagination even to devise a question about it, let alone to search for a different answer. For centuries, for example, astronomers had accepted that the Earth stayed still and the Sun revolved around it – the Bible itself dictated this to be so.

Consider the profound change to that view brought about by the amateur mathematician, Nicolaus Copernicus (1473–1543). He was a Church administrator in Olsztyn, now in northern Poland, who spent most of his working life collecting rents from peasants, looking after the health of colleagues and keeping an eye on local military defences. Concerned about accurately predicting holy days such as Easter and Christmas, he spent his spare time on mathematical calculations about the movement of the heavens. It led him to a model of the universe in which

The Scientific Method

If the new knowledge was as much about method as ideas, the career of Francis Bacon (1561–1626) embodied an important part of the scientific temperament of the period. At first glance, he was not an obvious candidate for the praise lavished on him by later thinkers. He was the consummate politician and bureaucrat who served James I as Attorney General and Lord Chancellor until, in 1621 at the age of 60, he was convicted of bribery and corruption.

Bacon wanted to change the whole way men thought. Not only was the purpose of natural philosophy to contribute to the well-being of humanity but, most importantly, its work had to be done by many men working together. This collaborative community of science was to be achieved by establishing appropriate institutions, as well as publishing and circulating their discoveries in plain language. Bacon's vision of the ideal such society was outlined in New Atlantis, a Utopian novel set, tellingly, in the South Seas. He clearly recognized that the exploration of new lands was bringing new knowledge. The frontispiece to his book the Great Instauration is one of the most famous iconographic statements of the new science of the 17th century. It depicts a boat sailing out of the Mediterranean through the Pillars of Hercules, which symbolized the edge of the known world. And his ideal institution, Salomon's House, was to be run and funded by government, an omen for big science today.

'Human knowledge,' Bacon said famously, 'and human power meet in one.' His state-funded science was to be in the service of the state. This went far beyond the courtly patronage of Renaissance princes looking for knowledge as adornment, as one more glittering prize. Bacon's knowledge was the furthering of state power – both in the practical sense that improved technology would bring commercial prosperity and military strength, and in the more dangerous sense that the control of knowledge would be kept in the government's 'safe' hands. Not for nothing had Bacon been a king's spy-master.

For all that he recognized the importance of practical experiments, Bacon's own were less than successful. Most famously, his attempt to freeze chickens by stuffing them with snow failed when he caught a chill and died.

Frontispiece to the Great Instauration. Set in the mythical land of Bensalem, the author's real purpose was to impose order on the new science. Bacon inspired the Royal Society, founded in 1660, which made the production of knowledge a vital part of the newly emerging civil society.

the Sun was motionless and the Earth travelled around it. You can see the threatening implications in Copernicus' account: far from being the very centre and purpose of God's creation, the Earth might be just another planet like any other.

Isaac Newton was the apotheosis of the new science, which was expected to be subject to fully reported and verifiable experiments. Newton's dealings with the Royal Society were often sketchy, and his notebooks reveal more commitment to theories than he let on.

The World as a Machine

Bacon may have supplied the method, but for natural philosophy to become modern science, it needed a transformation inside the minds of the scientists themselves. René Descartes' (1596–1650) search for a foundation of knowledge that he could trust beyond all doubt, started with the one underlying certainty that he could rescue: Cogito ergo sum – I think, therefore I am.

In Descartes' world, there was thinking stuff and there was matter. The body was matter, the universe was matter and all space was taken up by atoms or particles that moved as they bumped into one another. This was a whole new mechanical system of explanation.

Descartes likened the workings of the universe to trying to understand the motion of the hands of a clock. You see the hands, but that is all you see because the internal mechanism is hidden. For Descartes, the universe was a machine, and matter was inert and lifeless. In his account, the universe was held together by the constant impact of particle upon particle, atom upon atom, and that explained how mountains were formed, how a magnet worked or the phenomena of light.

There were problems with his system – not least that you cannot prove, nor see nor even square Descartes' mechanical philosophy with the facts of life. Where are the experiments to prove it right or wrong? But his philosophy was exhilarating and inspiring to the thinkers of his age, and increasingly textbooks were printed of and about his writings, which were used in universities as well as reaching a wide, popular audience.

Since he viewed the body as a machine, Descartes reckoned that by taking care of his health, he could live to be 100. In 1649, he was invited to teach philosophy to the young queen of Sweden, who wanted her lessons in the cold, dark pre-dawn at five o' clock in the morning. Descartes caught a chill and died.

Copernicus was so nervous and tentative about his theory, that his great book, De Revolutionibus, was only published in 1453, as he lay dying. It is hard to imagine what he felt on his death bed, receiving a printed copy of his masterpiece. It was seen as so dangerous that in 1616, it was put on the Catholic Church's Index of Prohibited Books.

By that time, Galileo Galilei (1564–1642) had already been condemned by the Church for defending the Copernican theory and had been forced to recant by the Inquisition. Galileo went even further than Copernicus – he claimed not only that the Earth revolved around the Sun, but also that stars showed observable cycles of change, and that the Sun itself was subject to changing sunspots, and so not eternally constant at all. Galileo, like Copernicus, used mathematical methods to formulate his discoveries, including his famous law of falling bodies.

The development and application of mathematics to explain the workings of the physical world is perhaps the clearest way to explain the importance of the Scientific Revolution. Even so, it had to wait another hundred years before Isaac Newton (1643–1727), the apotheosis of the new science, grasped the universal gravitational force that held Galileo's glimpsed world in place.

The Triumph of Science

It is only with hindsight that the natural philosophy of five and six hundred years ago can be seen as the milestone leading towards modern science as we know it. Nevertheless, by 1700 there were generally accepted assumptions about science: that it had to be based on systematic, first-hand observation of the real world; that it had to be subjected to controlled, repeatable experiment so that it could be proved to work (or not); and that it had to be explained by mathematical principals so it could be quantified. This last assumption was perhaps the beginning of science as beyond the grasp of most educated people. Isaac Newton's 1687 Principia Mathematica, the culmination of the Scientific Revolution and its endeavours, was probably read in its entirety by fewer than 100 of his peers, of whom perhaps only a handful could fully understand it.

The emerging community of scientists saw themselves as new men. They were self-consciously innovative and driven by a crusading desire to escape the shackles of the old ideas.

19: The Revolutionary Ideal

The French Revolution was essentially ideological, driven by ideas and emotions, by the idea of equality among citizens. It marked the moment that a newly-created public opinion escaped from the control of authoritarian power and captured a hollowed-out state.

Above: the storming of the Bastille had massive symbolic importance. However, Bastille Day, July 14, was not a national festival until 1880, when it was invented by the Third Republic to lend the ruling power revolutionary credentials and legitimacy.

There were revolutions before 1789 and have been many since – not least Russia (1917) and China (1948) – but none stirred the world with its ideas more dramatically than one of the most gigantic crashes in history – a crash that became the French Revolution. It was the first mass social explosion, the first great movement imbued with the ideology of the modern world. 'Men are born and remain free and equal in rights,' said the first article of the famous Declaration of the Rights of Man. It was not just a breakdown of an old regime; it was a fundamental reordering of how society should work.

The Birth of Nationalism

It was also the first great example of nationalism – the idea of 'the people' tied to a particular place, of government pursued in the name of the people and for the people (if only in name) and conducted in the language of nationalism, and a new society based on ideals of virtue, truth and love of the homeland. It created the idea of citizens instead of subjects, and, with the introduction of mass conscription, the idea that a citizen's life could be sacrificed not for money but for glory, the glory of France. It created nationalism as a new, secular religion.

The soldiers and bourgeoisie ('middle classes', as a term, came later) who supported the French Revolution were in part inspired by the American Revolution of 1776, but that country's break was basically with the English king. After independence, the country continued to exist much as it had before. Besides, the newly formed United States of America were then still too weak to be the milestone that they now seem from this distance. Few outsiders at the time could have guessed that a scattering of mostly farming communities, bickering still among themselves despite the grandeur of the Declaration of Independence and brilliance of its Constitution, was to become the mighty industrial and global giant of the future. But 18th-century France when its monarchy fell was the largest, most powerful country in Europe; one in five Europeans lived there.

In reality, of course, the ramshackle, chaotic French state had already withered from within. The king's extravagance, the greed of public officials who bought and sold their positions as private property, and a whole series of disastrous foreign wars had almost bankrupted the country. Even the weather turned against the monarchy, as peasants suffered through years of bad harvests, rising prices and hunger. And this time saw the dawn of modern media – in Paris, print created a whole new civil society. It existed in clubs, salons and in the pages of its newspapers. Posters and street songs whipped up public opinion and fired the mob, which in the end damned the weak if well-meaning king and his frivolous queen.

When it came, the Revolution heralded years of political instability and a series of endless wars fought across Europe. But behind the scenes, underlying the political turmoil and the ebb and flow of political fortunes, the Revolution laid down the foundations for the modern nation states that make up today's world – its legacy is the global 'club' of today, the United Nations, in which only states get to be members.

The constant wars increased the size and prestige of the army and of its officers, and marked the arrival of new, educated and energetic young men, hailed as heroes – the greatest of whom was Napoleon Bonaparte. Over the years, he created a new political system, which he exported through Europe as his army spread across Germany and down into Italy and beyond. He swept away monarchies and the privileged, rigid governments that served them. In their place, he set in motion a process of modernization, of new ways of ruling and running a country. 'He threw himself upon the universe, and shook it', as the writer Chateaubriand put it.

Napoleon was a military man through and through; he was a fanatic for uniformity, order and organization. Where the provinces of old France had each had their own ways of doing things and in which the king's rule was unpredictable and spasmodic, Napoleon reorganized and established an immense administrative structure ruled from Paris, in which the chain of command ran directly from the top to the bottom. The administration was the nervous system of the state: it had to function like a machine. Unlike anything that came before, he made government uniform; it had to work the same way through the whole of France.

A Meritocratic State

France was served now not by nobles but by notables. A new elite was restructured and broadened, giving opportunities to men of energy and drive. New landowners emerged who had benefited from taking

over the estates of emigrating or executed aristocrats. Professionals, such as lawyers, businessmen, government officials and army officers were quickly promoted through the ranks when they demonstrated ability.

The state was still repressive, but was founded on the creation of popular consent through carefully contrived referenda – in which the people voted on issues, the outcome of which had already been decided. And where Napoleon occupied countries such as Germany and Italy, this new form of state was exported along with his armies and officials. Even countries that were fearful of Napoleon's armies and of France's revolutionary ideas copied and imitated many of his innovations.

Napoleon established a secondary school system (the lycées) subject to state control and regulation. Every school in France was handed an identical curriculum, exam system, disciplinary procedures and uniform – even their libraries were told which texts to stock. Imagine how much easier it is to run a country when its future executives have all been educated the same way, with the same values, and in the same language. This was education not as welfare, but as discipline.

Napoleon formulated a new code of laws known as the Napoleonic Code, which transformed the legal and criminal justice system of France and confirmed the Revolution's ideals that everyone is equal before the law – well, everyone who was a man that is, since it did not always apply to women. There was now one single law for one nation. The administrative state was based on universal laws, not on special interest groups or privileges. When the legal system operates rationally and efficiently, it is not about justice: it is about predictability. Predictability is what makes trade and commerce possible.

There is a paradox – and an omen – in the career of Napoleon Bonaparte. It concerns the importance of personal liberty to the individual. While 'the people' in Napoleon's France were now sovereign and everything he did was done in the name of 'the people', the state was in the hands of an absolute despot. Despite all the high ideals for which the Revolution had been fought, given the choice between liberty and uncertainty, or tyranny and order – France's citizens preferred Napoleon's tyrannical law and order. Liberty revealed itself, as it so often has, as a fragile and luxurious flower.

Napoleon's Legacy to Europe

Napoleon's legacy survived him: some innovations helped to advance the Industrial Revolution. Others had their negative aspect, as fear and hatred of France accentuated the nationalisms of other countries. Even while France was creating its own new mythology,

Left: L'Arc de Triomphe in Paris was instigated in 1806 by Napoleon. However, this frieze of an allegorical France summoning her people to glory in 1792 was not commissioned until the 1830 Revolution sought to legitimize its new citizen-king Louis-Philippe, by identifying him with the Republic.

Below: A diagram demonstrates how many men Napoleon led into Russia in 1812 (422,000, light brown) and how few returned (10,000, dark brown). In the name of 'the people' and 'the nation', the Emperor achieved what no absolutist monarch could attempt – organized mass conscription.

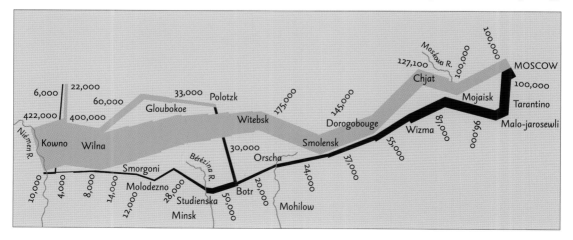

Napoleon's Empire c. 1812

By no means for the last time in history, a superior military force saw its advances into other territories not as imperialism but as liberation. Many of the reforms Napoleon brought with him were popular at first: the introduction of his civilian code of law, for example. Local industries responded to the call for French uniforms, guns, supplies. But as wealth was extracted and taken back to France, it set off revolts, repression and the growth of local nationalisms.

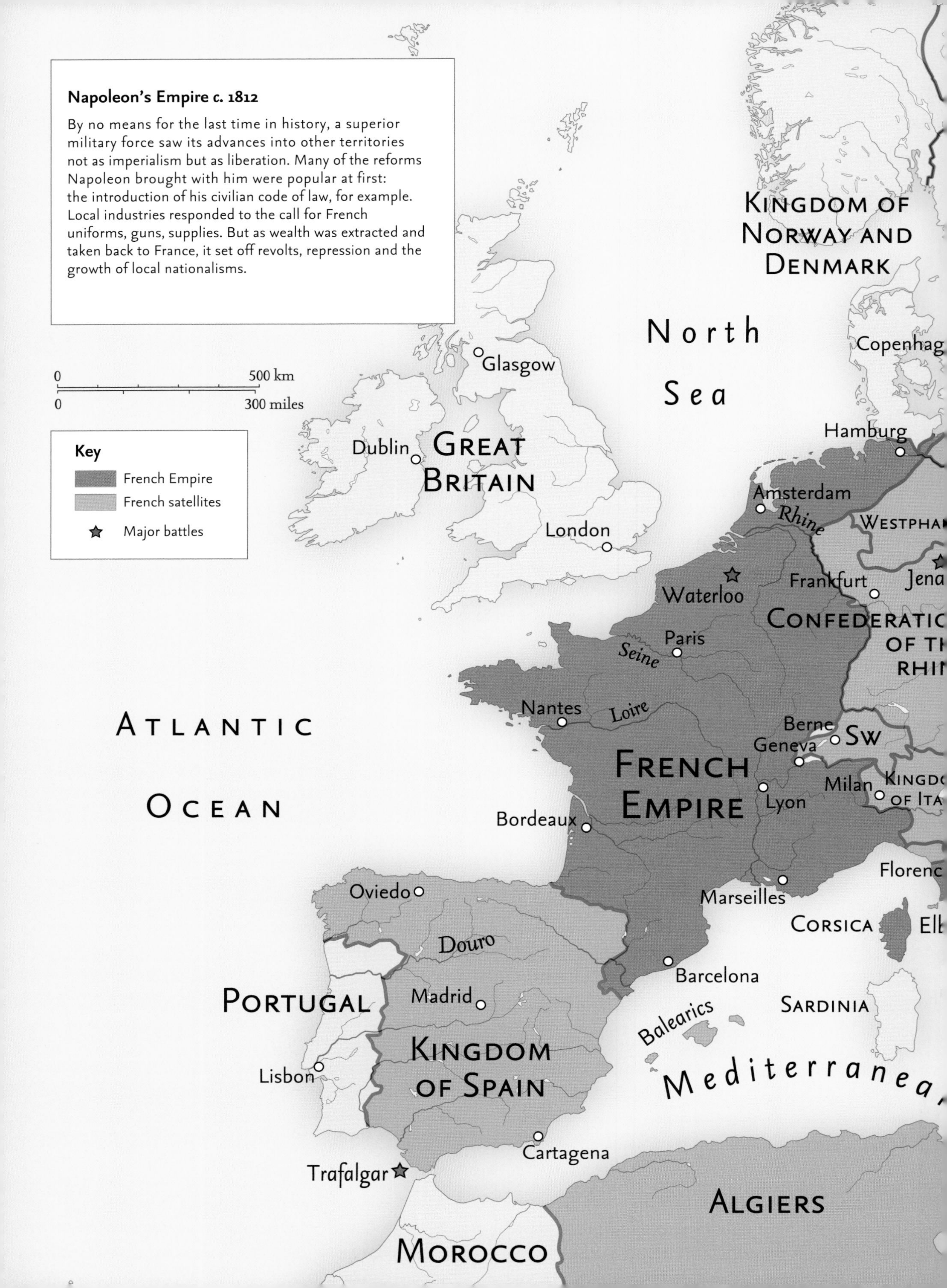

0 ———————————— **500 km**
0 ———————————— **300 miles**

Key

- French Empire
- French satellites
- ★ Major battles

KINGDOM OF NORWAY AND DENMARK

North Sea

Copenhag

Hamburg

Amsterdam

Rhine

WESTPHA

Frankfurt

Jena

Glasgow

GREAT BRITAIN

Dublin

London

Waterloo

Paris

Seine

CONFEDERATIO OF THE RHIN

ATLANTIC

OCEAN

Nantes

Loire

FRENCH EMPIRE

Berne

Geneva

Sw

Bordeaux

Lyon

Milan

KINGDO OF ITA

Marseilles

Florenc

CORSICA

El

Oviedo

Douro

PORTUGAL

Madrid

KINGDOM OF SPAIN

Barcelona

Balearics

SARDINIA

Lisbon

Mediterranea

Trafalgar

Cartagena

ALGIERS

MOROCCO

other countries were reinventing their history in legends and fairytales. The idea of a spiritual destiny shared by people who had never met or known each other, but who were united by blood or soil, language, culture or a geographical space took root. In Germany, opposition to French domination spurred the Romantic German ideal of the *volk*, 'the people'. 'In the beginning was Napoleon.' So the historian, Thomas Nipperdey (1927–92), began his history – not a history of France, but of Germany. Nationalism as a potent force had been unleashed, with immense consequences for the future.

Napoleon and Propaganda

On July 14 1789, the mob stormed the Bastille, a terrifying symbol of the old, royal regime. At the time it was almost empty, but the release of its seven prisoners and the pulling down of the building symbolized the destruction of the old regime itself. The news travelled like wildfire, and far beyond Paris. For the first time, the newspaper was the medium by which the revolutionary experience spread not only through France, but across the world. The French Revolution did not invent propaganda, but used and controlled it in a new and potent way to create the idea of 'the nation'. Its red, white and blue tricolour was incorporated in the Declaration of the Rights of Man, as was the freedom to speak, write and print freely. The flag is still the symbol of France: press liberty lasted barely three years, however, and what little survived was crushed by Napoleon.

Napoleon was the first master of modern propaganda. He had absorbed the importance of symbols as a Royalist army officer – think of the gold braid and stars on an officer's uniform, and the fact that striking a man wearing them was an automatic death sentence for an ordinary soldier. Once he took power, he controlled every aspect of his public image. His portrait was everywhere, together with the gold eagle of the great Roman empire – a symbol which he quickly appropriated and identified with himself.

By 1799, when he seized power, Napoleon had witnessed the invention of a new political culture and the construction of an entirely new community of citizens. There had been an explosion of new publications, with at least 250 newspapers founded in the last six months of 1789 alone. The female cook who, in 1791, professed to read four newspapers, was probably not unusual. In giving legitimacy to the Revolution by delivering its lawmaking and radical reforms into the 'possession' of a literate public, by relentless invoking of such magical terms as *liberte, fraternite, patrie, peuple* and *citoyen*, the print industry potentially created an independent public sphere. 'Four hostile newspapers,' declared Napoleon, 'are more to be feared than 100,000 bayonets.'

When he commissioned a portrait of his crossing of the Alps on his way to the Battle of Marengo, Napoleon instructed Jacques-Louis David to paint him 'calm upon a fiery horse'. No matter that, in fact, he had crossed the St Bernard Pass on a mule; kings had always been painted on horseback. So was born the image of the heroic commander on the tempestuous white horse. In the painting, storm-clouds rage in the background as Napoleon points the way forward – who could miss the message that in such troubled times, Napoleon alone could lead France through them?

Equally telling is David's painting of Napoleon's coronation as Emperor of France (an elevation supported by no less than 95 per cent of a referendum vote). It shows the moment when Napoleon – dressed in gold and an ermine-lined cloak, holding for himself the symbols of power, the golden laurel on his head, and the hand of justice – stepped up and crowned himself while the Pope stood by, impotent. It was a declaration that he was nobody's man – except that of France itself, confirmed and legitimized by successive public votes. Napoleon's use of the predetermined and manipulated referendum has lived on and been used since by many a dictator.

Napoleon's propaganda techniques worked so well that his legend grew even stronger after his death in 1821. So much so that, in 1840, his body was brought back to Paris from the remote island of St Helena and given a magnificent funeral. Nearly a million people lined the route as he was carried to his specially built tomb in the Hotel des Invalides – a place of pilgrimage ever since. The man who crowned himself Emperor has become a symbol of the French Republic. Such is the power of spin.

In Jacques-Louis David's portrait *Napoleon on Horseback at the St Bernard Pass* (1801), painted to commemorate his brilliant victory over the Austrians at Marengo, Napoleon borrowed from the past to play on symbolic imperial images identifying him with both Hannibal and Charlemagne heroically crossing the alps.

20: The Industrialization of War

The concept of 'total war' was not new to the West. What was new was the unprecedented intensity and reach brought to warfare by industrialization and mechanization. As Winston Churchill was to say in 1940: 'The front line runs through the factories. The workmen are soldiers with different weapons.'

Above: La Gloire, the first modern iron-clad battleship, launched in 1859. In an increasingly militaristic atmosphere, an arms race developed and welfare provisions were introduced – not necessarily in the cause of social justice, but to serve states needing healthy workers and soldiers.

A soldier from any battle of the 16th century could turn up at Sevastopol in 1854 and, after a day wandering about, could pretty much have fitted in. Warfare had stagnated. But had he found himself, instead, at Gettysburg only nine years later, he would have been in a strange, new hell. In the American Civil War, 622,000 soldiers were killed. It was the first taste of the next military revolution, which revealed itself in all its horror half a century later when, in the first six weeks of World War I, a third of a million soldiers died. They were not bayoneted to death in hand-to-hand combat. They were shelled, buried in concrete or drowned in liquid mud beneath a hail of bullets. This milestone marked the impact of industrialization.

The Rate of Fire

The first important change in warfare came in the 1850s with the development of rifles that really worked. The soldier armed with an old-fashioned gun had to tap down the gunpowder with a hammer. If he was skilled and kept a cool head, he could fire three times a minute. In the early 19th century, a cartridge was invented that could be fired quickly. It was easy to put the bullet in the barrel – and it worked. Now a soldier could fire 10 times a minute.

The Americans came up with a system of mass production, which could produce a constant supply of standardized, interchangeable parts. Guns became more reliable and predictable, and worked better. Rapid-firing, breech-loaded rifles increased the rate of fire and the range of distance. The result can be seen in the ferocious battle at Gettysburg, where the Confederate troops rushed on Union lines and were wiped out. The order of battle had been changed.

In 1884, Sir Hiram Maxim developed the first truly automatic machine gun, which could soon fire 600 rounds a minute at a range of 1.37 kilometres (0.85 miles). Now the job of closing with the enemy became almost impossible. The result? In the battle of Omdurman in 1898, the British lost 48 men and the Mahdi lost 11,000. The British mowed down the enemy; it was a massacre.

It was not only small arms that changed and became lethally effective. The Swedish inventor Alfred Nobel's refinement of nitro-glycerine, when adapted to military uses, meant that the size of ammunition could be reduced while its range more than doubled. The old fog and smoke of war gave way to a more lethally effective battlefield. In the 1850s, the largest cannon had a range of 1 kilometre (0.6 miles) – the new siege cannons weighed three times as much with a range six times further. The

The silent monuments erected by war's victors rarely hint at the reality experienced by those they honour. In the American Civil War, which this statue commemorates, over half a million soldiers died. In the three-day battle of Gettysburg alone, 50,000 soldiers were mown down.

old fortresses became obsolete and the only resistance to the huge new cannons were underground concrete bunkers. So the Industrial Revolution, which had spread through Europe and the United States, left only one option in war: to bleed the enemy into surrender.

The Scale of War

Half a million soldiers had died on their way to and in the Crimean War. They were not shot; they died of starvation and disease. The building of railways made marching to war a thing of the past and brought about mass mobilization on a bigger scale than ever before. In 1850, there were 32,000 kilometres (20,000 miles) of railway in the world. Thirty years later, there were 160,000 (100,000). If an army marched for 16 kilometres (10 miles) a day, it could take months to reach the frontier. With railways, large armies could be mobilized and put into the field in weeks. Once it was possible to move such armies, feeding them was key and that brought about canning and the possibility of storing food – and of fighting on for years.

With so many soldiers in the field, communication became even more crucial. The invention of the telegraph was a radical development. For the first time in human history, information could be transmitted across distance in real time. By the 1860s, there were 240,000 kilometres (150,000 miles) of telegraph cable covering the world. When Samuel Morse inaugurated his telegraph system in 1844, he transmitted the message 'What hath God wrought?' The answer was that it had injected control into warfare. Now there was an immediate information network, a new way of co-ordinating army movements. Without telegraphs, the railways were a disconnected series of lines – sending information in real time meant that it was possible to co-ordinate them.

As a result, the regulation of time acquired new importance. It was literally a matter of life and death to know exactly when trains departed, arrived and passed each other. New precision machine tools could produce uniform clocks and watches. To understand the enormity of all this change, picture our 16th-century soldier who measured life by the sun and seasons, and could travel no faster than his own legs, an animal or a sailing ship could carry him.

Steam Power

If we take a galleon in the Spanish Armada and compare it to a ship in 1830, there is not much difference between them. They were both large and wooden, both depended on wind propulsion. Then came steam engines. Now navies could sail and get from A to B in a straight line, even when the wind was not with them or blowing at all. The first modern ironclad battleship, *La Gloire*, was built by the French in 1859 but was obsolete almost as soon as it was completed, so rapid was the onslaught of technological advances. By 1900, a steel-built battleship could travel at 48 kilometres (30 miles) an hour for about 8,000 kilometres (5,000 miles) on coal and its guns could fire their shells to a range of 19 kilometres (12 miles). This was a quantum leap.

Once the industrialized states entered the armaments race, it had the unintended consequence that total war reduced any army's ability to defeat the enemy decisively. In 1914, the French sent their shipyard workers and arms manufacturers to the front in the first weeks, on the assumption that war could not last longer than six months because there would be a

In 1881, a non-drinking, non-smoking, agnostic American inventor, Sir Hiram Maxim, sailed to Europe to demonstrate his electrical current regulator. He stayed on to sell to the British forces the first automatic portable machine gun – the Maxim.

collapse of civilization and society. Instead, war became defensive, a matter of attrition and endurance in a miles-long siege of continuous trench-lines dug ever deeper. In the bitterest irony of all, industrialization actually increased the reliance of the First World War soldier upon the shovel, spade and pick.

Industry in Peace Time

While decades of experiment to create a system of industrial efficiency produced ever-deadlier weapons, it was quickly put to other uses. Canning reduced a household's reliance on fresh and seasonal food during times of scarcity. The modern manufacturing system applied by Colt to revolvers was also applied by Singer to sewing machines, and McCormick to agricultural machinery. The race to fine-tune the manufacture of cheaper steel made possible the building of skyscrapers – the first was the Leitner Building in Chicago in 1879 but others quickly followed. As the main driver of capitalism and consumerism, it seemed as if the USA would turn away from military confrontation. It did, for a while. However, anarchy entails violence. A world system that is basically anarchic seems to make war endemic to it.

The Sun Rises in the East

The humiliating defeat Japan inflicted on Russia in 1905 stunned the rest of the world. It signalled the sudden arrival of a new great power. The taking of the vital warm-weather port, Port Arthur, from the mighty Russian army, despite absorbing 20,000 casualties, demonstrated that for all the modern technology, superior will could prevail. Here was nationalism in action at its most aggressive.

The victory was all the more unexpected because for 300 years, Japan had been a closed society dominated by its traditional warrior nobility, in which the possession of weapons by anyone other than a samurai was a capital offence. The Dutch were granted a small trading post at Nagasaki in 1641, but otherwise foreigners and Japanese alike entered and left the country on pain of death. Within 30 years of the Meiji rebellion (the so-called Restoration) in 1868, the country had borrowed enough of the secrets of western technology to industrialize and expand its own arms industry and to put in place the infrastructure of a modern state. It built its first railway and launched its first newspaper and ministry of education.

Borrowed was the operative word. Japan's great leap forward was folded into its own traditional civilization. The emperor re-emerged from centuries of ceremonial seclusion as a focal point for a nationalism spurred by the passionate desire of literate Japanese to escape 'shameful inferiority' to the west. The conservative samurai were co-opted to lead a modern army of conscripts. Schools taught children the traditional Confucian duties of obedience to parents and sacrifice to the state if needed.

Spin forward half a century to River Rouge, Michigan. A young Japanese engineer was sent by his family to work in the Ford motor plant, which, with its moving assembly lines and integrated mass production, was able to turn out 7,000 cars a day. The Ford factory was then a symbol of the supremacy of American modernism. When Aldous Huxley (1894–1963) wrote *Brave New World*, he dated its creation from the Ford Assembly line.

In 1950, when Eiji Toyota was sent to River Rouge, his family car factory was 13 years old and could not produce half as many cars as Ford. When he went home, he borrowed what he had learned in America but rethought the entire process to create a new method of production. Toyota's 'lean production', as it came to be known, used only half the floor space, tools, workers and time, while imposing a tighter quality control than the American industry. In part, this was possible because Japan had retained much of its own disciplined, hierarchical culture. By 1987, a Toyota plant in Japan could produce a car in 16 hours, half the time of the biggest manufacturer in America.

It was a reminder that the West did not have a monopoly on modernity, and that modernity in itself did not define civilization.

Toyota's 'lean production' cuts out excess and unnecessary inventory, so the assembly line can change quickly to match market demands. This is how Toyota scooped the industry in 1997, when it delivered the world's first mass-produced hybrid electric-petrol car.

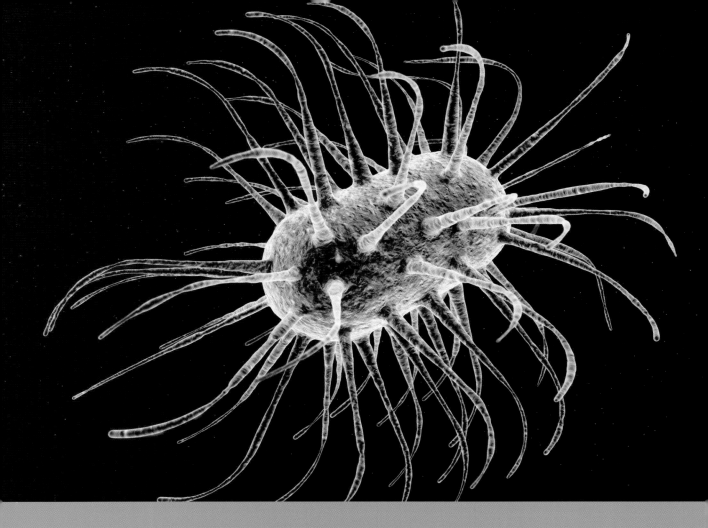

21: The Medical Revolution

Epidemics and disease are the ever-present companions of civilization. What has changed is the way science has organized the fight against them. If there has been one major milestone in medical practice, it would be the development of bacteriology – the study of the germs that cause disease.

Above: When Oxford University's Florey and Chain pursued Fleming's earlier work on how penicillin killed bacteria such as this, they did not patent their discoveries as it was thought to be unethical. Instead, drug companies reaped the fortunes, an early instance of the debate about ownership of life-saving medicines.

The idea that diseases were infectious was not in itself new; everyone knew as long ago as the 16th century that syphilis was passed through sexual intercourse. How it happened was not known exactly. At about the same time, miniscule, moving entities had been seen through the first microscopes. It was too great a leap to recognize in them the cause of infection, let alone to grasp the idea that each infection had its own cause. Yes, rotting meat could be seen to have maggots crawling over it – but did the maggots cause the decay or was it the other way around? In an era when it was accepted that only God could create life, these were huge mysteries.

Pioneers of Germ Theory

One clue emerged in the late 18th century, when an Italian estate manager made a connection between a fungus on mulberry bushes and the disease wiping out his silkworms. His findings inspired a Swiss researcher who, in 1839, demonstrated that a different sort of fungus was the cause of ringworm. Twenty years later in Paris, the experiments of Louis Pasteur (1822–95) with the fermentation of sugar into alcohol convinced him that fermentation was biological rather than chemical and that it depended on and could be spoiled by minute, living organisms. He found that heating wine to about 50 degrees Celsius (122 degrees Fahrenheit) stopped it from spoiling – a process now called pasteurization. He had carried out this research at the behest of an industrialist, but as a result he conceived the suspicion that living organisms could also cause infectious diseases. Pasteur had the beginnings of the germ theory – it would take him another 20 years to develop it.

Progress is often piecemeal, but medicine can make progress even while the science behind it is still a conundrum. Practice can, and often does, precede theory. The experiences of two 19th-century pioneers – Ignaz Semmelweis (1818–65) and Joseph Lister (1827–1912) – are perfect examples. Most doctors understood that person-to-person contact spread disease. The rest still shared the traditional 'miasmic' view of infection – that there were poisons in the air, which came from decaying vegetation, from the earth or stagnant water. There was not much to be done about the very air itself.

In 1847, Semmelweis was running the largest maternity wards in the world at Vienna's general

Lister's antiseptic practices not only included treating the wound during and after surgery but also spraying the operating theatre itself. Notice the absence of protective clothing on the medical staff: doctors discarded reluctantly the imposing black 'uniforms' of their profession.

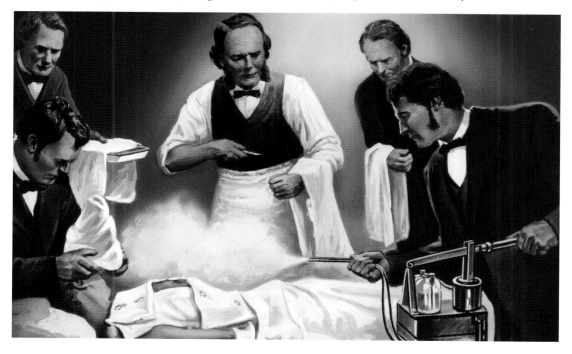

hospital. Ward 1, staffed by medical students, had a catastrophic death rate. In Ward 2, which was staffed by midwives, only three per cent of the new mothers died. Semmelweis was mystified by the discrepancy so he made the staff swap wards. The death rate followed the medical students. The inferior social standing of midwives in relation to doctors at the time was such that this in itself was a shock. It took a while before Semmelweis made the vital connection: the trainee doctors were coming to deliver babies straight from performing autopsies, and were bringing infection with them. Semmelweis ordered all staff to wash their hands with chlorinated water before deliveries, and death rates in both wards fell dramatically. When his colleagues refused to accept this practice, he took a job as head of obstetrics in Budapest. Under his direction, the death rate there plummeted to one per cent.

Meanwhile, in 1847 in Glasgow, Joseph Lister was encountering similar problems. Lister was a general surgeon who saw – as did the best of surgeons at the time – half his amputation patients die from post-operative infections. From experiments in the hospital's laboratory, he could tell that gangrene was part of a process of rotting, but it was not until he read Pasteur's early results on the existence of germs that he made the vital leap – it was not rotten air that infected his patients, but the invisible germs carried in the air.

Fighting Infection

In 1865, Lister experimented with carbolic acid, which had been discovered in Germany 30 years earlier and was being used to treat the toxins in raw sewage. He devised an elaborate routine to fight infection (sepsis) by keeping the wound clean during and after surgery. Within two years, he had operated on 11 patients with his regime and none had died of infection. When he published his results in the esteemed medical journal, The Lancet, his theory advancing antiseptic routines as

India's Jaipur Foot

Scientific medicine is usually seen as irreconcilable with traditional practices, and vastly 'superior'. However, it clearly does not work everywhere or for all cultures. How do you tell people who do not measure time by the clock to take pills every four hours? How do you dispense pills to them at all when roads are poor, and when the patient may have to walk miles to reach their nearest source of healthcare?

And what if they have no feet in the first place? Landmines have left untold millions missing one foot or both in some of the poorest countries in the world. The invention of the humble, artificial Jaipur Foot is a reminder that the small and personal milestones of everyday life also build civilizations. It demonstrates too what can happen when conventional modern medicine is sensitive to cultural context.

The orthopaedic surgeon Dr Parmod Karan Sethi and the sculptor Ram Chandra met in the corridor of Jaipur's teeming SMS hospital in the late 1960s. The surgeon was teaching his amputees to totter along on crutches; the semi-literate artist was teaching crafts to lepers. Why crutches? Because SMS could turn out only five or six artificial limbs a year and Western prostheses cost thousands of dollars. Besides, they were a cultural mismatch for people who sit, sleep and worship on the floor, all without shoes. Here was another hitch: the Western prosthesis came with a shoe attached, which turned to sponge on a farmer working in sodden fields.

The surgeon taught the craftsman the precise anatomy of the foot. Chandra came up with a vulcanized rubber, wood and aluminium model, which even now costs no more than $35 and takes only 45 minutes to make. It can be fitted in temporary camps by technicians, many of whom are amputees themselves. Because they are so low-tech, in Cambodia, where roughly one out of every 380 people is a war amputee, part of the foot's rubber components are scavenged from truck tires. In Afghanistan, they are hammered together out of spent artillery shells.

Chandra sculpted a foot so realistic that it is hard to spot, and because it is made of light rubber and supple, those who wear it can run, climb trees, ride bicycles and, yes, work in the fields. Meanwhile, India's Space Research Organization is testing out material used in rockets and satellites to help improve its durability. Science and the modest Jaipur Foot is an unlikely but inspiring partnership.

The Jaipur foot raises the ethical problem of how inequitably distributed are the benefits of modern medicine, and how rarely affordable alternatives are sought or funded. The Jaipur foot was developed by individuals and is dependent on a local charity.

protection against bacteria met much the same resistance among senior colleagues as Semmelweis had encountered in Vienna. 'Where are the little beasts?' scoffed one professor about Lister's germs. 'Show them to us, and we shall believe in them.'

Lister's regime took time to be accepted – first by a few surgeons in Germany, then a few in France and even more slowly in North America. The brilliant New York surgeon William S. Halstead (1852–1922) had to operate in a tent in the garden of Bellevue Hospital because his colleagues could not bear the smell of the carbolic acid he insisted on using in the operating theatre.

In a period of transition, the old ways and the new overlap. Lister was scrupulous about treating and protecting wounds during and after surgery, even spraying the operating theatre with antiseptics. However, he carried on operating in whatever street clothes he was wearing when he entered the hospital. It was not until 1886 that a German surgeon introduced the steam sterilization of surgical instruments in his clinics. It was even later before the first surgeon put on a face mask.

The Birth of Bacteriology

It took until the 1880s, when Robert Koch was able to identify a specific bacillus as the cause of TB that the discipline of bacteriology developed. One by one, there was a more precise understanding of which germs caused which diseases. Even so, Florence Nightingale, the famous 'Lady with the Lamp', whose passion for cleanliness and orderliness was transmitted to a generation of nurses trained to her exacting standards, never accepted the existence of bacteria. Her passion for fresh air in hospital wards sprang from her continuing commitment to the 'miasma' theory.

Antiseptics revolutionized surgery but it was the discovery of antibiotics (which literally means 'destructive of life') that produced the 'miracle' cures with which to fight infection. Alexander Fleming (1881–1955) was a Scottish bacteriologist who had worked on wounded soldiers during World War I, and had demonstrated that not only were harsh chemical antiseptics damaging to the body's natural defences but also that they failed to destroy the bacteria that caused the infections. After the war, he worked for years to identify, isolate and reproduce what it was the body did itself to fight infection.

Nobel laureates 1945: The bitter irony of receiving the prize for his work on life-saving penicillin six months after the opening of Germany's concentration camps was not lost on refugee Ernst Chain (centre, with Fleming. Florey is on the far right), who referred to it in his speech.

Fleming first identified penicillin in 1928, when he found that the mould that had grown in a dish of bacteria had killed it.

His discovery was largely ignored by the medical profession because early penicillin was unstable and hard to mass produce. It was not until a team of young scientists at Oxford led by Howard Florey (1898–1968) and Ernst Chain (1906–79), a refugee from Nazi Germany, developed ways of stabilizing and producing Fleming's penicillin that its life-saving qualities were recognized. Even so, Florey had to go to America for funding from drug companies. In 1945, 20 years after his discovery, Fleming shared the Nobel Prize with Florey and Chain.

Public Reaction

If the medical profession was instinctively conservative, so too were its patients. It was not until it became known that Queen Victoria took chloroform, during the birth of her son in 1853, that its use was accepted as anaesthesia. Even so, The Lancet attacked it on grounds of safety. Others objected on religious grounds, citing the Bible's decree that a woman was to bring forth her child in pain. As unreasonable as this might seem today, there were many who felt ethically if

China's Barefoot Doctors

China's barefoot doctors are important as a reminder that there is no such thing as neutral science – medicine is often no more than a snapshot of the political climate in which it operates. When Mao Zedong sent these rural practitioners out into the field in the mid 1960s, they reflected his embrace of Chinese-ness and signalled the Cultural Revolution's demotion of the country's health ministry, dominated as it was by Western-style doctors.

The barefoot doctors were farmers, some with some education, others barely literate. They were given training, some for three months, some for up to two years. They were then sent back to their villages to continue farming while offering simple health care. This took in a wide range of traditional practices, such as herbal remedies and acupuncture, but also included immunization and even surgery.

For Western liberals, these doctors were a symbol of the empowerment of the poor. They were thought to be responsible for reducing by 90 per cent the incidence of such diseases as bilharzias ('big belly'). Conservative Western, public-health consultants tended to dismiss them as a political symbol, and put the reduction in disease down to public-health projects, such as the increased availability of clean water and sanitation.

In 1981, China abolished its agricultural communes and the barefoot doctor network went with them. Medicine was privatized in China's embrace of economic modernization. It is estimated that today over 60 per cent of China's rural population cannot afford medical treatment either in the villages or in hospitals. Whether or not the reappearance of bilharzias is put down to the impossibility of fighting any such disease in a large, newly mobile population, or the dangers of a medical system dictated by economics alone, obviously depends on the political standpoint of the person making the evaluation.

The barefoot doctors or rural practitioners were a major inspiration behind the World Health Organization's enthusiasm in the late 1970s for primary health care for developing countries.

not religiously uncertain when Louise Brown – the first 'test-tube' baby, conceived outside her mother's body – was born in 1978. (Actually, she was conceived in a dish.) Nor, more recently, could many people accept a test-tube baby being born to a woman old enough to qualify for a pension. Today, embryos are routinely fertilized in dishes and even from a dead husband's frozen sperm, while the cloned Dolly the Sheep conjures the possibility of replicating human life itself in a laboratory.

The thrill of new scientific triumphs and the euphoria surrounding 'magic bullets' for every killer disease may have worn off somewhat now, with the fear of drug-resistant super-bugs and the threat of new diseases such as Ebola fever and Bird Flu. The possible link between the deadly Creutzfeldt-Jakob disease (CJD) and its source in infected beef has sparked new scares about killers invading the food chain.

On the other hand, human beings have always had to deal with the threat of illness and disease. Different civilizations have found their own way to meet that threat, whether with herbs, chemicals, sorcery, religion or scientific medicine, whether holistically through addressing and balancing the whole body, or in pieces through surgery, which is as old as man himself.

Millions of Lives Saved

One fact is certain; in the last hundred years, the advances made in bacteriology have revolutionized medicine. Antibiotics have saved millions of lives and made possible surgeries unthinkable in Lister's time. In 1968, the South African surgeon Christian Barnard performed the world's first heart transplant. The patient died 18 days later, as did two thirds of the early transplant patients. But it took less than four years for science to come up with the immunosuppressant drug cyclosporine, which made it possible to prevent the body's own immune system rejecting the transplanted organ. This was just the first in another generation of 'magic bullets'. Today, liver and kidney transplants are routine, new hips and knees are commonplace.

Vaccines have liberated whole populations from a myriad of diseases; surgery and medicine have made people safe in ways our ancestors could not have dreamed of. Seventy years ago, a woman going into a London hospital to deliver a baby had a 1 in 250 chance of coming out in her coffin. Today, she has a 9,999 chance in 10,000 of coming out alive and well.

22: The Origins of Man

Until the mid 19th century, the problem of man's creation was almost exclusively a theological one. Human life was understood to transcend animal life and the gifts of reason and free will to bear the fingerprints of God. In 1859, Charles Darwin made claims that destroyed the bedrock of such beliefs...

Above: In 1848, before the Industrial Revolution covered the land with soot from coal-burning factories, 98 per cent of peppered moths were light coloured. By 1895, 98 per cent seemed to be black. As tree bark darkened, those moths that adapted, survived.

The mid 19th century was an era of such mighty European confidence that a few hundred colonial officers instilled with the values of 'muscular Christianity' could impose their will on millions of subjected people and paper over them an alien culture. But it was the very contact with those other civilizations that was to shake to the core European conviction in its own Godly mission. The evidence that Charles Darwin (1809–82) amassed on his five-year expedition around the world on the British ship HMS Beagle from 1828–33 led to a momentous event. As we have often seen, ideas can change history – in this case, the idea was his theory of evolution.

How Natural Selection Works

What Darwin claimed in 1859 with his book On the Origin of Species by Natural Selection and, 12 years later, even more explicitly, in The Descent of Man, and Selection in Relation to Sex, was that nature inadvertently breeds species that are better equipped to survive. Every species lives in a particular and changing environment and faces different threats or 'selection pressures'. If certain traits help a living organism to survive, these adaptations can be passed on to successive generations. Darwin's evolution is often misunderstood – or deliberately misinterpreted – so we should be clear about its claims. Natural selection is not preordained; it is not part of a plan working towards some desirable end-goal – it is random. It is not 'progress', there is no direction to it, nor does it make one species better or fitter than another. It is just a way that some living things adapt biologically to different conditions.

Natural selection, said Darwin, worked in favour of characteristics for survival by passing them on to future generations. Individuals who survived were more likely to reproduce and become the dominant strain and so, over time, natural selection could and had produced entirely new species. Adaptation for survival might or might not occur. (Besides, you do not need to be a scientist to know that you cannot count on any species' mating habits.) But, over time, the weakest die off – only the best-adapted survive and the adaptations that are favourable became fixed. 'From the war of nature', Darwin wrote 'from famine and from death, the production of higher animals directly follows.'

Perhaps the clearest example of natural selection is the mottled black-and-white peppered moth. In the middle of the 19th century, when soot and grime blackened the trunks of trees in industrial Britain, the all-black form of peppered moths became more common. The adaptation made it harder for birds to see the moths in order to pick them off and eat them, so more survived. When the Clean Air Acts (1956 and 1968, respectively) were passed and industrial pollution declined, lo and behold, the peppered moth adapted and re-appeared in its earlier, more typical, pale form. This gave it a better chance of escaping the notice of birds on the cleaner, lighter tree barks. There was not a 'higher' or 'lower', 'better' or 'worse' peppered moth – the species simply adapted to the changed environment and so improved its chances of survival.

The Context of Evolutionary Theory

In order to understand the impact of Darwin's theory – a theory as abstract, impersonal and universal as any law of physics – it helps to understand the 19th-century world into which it burst. Europeans of Darwin's time saw themselves as uniquely responsible for the triumph of reason and science. From this viewpoint, how did they look at the rest of the world? As they encountered 'primitives' who were pre-literate, they encountered people who did not have writing, who had not developed as they had. How were they to explain this?

They knew that the world outside Europe included ancient, oriental civilizations such as China, which were fascinating but barely known. Since the times of ancient Greece, there had been intimate, close connections with the Arabs and their grasp of a complex cosmos. Early science, philosophy and mathematics all came to Europe from the Arab world. But, viewed from a 19th-century European perspective, these ancient civilizations did not achieve reason or fully develop science and the scientific way of thinking as Europe had. So, roughly speaking, Europe dismissed the world of 'the primitive' as savage or barbaric and inferior, and ignored the rich traditions of the little-known Orient. Europeans reserved their admiration for a West with its Industrial Revolution, which had

Thomas Nast's cartoon from Harper's Weekly, 1871:
The Defrauded Gorilla: 'That Man wants to claim my Pedigree. He says he is one of my Descendants.'
Mr Bergh (founder of the American Society for the Prevention of Cruelty to Animals): 'Now, Mr Darwin, how could you insult him so?'

The Origins of Modern Woman

On the *Origins of Species* was published in an era of rapid change, spectacular achievement and social confusion in the Western world. The ruling classes and new middle class faced unprecedented demands from organized labour and radical political parties. Just as they were recoiling from the idea that their ancestors had emerged from the primordial slime, they were confronted by the beginning of a women's rights movement that was to turn Western society upside down. In 1837, the Utopian socialist, Charles Fourier gave it its name – 'feminism'.

Repressive Victorian domestic norms were one response to the changes challenging an elitist, patriarchal society. As so often through history, 'civilized' men acted out their anxiety on women – literally, in the restricting clothes respectable women were expected to wear, and, legally, in the total power granted to them over their wives.

Intriguingly – and modern feminists would say not by coincidence – it was precisely the repressive nature of respectable, educated society that set off both the rise of feminism and a curious epidemic of what the medical profession called 'hysteria'. They can be seen as two sides of the same coin – reactions to the suffocating position of women in an increasingly rigid society.

Hysteria – so named from the Greek term for a woman's womb, *hystera* – was seen by physicians as the result of a woman's inability to accept her proper place in the world.

She was too intellectual, too abstemious or too sexually indulgent. No longer a valid medical diagnosis, hysteria was considered one of the most common female disorders of the 19th century. Doctors advised parents not to let their daughters go horse-riding, eat vanilla or read novels in case they developed the condition. For those woman diagnosed with the disorder – often the brightest and most creative of their sex – doctors built spas, prescribed rest in darkened rooms, and often administered painful electric therapy. To the medical men, the roots of the problem remained elusive – since assertiveness was denied to women and vulnerability was admired, the hysterical woman retreated into illness.

Modern feminists link this 'outbreak' of hysteria with the early stirrings of organized feminism. In 1848, a group of New York housewives put together the Women's Rights Convention, the first ever such public meeting organized by women. It called for property rights for married women, legal power and political representation. Imagine the shock to a society that only three years later would be entirely untroubled by the passing of a Prussian law forbidding women from joining political parties or attending meetings where politics were discussed.

Manet's *Olympia* stares boldly and without shame from the canvas. The model, Victorine Meurent, is known to us. Not so the black servant girl, who is left unremarked and anonymous.

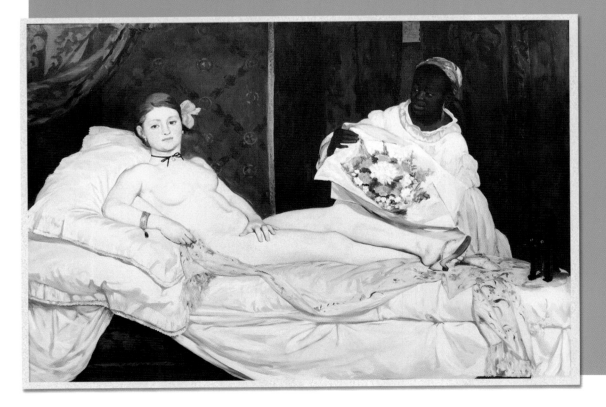

The same face, the same unswerving stare in *Gare Saint-Lazare*, but now Manet clads Meurent in the drab habit of domesticity as her charge turns away from us rattling the bars that will cage her, too.

Two paintings by Edouard Manet (1832–83) illustrate the prevalent attitudes that early female pioneers faced and show how obstacles existed even in the traditionally progressive realm of art. In 1878, Manet's *Gare Saint-Lazare* used as its model the gifted painter, Victorine Meurent. Manet chose to portray her as weighed down in a heavy, black outfit, the epitome of the respectable mother. Yet only 13 years before, *Olympia*, Manet's portrait of Meurent apparently taking pride in her naked body, had caused such outrage that two guards had to be put on the painting when it was exhibited. If her blatant sexuality could be shown at all, it was only because Meurent was dismissed as a life-model, and therefore outside society.

Later feminists have made a telling connection between the two paintings. They see the way that Manet 'imprisoned' Meurent in the deadening domesticity of *Gare Saint-Lazare* as an act of revenge – her crime was that the Paris Salon had accepted one of Meurent's paintings while rejecting Manet's submission. The portrayal of Meurent's sexuality as subversive,

and the subsequent taming of her body in the uniform of respectability, was more than acceptable to a patriarchal society that held a woman responsible for the original Fall from God's grace. That she was a talented female artist was too much of a threat. She was a woman who had lost her place – and here is the link to the epidemic of 'hysteria', which took its name from the Greek image of a lost and wandering womb.

The fight for creative recognition or the right to participate in the political process were preoccupations of women in white, privileged society. To some women, the challenges were greater. In 1851, at the Ohio Women's Rights Convention, a black woman got up and made a speech that spoke of a far more desperate plight. Sojourner Truth had been born into slavery and had been sold on four times to different owners. 'I could work as much and eat as much as a man – when I could get it – and bear the lash as well. And ain't I a woman? I have born 13 children, and seen most all sold off to slavery, and when I cried out with my mother's grief, none but Jesus hear me. And ain't I a woman?'

Some milestones mark change that comes all too slowly. This was one of them. In 1893, New Zealand became the first country to give women the vote. It took until 1965 for black women in the USA to be fully enfranchised by law.

delivered modernity, wealth, the harnessing of energy and the mass production of goods.

This pride in the modern world drew strength from a religious belief in the Bible as a representation of the literal truth. God made all the beings on Earth at the beginning of the world, which he created in its entirety only a few thousand years ago. All the species on Earth came into being at once. No living creature could become anything other than that God had designated. In this scheme of events, the so-called primitives fitted in at the bottom of a long ladder of progress; on the top rung of this ladder was European, modern, capitalist society. Since this was deemed to be God's will, the whole triumphant, modern European project carried a sense of spiritual purpose alongside the commercial. It was this certainty that Darwin's theories undermined.

A Scandalous Idea

Darwin's evolution had no pattern to it, no necessary scheme of things and – here was the shocker for his time – if it is all random, there is no creator. This was seen as a killer for Christianity – or at least, for the religious way of seeing the world. The only order in Darwin's universe was a coincidental by-product of brutal competition and the struggle for reproductive success. So much for nature as the creation of a benevolent God. Far from being the children of the all-powerful father created in his own image, we are merely a better-adapted ape. The idea that man was descended from an ape at all was utterly scandalous and shocking. We take it for granted now that we are another kind of animal that evolved like all the others, but, at the time, it was the last blow to the idea of human beings as uniquely created and standing at the very centre of the universe.

Although Christianity underpinned it, this outwardly unassailable capitalist society was not without dark, unresolved tensions. Consider those of four-times British Prime Minister, William Gladstone. His father, usually described as a 'prosperous merchant' made a fortune from slave plantations while Gladstone, an Evangelical, abhorred slavery. He was obsessed with 'fallen women' but tortured himself about it. The man was the microcosm of his society. Both appeared to be rock-solid and confident while beginning to sense danger and competition. Darwin's theory threatened this society with nothing less than the loss of its place as God's higher purpose.

The Hijack of Evolutionary Theory

Perhaps it was inevitable that notions of 'survival of the fittest' were misinterpreted. They justified the European empire-building impetus, for a start. Just when white power was sweeping the globe, science was used to give justification to racism. And if the weakest were going to die out anyway, why wait for natural selection? Why could humans not help it along, and make sure it was not so random? You can see where this was going. Why let inferior strains into the breeding pool? Social Darwinism, as it came to be known, was used as a basis for the eugenics laws used to reduce inferior stock through such policies as the compulsory sterilization of the 'feeble-minded'. By the 1930s, more than 30 American states had them in place. This twisted interpretation of the theory of evolution found its ghastly, logical conclusion in Hitler's Germany, with its breeding programmes of the 'purest' Aryan race, and death camps established for 'inferior' types such as Jews, Slavs, homosexuals and gypsies.

What was forgotten in this warped interpretation of Darwin's theories was that it did not privilege the development of one kind of human being over another. In part that was because Darwin could not identify the biological mechanism by which living beings adapted and evolved.

DNA – The Final Piece in the Jigsaw

Knowledge of the inheritance of different characteristics had been implicitly recognized since the beginnings of civilization – crops were manipulated to produce better harvests, animals were bred to be stronger or faster. It took a mild-mannered and patient monk from what is now the Slovak Republic to produce the first scientific evidence of inheritance. Gregor Mendel (1822–84), 'the father of genetics', spent seven years testing 29,000 pea plants in order to identify the traits that were passed on. His findings, published in 1865, were overlooked at the time but, when they were re-discovered in the early 1900s, it marked the birth of modern gene theory.

A century after On the Origin of Species, four British scientists finally established how information in the form of a three letter code (DNA – deoxyribonucleic acid) directs the development of all living creatures (well, almost – some viruses still escape us, as we know). The revolution Darwin's seminal book started in 1859 led science to the very stuff of life; but that, too, is another story.

23: The Museum's Gaze

The museum is a mirror of civilization. It reflects who we are, or who we like to think we are. On a grand scale, it is the celebration of the collective 'I'. Its silent objects gaze back at us and by their collection and presentation they both freeze the past, and soothe away troubling questions of identity.

Above: Frank Gehry's stunning Guggenheim Museum in Bilbao, opened in 1997, is a free-flowing sculpture of titanium sheathing, which glimmers in the sunlight. Is it 'the greatest building of our time' or 'the world's largest toy'? It has been called both.

Where else in a modern city will you find such calm confidence and complacency? Perhaps this explains why, amid growing urban turmoil, half the museums in the world have been opened in the last 50 years. For every one museum that existed half a century ago in Europe, there are now four. Not hospitals, not schools, but museums. It is because of what it tells us about civilization at any particular time that the museum has become, in itself, a milestone – every country has to have one, or several. The United States has 25,000.

Of them all, the 'star' is the Guggenheim museum in Bilbao. It is the only one that has achieved that prize of the age of media – celebrity status. It may well be the most written about structure in architectural history.

Lord Elgin shipped sculptures from the Parthenon and presented them in 1816 to the British Museum in London, which still refuses the Greek government's request to return them, insisting that they are 'integral to the Museum's purpose as a world museum telling the story of human cultural achievement'. The question is: can any one national museum still claim to 'own' or present such a story on either moral, artistic or legal grounds?

Philip Johnson, no mean architect himself, has called it 'the greatest building of our time'. The novelist J.G. Ballard called it 'part train crash and part explosion in a bullion factory'. The fact that it is an art gallery seems almost irrelevant.

Museums are Big Business

Twenty years ago, Bilbao, a city of one million people in northern Spain, was suffering under the weight of economic and environmental disaster. Up to half of its rusting, industrial heartland lay in ruins, much of it devastated by pollution. It had lost mining, steel and shipbuilding industries, as well as 20 per cent of its population and 47 per cent of its industrial jobs. It was the centre of the Basque country, home to a militant separatist movement that had already claimed nearly 1,000 lives. The regional government put its faith in Bilbao's revival not in new factories or service centres but in a museum – and not any museum, not even a Spanish museum, but one imported from New York.

The Guggenheim Bilbao Museoa is part of a chain, a franchise; it is 'McGuggenheim', centred on

the contemporary art museum on Fifth Avenue in Manhattan, which is in the business of licensing itself all over the world. Its branches reach from Berlin to Las Vegas – where it is tucked into the lobby of a casino that recreates Venice, complete with gondolas. 'Growth is almost a law,' the director of the main Guggenheim has said 'Either you grow and you change, or you die.' Here is the museum truly reflecting its time – an era of fund-raising, glittering openings of blockbuster exhibitions, acres of press coverage and the museum shop on the web. 'Relish each view of the Guggenheim on the wrappers of our dark chocolate squares,' $14.

Online today, you can buy posters of works by Kandinsky, Van Gogh and Picasso, or T-shirts with the Guggenheim logo. ('Been there, done that, got the T-shirt,' being the new call of civilized ennui.) The entrepreneurial museum reflects the power of shopping and branding in a civilization dependent on consumption and underwritten by global tourism.

Royalty – The Early Collections

The idea of the museum open to the public gaze is a relatively new one. Its early precursor was the studioli of the Renaissance princes, the closed and windowless rooms and cabinets, often secret, in which were kept curiosities brought from far and wide in the known world. Such collections were about displaying power, as well as the search for knowledge that was integral to it. These priceless curios were not to be shared indiscriminately. Even when princes were no longer regarded as divine, nor their rule absolute, the great works of civilization in their private collections were emblematic of their status. The princely gallery spoke for and about the prince.

It was not merely as an afterthought that the French Revolutionaries seized the Louvre palace from the dethroned king, Louis XVI, and, rather than pulling it down, in 1793 transformed it into their national gallery. Suddenly, the treasures of civilization embodied in visible form not the power of the king but that of the new state. Gazing upon its paintings was intended to uplift French citizens and inspire them with loyalty to the new republic. It was another way of creating and re-enforcing national identity.

A Civilizing Influence

It was not only the radicals who saw in a national museum a way to bind the unruly masses into the nation. The spate of museum development in mid-19th-century Britain owed much to what was seen as the 'civilizing' effects of art. That most realistic of Victorian prime ministers, William Gladstone (1809–98), claimed that the arts as 'the highest instruments of human cultivation are also the guarantee of public order'. Certainly, the silent, awed walk through the public galleries beneath the vigilant attention of museum guards was intended as a discipline in itself. As if that was not warning enough, the 1845 Museums Bill stipulated imprisonment, hard labour and whipping for anyone attempting to damage works of art in public collections.

Art museums were intended to remove the visitors from everyday life. The noise and urgency of the street was stilled in windowless galleries. The objects displayed were meant to lift those who looked upon them to a higher aesthetic and even moral plane. They were, for the Industrial Age, the equivalent of stained-glass windows in the great Gothic cathedrals – the truth-bearers, telling stories of beauty and sacrifice.

They created a distance from the material world of necessity and struggle. The museum's artefacts were not for sale; they were unique, rendered priceless and removed from economic consideration.

Culture as Tourism

There is no such cultural solemnity to that iconic building by the Californian architect, Frank O. Gehry, which stands on the banks of the Nervion river in Bilbao. According to The New York Times, it is: 'A shimmering, Looney Tunes, post-industrial, post-everything burst of American optimism wrapped in titanium'. Put it another way, in a highly nationalistic region full of prickly independence, only 10 per cent of the Guggenheim's visitors are locals. Ninety per cent are tourists. It is a museum both intended for and accommodating the comfort of international travellers. Café, restaurant, shop: these are the essentials of the modern, competitive museum. Hence also the sleek new international airport designed by Santiago Calatrava and Sir Norman Foster's new metro system.

Bilbao is full of contradiction and complication. Not least is the still open question about whether new industries will follow this cultural trail into the city, bringing jobs and prosperity. Is Gehry's curvaceous building – the new Marilyn Monroe, as it has been called – the point of the museum, or the works of art it contains? Further, is art one of civilization's treasures

Reassembling the Fragments

The very idea of the 'nation' is in the singular. It has its own singular identity. Its civilization was long understood as a purposeful journey of one particular national identity towards the present. What happens, though, when both nation and civilization in general develop so many identities that neither presents only one face, represents only one experience?

The new National Museum of Australia in Canberra is a casebook example. While it must represent the nation, the very question of Australian-ness is thorny and contested. Trying to place the first Australians – that is, the Aborigines or Indigenous Australians – within the reality of the present, let alone the past, has stirred contentious debates. For Aborigines, the invasion and loss of their land, the massacres and forced removal of their children ('the stolen children') are painful issues. How could they be acknowledged properly in the national museum when the then-long-serving prime minister had always refused to apologize for the injustices of the past?

The National Ethnographic Collection of Aboriginal objects had been housed in the Institute of Anatomy, together with the National War Wounds Collection (the odd choice of its placing is telling in itself). These objects, variously collected by white settler-researchers and government officers, mostly date from the Aboriginal hunter-gatherer past. Today, Indigenous Australians are lawyers, civil servants and professionals, living in a modern world. Too past-oriented a presentation of their hunter-gatherer ancestors would be an unwelcome reminder of centuries of disdain. To ignore all evidence of the past would be to lose a rich and spiritual part of Aboriginal culture. There is a further wrinkle in that wrinkle; Indigenous Australians were never one people with one uniform culture: they were many peoples. Their stories were different; they were colonized at different times and their legal battles continue on different paths to this day.

The challenges faced in that sleek, modern building in Australia are common to all new museums of conscience around the world, whether museums of slavery, the Holocaust or indigenous peoples. In telling the stories and displaying the artefacts of oppression, there is also the danger of perpetuating it – of keeping alive images, memories, and stereotypes. In a world where peoples have become largely rootless and disconnected from their own past, does the museum, in stirring memory, act as a warning, a weapon, a comfort or a wound?

To privilege one 'civilization' in a nation also risks making others invisible – what of more recent immigrants to Australia – from Asia for example? Where will their stories be told when future generations 'read' the new National Museum as the 'text' of today's Australian civilization?

One last question: who are such museums really aiming to attract as they attempt to reassemble the fragments of a splintered past? The clue is possibly on the homepage of the Australian National Museum website. The logo reads: 'Winner 2006 Australian Tourism Awards: Major Tourist Attractions'.

The Aboriginal didjeridu is a musical instrument used in ancient male rituals. Some Aboriginal cultures forbade women to hear, see or touch the didjeridu. How can such meaning resonate in a self-conscious museum setting?

Phnom Penh, Cambodia. What was the notorious Toul Sleng prison is now a museum of conscience and mourning. Clothing and photographs commemorate some of the 30,000 men and women who were tortured and died here. Ironically, Toul Sleng had been a school, a place of aspiration and hope; thus civilization mocks itself.

or is it another form of entertainment? If the building has more impact than the art hanging in it, is that art compromised and dispossessed?

Nowhere are these questions more knotty than in the plans for the latest Guggenheim branch, to be designed once again by Gehry. It is to be the anchor of a $27 billion cultural centre being erected in Abu Dhabi on a specially constructed spit of land jutting out into an ancient trade-travelled sea. Approached by a direct 10-lane highway from the airport, this man-made 'island' will also include 29 hotels, a marina for cruise ships and private yachts, and a performing arts centre with two concert halls, an opera house and two theatres. Besides the new Guggenheim, the French architect,

Jean Nouvel, is designing a branch of the Louvre, for which brand, honouring a democratic republic, the oil-rich government of a traditional and autocratic ruler is said to have paid a fortune in dollars to France.

To Whom Does Culture Belong?

The Prophet emerged from across the desert behind the United Arab Emirates bringing the message of Islam, held sacred by these Arab hosts. Does the milieu of high-end tourism and Western civilization at its most hedonistic hold any inherent contradiction in this centre of the Arab world? Does it mean that great art is universal and belongs anywhere, in any culture? Or does it mean that in a global civilization dedicated to consuming, art has no message beyond that of pleasure itself? Not so long ago, the novelist Iris Murdoch (1919–99) wrote that 'serious art is a continuous working of meaning in the light of the discovery of some truth.' Whether that claim is pertinent today must worry the directors of museums everywhere. At heart, it is not only a question about art, but about civilization itself.

24: Setting the Earth on Fire

'Globalization' was a buzz word of the late 20th century, but slowly it came to mean more than free trade and shared media images. Pollution, deforestation, desertification, destruction of ecosystems, flash flooding, water stress – these were challenges that crossed borders and sped around the turning planet.

Above: Not even half a century ago, the busy fishing waters of the Aral Sea lapped onto Kazakhstan in the north and Uzbekistan in the south. Today, the skeleton of an old ship rots on the desert that was once the fourth largest inland sea on Earth.

'Spring now comes unheralded by the return of the birds and the early mornings are strangely silent.'

RACHEL CARSON, THE SILENT SPRING (1962)

'Without realizing it, we have begun to wage war on the Earth itself. Now, we and the Earth's climate are locked in a relationship familiar to war planners: "Mutually assured destruction"'

AL GORE (NOBEL PEACE PRIZE SPEECH, 2007)

In 2007, 45 years after Rachel Carson's seminal book conjured the spectre of an America devoid of songbirds, The World Conservation Union issued a warning. Effective immediately, 16,306 species around the world were defined as vulnerable, endangered or critically endangered. In total, 51 per cent of invertebrate species, 39 per cent of fish, 31 per cent of reptiles and amphibians, 20 per cent of mammals and 12 per cent of birds are threatened with extinction. Only future generations will know whether the milestone of today's civilization turns out to be 'green' or the colour of scorched earth – either way, the problem is environmental damage and global warming.

Carbon dioxide and other gases warm the surface of the Earth by trapping the sun's heat in the atmosphere. Burning fossil fuels, such as coal, gas and oil, and clearing forests, which are the planet's lungs, have dramatically increased the amount of carbon dioxide in the atmosphere. Temperatures are rising. Changes are already happening: hurricanes, droughts, melting ice caps, wildfires, flooding, heat waves. Al Gore's Oscar-winning film, An Inconvenient Truth, in documenting such threats, was a call to arms for eco-warriors, a plea to work across national and political borders to save the planet's fragile ecology and biodiversity.

The belief that nature has a value of its own, that it is worth conserving for its own sake, has a long tradition in many of the world's religions – for Buddhists, Hindus, Jains, followers of the Tao. The secular, global environmentalism movement can now be added to that list. Devastation on the scale seen today is the work of modernity, of industrialization and intensive agriculture. It is the result either of humanity's naïve faith in nature's endless bounty or, as environmentalists would have it, of its arrogance and greed. There is still a chance to make amends, they say, but the challenge is daunting.

Pollution and Destruction

The vast central Asian republic of Kazakhstan stands as a casebook example of the immense task facing those who would reverse the damage. What has happened to the Aral Sea has been called the greatest environmental tragedy of the 20th century – and it had some stiff competition. The planet's fourth largest inland sea has been turned into mostly desert. When the former Soviet Union diverted the rivers that fed into it to grow cotton on the inhospitable desert steppes, it created an ecological and human disaster. The seabed today looks at first sight as if it is covered with snow; it is in fact a crust of salt, which the winds blow as far as the Himalayas.

Around the old sea, cancers, lung disease and infant mortality are 30 times higher than they used to be because the drinking water is heavily polluted with salt, cotton fertilizers and pesticides. Once-busy fishing villages have become the graveyards of rusting ships. Jobs, food, fish and children have died with the sea. The countries nearby have set up an organization to save what is left of the water. It will be years before the sea begins to grow again.

On the great steppes of this ancient land were set up heavily polluting industries such as lead and chemical plants, which drained the ground water and leached poison into what was left. Copper smelters were built in the 1930s on the shores of the 450-kilometre (280-mile) long Lake Balkhash. Bird and other lake life is practically extinct today while the drawing of drinking water supplies from the lake means that 40 per cent of Kazakhstan's population are drinking polluted water. In the north-west of the country, the enormous Ekibastuz power plant, running on low-grade coal, belched yet more pollution into the air while it supplied 27 per cent of the former Soviet Union's electricity.

Nuclear Fallout

North of Lake Balkhash is an even more treacherous legacy – the nuclear testing grounds of Semipalatinsk. From 1949, some 467 nuclear tests were carried out here – above ground until the 1963 Nuclear Test Ban Treaty, underground after that. Forty years of nuclear tests, the equivalent of thousands of Hiroshimas, during which years Kazakh nomads herding their animals round Semipalatinsk suffered massive doses of radioactive fallout. Children were born without arms or fingers, blind or deaf. Whole families died of cancer.

In 1991, soon after the demise of the Soviet Union and the independence of Kazakhstan, President Nazarayev's government closed down Semipalatinsk and declared the area around the site an ecological disaster zone. All agriculture was banned, and, to clear up the deadly nuclear heritage, the president called on the help of foreign specialists. A world of self-contained nation states has no meaning for nature.

Five years earlier, the planet had shared the effects of the worst ever nuclear accident. The fire at Ukraine's Chernobyl nuclear power plant sent a plume of highly radioactive fallout across the world from Japan to the edge of Europe and beyond. It had brought home a lesson: what blows with the winds and falls with the rain recognizes no political borders.

Toxic Waste

All industrially developed countries have such time bombs within them. In the United States, Love Canal is a byword for such threats. In 1979, 25 years after a large chemical company stopped using the canal by the picturesque Niagara river as an industrial dump, 82 different compounds, many of them known and suspected carcinogens, were found to be oozing upwards through the soil from rotting drum containers. The toxins seeped into the back yards and basements of a hundred homes and a public school built on the banks of the canal. Everywhere the air had a faint, choking smell, and children came in from playing outside with burns on their hands and faces. There were clusters of cancers, miscarriages and birth defects. In all, the government moved 200 families

The Aral Sea viewed from space: what was once a single body of water is now divided, but intervention by the Kazakh government appears to be saving the north lake – the water level has risen, salt levels have dropped and fish are gradually returning.

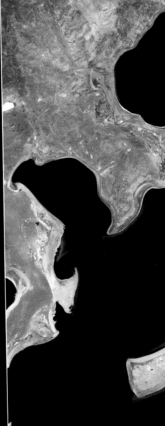

away and set about the challenge of detoxifying the area. There may be hundreds of such chemical dump sites all across the United States.

Limited Natural Resources

Such tragedies can be caused by negligent carelessness of consequences, by ignorance or by simple denial that the earth's natural resources are limited, scarce and delicate. Only 0.08 per cent of all the earth's water is accessible or suitable in its natural state for humans' use. Today, one person in five across the world has no access to safe drinking water. Where shortage is the problem, increasingly, irreplaceable underground aquifers are being drained. When emptied, they will buckle in on themselves – hence the surface subsidence in Bangkok, Mexico City and Venice.

For years, John Howard, Prime Minister of Australia, denied that the country's unprecedented and epic seven-year drought since 1999 had any connection with global warming. A hardened climate-change sceptic, he finally had to warn the country in 2007 that unless heavy rains arrived, the government would have to switch off the water supply to the Murray-Darling basin, the continent's food bowl. As it is, the mighty rivers feeding the basin have shrivelled into slow, muddy streams. The land of sweeping plains and bounty could easily be reduced to a dust bowl.

When Al Gore went to Australia with his documentary film, Howard refused to meet him. He ignored the report by the UN Intergovernmental Panel on Climate Change predicting bush fires, tropical cyclones and cataclysmic damage to the Great Barrier Reef. 'We must all hope and pray there is rain,' he said. A few months later, the Australian public voted Howard out of office after 10 years. The main concern cited was the environment, and the new government made solving the climate crisis its highest priority.

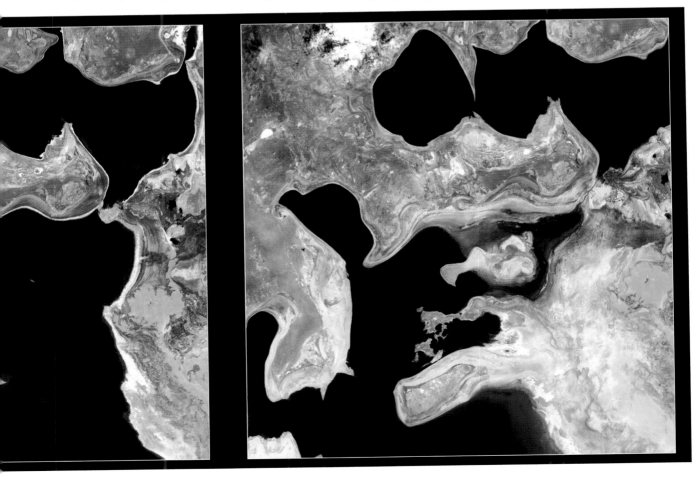

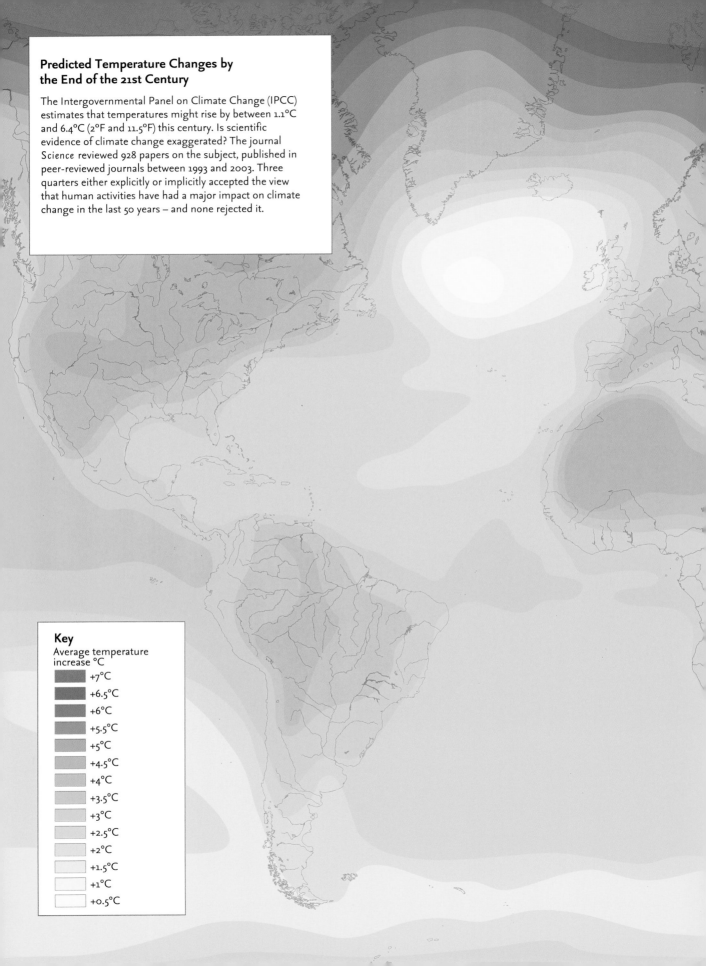

Predicted Temperature Changes by the End of the 21st Century

The Intergovernmental Panel on Climate Change (IPCC) estimates that temperatures might rise by between 1.1°C and 6.4°C (2°F and 11.5°F) this century. Is scientific evidence of climate change exaggerated? The journal *Science* reviewed 928 papers on the subject, published in peer-reviewed journals between 1993 and 2003. Three quarters either explicitly or implicitly accepted the view that human activities have had a major impact on climate change in the last 50 years – and none rejected it.

Key
Average temperature increase °C

- +7°C
- +6.5°C
- +6°C
- +5.5°C
- +5°C
- +4.5°C
- +4°C
- +3.5°C
- +3°C
- +2.5°C
- +2°C
- +1.5°C
- +1°C
- +0.5°C

The Challenge Today

When he accepted the Nobel Peace Prize, Gore finished his speech with a challenge. 'The future is knocking at our door right now,' he said. 'Make no mistake, the next generation will ask us one of two questions. Either they will ask: "What were you thinking; why didn't you act?" Or they will ask instead: "How did you find the moral courage to rise and successfully resolve a crisis that so many said was impossible to solve?"' There are signs that the peoples of the world are ready to respond to Gore's challenge. With enough determination, environmentalism could yet replace global warming as the milestone of our civilization today. Politics could still give the Earth a voice.

It is nearly 40 years since the first human stepped onto the desolate and empty Moon. The photograph the astronauts took of the earth, showed one tiny and unique globe revolving in a vast space. It is to be hoped that as you read this the Four Horsemen of the Apocalypse are not riding unchecked across its face.

The environment is not an add-on to civilization. Climate change is not alone in decimating the habitats of plants and animals, such as these kangaroos in Sturt National Park, Australia. Increasingly, governments are seeking to solve growing water shortages by tapping irreplaceable groundwater, which dries out the rivers, wetlands and lakes depending on it.

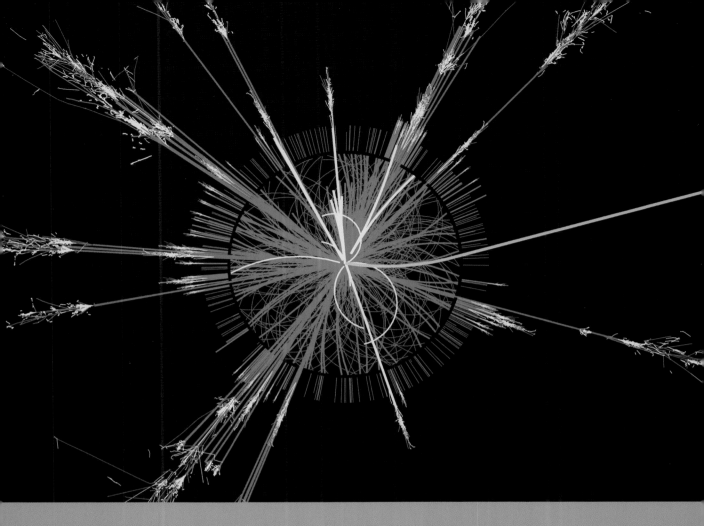

25: A Theory of Everything

There is a strong chance that the next milestone will come from the gaze of physicists into the existential loneliness of space. What are we seeking there? As Nobel laureate Leon Lederman puts it: 'If the universe is the answer, what is the question?'

Above: A simulated black hole, one of many cosmic mysteries. 'The more the universe seems comprehensible,' says one physicist, 'The more it seems pointless.' Perhaps our question is how to find meaning for and on this infinitesimal speck, Earth.

From the earliest times, ancient human remains have revealed humankind's interest in the surrounding universe, the question of the divine, the puzzling and sometimes terrifying power of the natural world. For centuries, early scientists – including Isaac Newton – believed that to know the true God was to know the true nature of the universe. Modern physics stands that assumption on its head: perhaps to know the true nature of the universe will be to know the true God.

At the CERN laboratory (CERN is the French acronym for the European Centre for Nuclear Research – a centre which, confusingly, does not do nuclear research), straddling the borders of Switzerland and France, the search is on for what has become known – for some in earnest and others in irony – as 'the God particle', the key to understanding our universe. At stake are some of physics' deepest problems: why is there mass in the universe? Why is there matter? Why is the universe hurtling outwards like a loaf of raisin bread leavened with a huge amount of yeast? What circumstances of physical law and cosmic history results in the world as we know it, including its thinking, questioning beings? In short, nothing less than a theory of everything.

The Particle Accelerator

At the time of writing, the CERN particle accelerator is months from being switched on. When it is, it will be the largest atom smasher in the world. It might deliver an understanding, at last, of the make-up of the subatomic particles that are the building blocks of all matter in the universe. The Large Hadron Collider is a giant machine, part of which is called Atlas, after the Greek god who carried the weight of the world on his shoulders. It is 46 metres (150 feet) long, 25 metres (82 feet) high and weighs 7,000 tons. It has been designed to measure particles so small you can fit hundreds of billions of them into a beam narrower than a human hair in width.

When it is switched on, two beams of invisible, massively energetic proton particles will travel in opposite directions around a 27-kilometre (17-mile) ring some 90 metres (300 feet) under the earth's surface. Travelling in a vacuum colder than deep space

– -236°C (-393°F) – the beams will approach the speed of light, making 11,245 circuits a second. When the particles in the beam collide, each collision will create conditions that existed in the first fraction of a second after the Big Bang, the 'birth' of our universe, when it came fizzing and broiling into being. It will turn into a kind of time machine that, when it works, might give us a glimpse into the very structure of the universe. It might tell us what happened, but to what purpose is the question beyond even physics.

The God Particle

The particles are so small that at best only 40 or so of every 200 billion will crash head-on. Atlas can process 600 million such collisions a second, delivering raw data at a rate of around 40 million filing cabinets full of text every second. In this morass of information, among the many things the physicists are hoping to find, the prize would certainly be the God particle, the elusive Higgs Boson. Like most particles worth searching for, the Higgs Boson will remain undetectable, even assuming it exists. All that will be visible to the massive Atlas will be the stream of debris it leaves behind. In short, there will be ghosts in the machine. To get some idea of the faith, intellectual curiosity and courage involved in this £8 billion enterprise, Sir John Adams, the pioneer of this giant particle accelerator, once likened atom-smashing to trying to understand how a watch works by hanging it in a dark room and hurling cricket balls at it.

The Higgs Boson was the idea of an Edinburgh physicist, Peter Higgs. While many were dancing at Woodstock and celebrating hippy freedom in the 1960s, he was trying to understand what gives matter its mass or weight. He theorized that as particles travelled in space through what is now known as the Higgs field, those that collided frequently with it gained heavy mass. The field tugs on matter, making it heavy. Imagine pulling a weightless pearl necklace through a jar of honey and how much heavier it will be afterwards – there you have something of the effect of the Higgs Boson. It is still only a theory, but there is one type of quark that was only discovered in 1995, 20

Atlas, CERN's Large Hadron Collider. The medieval cosmos was beautiful – simple, divine, as long as the bits that did not fit were fiddled and fudged. The current Standard Model of the universe relies on similar fiddling – maybe CERN will be able to deliver unity once more.

years after physicists had theorized about such a particle's existence.

Bosons, protons, neutrons, leptons, quarks – whatever happened to the lowly atom, once seen as the smallest particle of matter? Its very name comes from the Greek, meaning 'indivisible'. It turned out, of course, to be divisible. The atom is tiny; its nucleus of protons and neutrons is 10,000 times smaller than the atom. Quarks and electrons are 10,000 times even smaller than that. So far, physics has found about 200 particles. Worry not: the great Enrico Fermi (1901–54) (winner of the Nobel Prize for Physics in 1938) once said to his student, Leon Lederman (b. 1922) (himself a future Nobel laureate): 'Young man, if I could remember the names of these particles, I would have been a botanist.'

The New Frontiers of Physics

As recently as the 19th century, it seemed as if all that remained for physicists was to fill in minor gaps in the seemingly well-established body of knowledge. For two centuries, science had produced unassailable facts. It was the benchmark for what could be known about the world. In 1905, Albert Einstein and his theory of relativity started to shake it all up again: in defiance of common sense and centuries of the accepted laws of physics, he theorized that at speeds

Earth, a speck in a complex universe. Laureate Leon Lederman has a cartoon of a white-gowned deity, staring at a 'Universe Machine' with 20 encoded levers and a plunger marked 'Push to Create Universe'. Not, he argues, how a self-respecting God would create a universe.

The Information Age – from CERN with Love

Looking into the future, the French critic, Jean Baudrillard (1929–2007) once argued that 'power will belong to those peoples with no origins and no authenticity'. He was defining peoples living at one with their machines, living virtual lives sustained by gigabites of information in which fact and fiction become interchangeable, reality and unreality hard to distinguish, cybersex and pornography the experience of choice. Surfing down the superhighway past the milestone of a thousand such alienated tomorrows can sound more like a bleak threat than an attractive promise. When the World Wide Web (www) was created by a physicist at CERN two decades ago, it was presented to the world as a gift. Almost uniquely, it preserved intellectual freedom over personal profit.

Thanks to the World Wide Web, with a mouse, a modem and internet access, you can point and click anywhere in the world and be flooded with information. This invention was the work of one man: Tim Berners-Lee. He argued for years that it was possible; when he had no takers, he went on to do the job himself. His initial motivation was to organize the vast quantities of information stored in CERN's powerful but isolated computer systems to make it centrally accessible. When it worked, he went on to make it possible for computers all over the world to talk to each other using a 'language' he devised.

Thomas Edison is credited with the light bulb, but dozens of people in his laboratory worked on it. William Shockley is recognized for the invention of the transistor, but it was built by two of his research assistants. The World Wide Web is Berners-Lee's alone. He designed and built it when he was a fellow at CERN. Even more significantly, he persuaded CERN to keep his invention freely in the public domain – decentralized, non-proprietary, no restrictions, no royalties, no patent dues.

It is because of his idealistic vision that the World Wide Web is a completely open book. It has created a vast information space that knows no geographical boundaries. As of now, more than a billion people regularly access the internet – it has become an essential feature of global civilization.

Others made millions and billions in the dot.com boom that followed Berners-Lee's invention in 1991. Marc Andreesen, for example, who helped to write the first popular web browser, Mosaic, and went on to found Netscape, sold his company to AOL for $10 billion. Bill Gates of Microsoft became the richest man in the world, despite failing at first to predict the impact of the internet. Berners-Lee continued along the non-profit route. When he left CERN, he went into academia – to the University of Southampton in England and then to MIT (the Massachusetts Institute of Technology) where he works to guard the rules and development of the web. This last is a nice irony: as a physics undergraduate at Oxford, he was banned from using the university computer – for hacking.

He is often asked whether he minds that his invention is used for paedophilia as well as social networking, for smart wars and information on building bombs as well as on relativity. 'It's a universal medium and it's not itself a medium which inherently makes people do good things or bad things,' he has said. 'I see it as something on which humanity will do what humanity does.'

The World Wide Web, then, is another mirror of social relations in a civilization, of its weaknesses as well as its strengths. It throws up a reflection of the inequalities between nations; only two per cent of the world's population have regular access to it. What it will do for civilization is written in the future.

Sir Tim Berners-Lee, the gawky schoolboy turned geek, who refused to allow the World Wide Web to be patented, shown here with Kofi Annan, Nobel laureate. Will the human genome be subject to similar idealism? Not a chance, it seems.

approaching that of light, time slows down and distance shortens. Since then, there has been a crisis in physics that has turned it on its head, so that it has seemed at times as if all had became uncertainty, indeterminacy and random.

The Age of the Universe

Take the age paradox, for instance. The universe is thought to be (and even this is controversial) somewhere between eight and 12 billion years old, but some stars are 16 billion years old. How is it possible

'Einstein linked time with space, mass with energy, and the path of light past the sun with the flight of a bullet; and spent his dying years in trying to add to these likenesses another, which would find a single imaginative order,' said Jacob Bronowski. Such an order still eludes science.

that some bits of it are older than the universe itself? At the beginning, there was both matter and anti-matter and a symmetry between the two, they were equal but opposite. So why is there so much more matter left now in the universe than anti-matter? Physicists do not yet know. What is dark matter? What is dark energy? About 96 per cent of the mass of the universe – dark, not as in black or sinister, but as in ignorance, in what is not known. Slowly, stealthily, within their own world for the most part, physicists are amassing pieces of a jigsaw for which, as yet, they have no picture on the front of the box. Each piece of this jigsaw is both infinitesimal and huge. For most of us, too huge even to imagine.

The Biggest Milestone of All?

Why then is this to be such a milestone of civilization? On the largest scale of all, it is because CERN is driven by the very intellectual curiosity that is the mark of all civilization's advances and knowledge. Many years ago, the physicist Robert Wilson (1914–2000), a leading accelerator designer, was called to testify before the US Congressional Joint Committee on Atomic Energy. What, he was asked, would an accelerator do for the defence of the United States? 'It has only to do with the respect with which we regard one another, the dignity of men, our love of culture,' he answered 'It has nothing to do directly with defending our country – except to make it worth defending.'

Whether or not the Higgs Boson is found, perhaps the deepest meaning of CERN for the rest of us is in its very existence. CERN has at work around 1,000 scientists and 100 nationalities. Where else in the world is there an institution so truly global, working with openness and trust? At any one time, more than 50 per cent of all the active particle physicists in the world are participating at CERN in more than 120 research projects, sharing their exploration, their discoveries and their faith that the universe will turn out to be ordered, elegant – to make sense. As Albert Einstein famously insisted: God does not play dice with the universe. On the other hand, when Einstein revolutionized physics with his theory of relativity E $=MC^2$ (energy = mass x the speed of light squared) he was working as an obscure technical officer in a patent office in Bern, not in a $300-million-a-year laboratory. What modern astrophysics is waiting for now is either hard evidence from CERN – or the single mind of a genius.

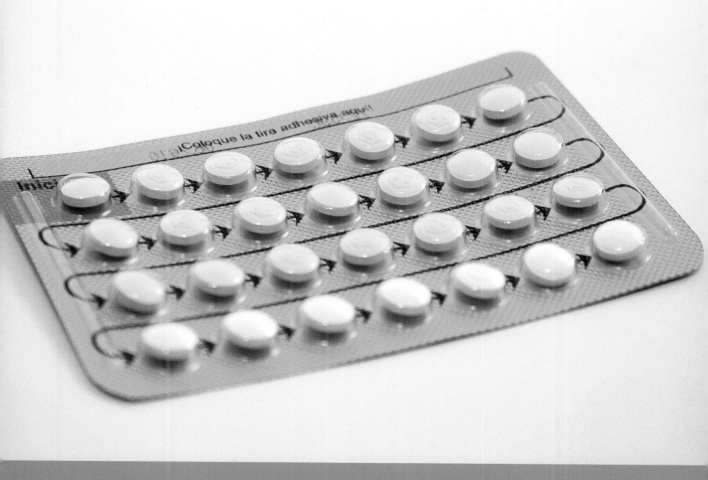

26: Burying the Present

Civilization flows and changes. Values, ideals and practices wax and wane, maybe vanish, maybe come around again. Cultures are like comets travelling across history, sometimes known only by the trail they leave behind. If we were to bury a time capsule that presents ourselves to some future civilization, what should we include that captures something significant about our present reality and, maybe, a reminder of our better selves?

Above: There is only one drug so famous that it is known simply as 'The Pill'. Marketed as a contraceptive in 1960, it was probably the first ever to be designed for social rather than therapeutic purposes. In 1993, the British weekly The Economist listed it as one of the seven wonders of the world.

The Nobel Peace Prize

When the industrialist and weapons manufacturer Alfred Nobel died in 1896, he left most of his wealth to be used for five prizes including one for peace. Four were to be decided in Sweden; the peace prize, uniquely, was to be awarded by a committee elected by the Norwegian Storting or parliament. Norway, a small European country admired for its quiet attempts at international bridge-building, has administered the world's most prestigious (and valuable) peace prize ever since. Each year the prize marks the journey across the bumpy landscape of humankind: what are the current concerns of the civilized world, what its progress? As such, it is a crucial milestone – a benchmark of our civilization today.

Through history, war has set many once-great civilizations on their path to ruin. In the 20th century, a century racked by global blood-letting, the definition of what constitutes peace, let alone its preservation, was always controversial. To read the list of the prizes awarded – or sometimes not – is to read civilization's tortuous search for the ethical values underpinning peace, its successes and its failures.

The idealism and hopes of internationalist movements shone through the years that led up to 1914 and 1939. Disappointments abounded – the prizes for political peace-making which never came to fruition, for the promise of nuclear disarmament that left a world still full of such weapons. Watch, though, at the changes as a new century opened and global and humanitarian concerns were mirrored by the choice of prize laureates. Hope is part of civilization too.

The Nobel Peace Prize Winners of the 21st Century

2007 – Al Gore and the Intergovernmental Panel on Climate Change

2006 – Muhammad Yunus, Grameen Bank
Yunus, 'banker to the poor' in Bangladesh, is the pioneer of microlending who founded the Grameen Bank after seeing the effect of his personal loans of small amounts to destitute basketweavers in the mid 1970s.

2005 – Mohamed El Baradei, International Atomic Energy Agency
El Baradei, Egyptian lawyer and diplomat, tried to set down protocols and inspections by the IAEA to prevent nuclear energy being used for military purposes.

2004 – Wangari Maathai
Maathai is the Kenyan founder of the Green Belt Movement, which has planted 30 million trees on farms, schools and church compounds with women's groups, both to conserve the environment and improve the quality of their lives.

2003 – Shiran Ebadi
This Iranian former judge, dismissed from the bench after the Islamic revolution, has led the struggle for the rights of women and children in her country.

2002 – Jimmy Carter
Two decades after the end of his US presidency, Carter won the prize for his work in conflict mediation, quietly monitoring elections all over the world, physically building houses for Habitat for Humanity, almost always out of the spotlight.

2001 – Kofi Annan, The United Nations
For all its imperfections, this international institution marries idealism, realism and sheer pragmatism, and keeps the 188 member countries talking.

2000 – Kim Dae-jung
This president of South Korea won the prize for his attempts to establish peace and reconciliation with North Korea, the latest global outlaw.

Wangari Maathai, Professor of Veterinary Anatomy, who developed a grass-roots tree-planting movement for women.

Landmark laureate: Nelson Mandela (Nobel Peace Prize, 1993)

In 1964, Nelson Mandela was sentenced to life imprisonment for plotting to overthrow the South African government by violence. He was incarcerated for 27 years – 18 of them on Robben Island. During those years he was widely accepted as the most significant black leader in South Africa, a powerful symbol of resistance.

What happened in the years following his release will forever be marked by the enormity of his forgiveness. The son of a tribal chief, he worked for an African country that put aside tribalism. The leader of a violent, black political movement, he sought a non-racist South Africa built around 'a rainbow coalition'. He became president of a country unified by a constitution that, together with that of the French and American Revolutions, must stand as a milestone of democracy and humanity, whatever the future may bring.

The Preamble to the South African Constitution of 1996

'We, the people of South Africa,
Recognise the injustices of our past;
Honour those who suffered for justice and freedom in our land;
Respect those who have worked to build and develop our country;
And believe that South Africa belongs to all who live in it, united in our diversity.'

Here UN Peacekeepers safeguard food supplies. What happens when there is no peace to keep? In the Congo, for example, 16,000 troops from 100 countries were expected to impose peace on a civil war in which 3 million had already died, mostly civilians.

Landmark laureate: the Blue Berets, also known as the United Nations Peacekeeping Forces (Nobel Peace Prize, 1988)

It seemed an oxymoron: a peace prize awarded to what was, in large part, a military force. When it was presented, 733 UN soldiers had already sacrificed their lives. Since then, another 1,682 UN personnel have died in the service of furthering 'peaceful' solutions to conflicts. Are they peacekeepers – or peacemakers? Do they hold the ring or enter it? Should they be (let alone are they?) unarmed observers or active participants? And, importantly, what can it say about civilization that it needs soldiers to stand guard over its peace? It says that even at its most civilized, our world is no Utopia, and never has been. Our best efforts, while flawed and subject to human frailty and political weakness, must speak for us as loudly as our worst.

At the time of writing, there are approaching 100,000 blue berets on duty throughout the world – their weapons, support systems, even their very food and drink depend on member states of the United Nations, which may or may not deliver promised provisions on time, or ever, but many of them do.

In a dangerous, anarchic world where co-operation, consensus and alliances are constantly shifting, it is perhaps a miracle that an international military force can be sustained, fifty years from its inception. Its failures are a stain on the world's conscience: the 1994 Rwandan genocide, the betrayal that led to the 1995 massacre in Sebrenica. Its successes show that despite these failures, it is underpinned, however reluctantly, by ethical values. UN peacekeeping forces have not, for instance, stood aside from the disaster that is Darfur, despite the bitter opposition of the Sudanese government.

Today, 17,000 blue berets are at work in the Congo, a country in which four million people died in five years of civil wars, in which 20 per cent of children die before the age of five and 38 per cent suffer from malnutrition. Those who would dismiss the UN peacekeepers as corrupt, hypocritical or merely ineffective should perhaps have to stand up for peace where the blue berets stand; they are often all there is between the beasts of war and a threadbare civilization.

Landmark laureate: Médecins Sans Frontières (Nobel Peace Prize, 1999)

Bernard Kouchner, at the time of writing, is the unlikely Foreign Minister of France. Unlikely, because he was first celebrated for fishing Vietnamese boat people out of the China Sea and for shouldering sacks of rice in Operation Restore Hope in Somalia. Nelson Mandela once whispered to him: 'Thanks for intervening in matters that don't concern you.'

Kouchner, one of the original founders of MSF in 1971, reminds us how much difference one person's obstinate intervention can make. Altruism – so derided – can be a powerful driver. MSF is secular, humanitarian, independent and non-governmental. It does not keep quiet, it does not acquiesce. Its professional volunteers not only provide medical care in natural disasters and war-torn countries, they speak out, they obey what Kouchner has called 'the duty of international meddling'.

Not for the early MSF the mistake of the Red Cross from 1940–44, which distributed care packages to prisoners while keeping silent about the death camps in which Kouchner's grandparents perished. MSF insists on breaking the silence, which touches on an

Médecins Sans Frontières doctors work even as populations flee. In N'djamena, Chad, MSF doctors struggled to reach hospitals through streets choked with tens of thousands in flight. They withdrew from Somalia only after the brutal murders of their surgical team.

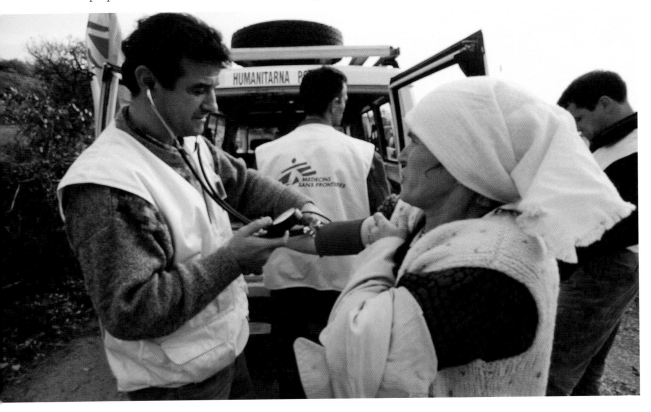

ongoing debate in the world – how far to co-operate with tyranny in the hope of softening it, how far to isolate it in its own cruelties?

Kouchner's own engagement was individual at first. He went to Nigeria during the civil war to provide medical relief. 'I ran to Biafra,' he once said, 'because I was too young for Guernica, Auschwitz, Oradour and Setif.' MSF emerged from the experience of Kouchner and other French doctors who were burned by the inhumanity they witnessed in Biafra, determined no longer to let the world stand by in the name of neutrality.

One cannot stop a genocide with doctors. But they can keep the hospitals open and start the healing process for those who survive.

The HIV Virus and AIDS

In 1969, the Surgeon General of the United States claimed that, 'the book of infectious diseases is now closed.' A decade later, doctors in New York and San Francisco started reporting cases of young homosexual men dying from a rare cancer, Karposi's Sarcoma. Within four years, 10,000 people in the United States alone had the disease, most of whom would die within two years. By then, 50 per cent of prostitutes in Africa's Kenya were infected by male lorry drivers carrying the disease along the main highways of the continent. A new global epidemic had arrived: AIDS. By the year 2000 it had caused 20 million deaths worldwide, and another 36 million people were estimated to be HIV positive.

What, then, should we put into our time capsule to help the future identify the new plague, which will, hopefully, by then have been overcome? Perhaps we should settle for a note defining it as a medical term, together with current figures? HIV is a retrovirus, which affects the white blood cells essential to the body's immune system. It is spread through the transmission of sexual fluids or blood, and can be passed by pregnant women to their foetus, and through breast milk to their babies. When the cells attacked by the HIV virus are reduced from a normal density of 1,000 per microlitre to the critical point around 200 – the patient is suffering from immune deficiency (AIDS), and is unable to fight against other invading viruses, infections, tumours, diseases of the nervous system.

Its historical origins are still uncertain but it seems to have crossed to humans from chimpanzees along the Congo river sometime during the 1970s or before.

In some ways the medical history of HIV and AIDS is a disgrace, but the fact that it is recognized as such speaks well of our ability to acknowledge failure and try to redeem it. The brazen competition between an American and a French scientist to identify the virus was mediated and halted by another (Linus Pauling); powerful drug companies were finally shamed into allowing anti-retroviral therapy treatment to be made cheaply available in poor countries; those involved were jailed following the death of 300 French haemophiliacs from infected blood banks. If greed and ambition among medical 'stars' is part of our civilization, so too is altruism and international conscience.

It is possible, though, that with hindsight our undetermined future might see a different milestone. The UN AIDS organization has just announced that global HIV has at last plateaued. Although AIDS is among the leading causes of death in the world and the primary cause of death in Africa (68 per cent of all the people in the world living with HIV are in sub-Saharan Africa), the number of new HIV infections is thought to have finally levelled off and dropped from its peak of more than three million a year to 2.5 million in 2007. Half a million people a year less is reason, perhaps, for hope – but it still means that as we close our time capsule, 6,800 people every day around the world are newly infected with a disease for which there is as yet neither cure nor vaccine.

Of Pills and Side Effects

Modern medicine and hygiene, however slow in coming, is perhaps the most welcome of benefits passed on by the rich countries of the world to the poorest. What they have brought with them, however, is a population explosion unprecedented in human history. In 1960, there were three billion people in the world; at the beginning of 2007, there were nearly seven billion. This alone is a milestone, which one scientist has called 'the introduction of death control without the introduction of life control'.

There is one discovery that has so transformed the lives of so many women that it figures on the list of the 'greatest' medical advances. As a 'medical miracle' it still needs to be viewed warily. It is the Pill. Within seven years of being licensed in 1962 in the United States, one in four American women were using it. This was a revolution indeed – especially considering that the contraceptive pill could not even be legally tested in the state in which it was developed. The anti-birth-control

The unequal distribution of AIDS and the lack of freely available drugs to manage HIV is a reminder that the bottom 20 per cent of the world's population shares less than a tenth of one per cent of the world's global income. What use drugs, however, without the means to distribute them?

laws in the state of Massachusetts were not struck down until 1972, and then by the nation's Supreme Court. Nothing to do with women's bodies as their own private property has ever been straightforward.

Why does the Pill, which has proved such a liberating milestone for Western women, still have to be viewed warily? First, because even apart from AIDS, there is an epidemic of other sexually transmitted diseases, some of which become life-threatening over time. Only the careful use of a condom prevents the communication of STDs and young women who are on the Pill and sexually active are often loathe to heed messages about 'safe sex'.

Once again, though, there is a rich/poor global divide: worldwide only 100 million women use the Pill in any form. Put this figure against the 128 million who use an intrauterine device because an IUD is cheap and once fitted can stay in place for up to 12 years. Where the pill is concerned, there are all the customary problems of prohibitive cost, difficulties of distribution and, often, religious opposition.

The Catholic Church is often cited as the enemy of effective contraception. It is not alone in this. Muslim clerics from the African countries that account for a third of all AIDS deaths met recently, with AIDS on the agenda. They could not agree on the use of condoms, let alone birth control for its own sake. Abstinence and/or fidelity may be fine ideals, but into the time capsule will surely go the Pill and a packet of condoms.

The Holy Books Go Global

Every year, over 100 million copies of the Bible are given away. Americans buy 20 million of them a year to add to the four the average American home has already. The Bible has been translated one way or another into nearly 2,500 languages and the international network of Bible societies has plans to put their 'good book' into the hands of every human being on earth.

While the American Bible Society has published 50 million bibles in China, Saudi Arabia has managed to give away 30 million copies of the Koran. At mosques and through Islamic societies and embassies, even through the internet (go to www. FreeKoran.com), the sacred and most widely read book in the Islamic world is made available to all. Reciting the Koran is the foundation of Muslim education; to be able to recite the entire sacred text by heart is to win the honoured title of 'hafiz'.

Christianity and Islam have gone global as never before. This might turn out to be a milestone of faith renewed and moral values regained – except for the fact that in the dark shadows of the battle of the books lurk 'the war on terror' and 'the holy jihad'.

Going to Market

McDonalds, Coca Cola, Google, Visa – what do these have in common? That they have been brought to global markets and either exist or can be recognized in almost every country on the globe. Welcome to the logo world – to the sign or symbol that speaks in place of words.

There are some not-for-profit emblems that most countries recognize – the Red Cross and the Red Crescent, for example. Mostly, though, the logo is about marketing and consumerism, often on a global scale: what more fitting milestone could we drop into our time capsule than a pair of $150 sneakers sold in New York, made in Chile or China, by a company in California, but recognized all over the world as a status symbol by the Nike Swoosh?

The greatest status symbol of all in the United States has doubled in value in the last decade, increasing to more than $260 billion: private charity and philanthropy. So perhaps, to right the balance, we could drop into the time capsule a cheque signed by any of the US billionaires who have given away their money…

Mobilizing the World

Less than 20 years ago, mobile phones were the expensive perk of business executives; now they are the landmark low-cost personal way for people to communicate all over the world. There are already countries that have more mobile phones than people. Half of all the children in the United States have one.

Thanks to pre-paid arrangements, the largest growth rates are in countries where communication has traditionally been difficult, if not impossible. Cell-phone use in developing countries has quadrupled in the last decade. When roads were non-existent, post offices unreliable or inaccessible and travel beyond the reach of families divided by exile or emigration virtually impossible, there could be silence for years. The cell phone breaks that silence across thousands of miles.

While the mobile phone has also facilitated organized crime, drug running or terrorism on the big city streets of the West, it has liberated millions just wanting a chance to participate. It makes small businesses possible. It is often the only way to have access to medical or legal services. No wonder that India has about six million new cell-phone users every month and expects to have 500 million subscribers by 2010. It may be merely another convenient gadget in some countries; in the developing world it is a milestone of its own.

The Personal Genome

At the time of writing, the era of personal genomics approaches. The first commercial service to provide people with an extensive look at their own DNA for under $1,000 has just been launched. All you have to do is send in a cheek swab and a company will test more than one million genetic variations to let you know whether you have specific variants associated with a whole raft of common diseases. It will then be up to you whether or not you want to know if you are genetically at risk of, say, Alzheimer's disease.

The human genome consists of the multi-billion-letter alphabet contained within the DNA helices (the DNA has a double-helix structure like two entwined spiral staircases as Crick and Watson discovered over 40 years ago), or, to put it more simply, 'the secret of life'. This is the new alchemy: the hope that by identifying faulty genes associated with disease, medicine will be able to correct them. There has been tremendous hype about the human genome project and all it promises.

One of the leaders in decoding that alphabet, Craig Venter, has analyzed and published the six billion chemical letters of his own personal genome. Probably more is known right now about his DNA than anyone else's in the world. But Venter himself has called the human genome project, 'only the race to the starting line'. At least he got that far. The next race will be to the development of gene therapy – replacing defective genes, matching treatments to genetic make-up, inserting new ones to help fight diseases such as cancer. Once again, the question remains to be answered: how will this miracle serve all humanity, rich and poor?

Further Reading

If you want to find out more about a topic, you may find these books a useful place to start:

PART 1: THE ELEMENTS OF CIVILIZATION

For general background and history
Cotterell, Arthur, (ed.), The Penguin Encyclopedia of Ancient Civilizations, new edition (Penguin, 1989)
Cotterell, Arthur, (ed.), The Penguin Encyclopaedia of Classical Civilizations (Viking, 1993)
Diamond, Jared, Guns, Germs and Steel: The Fates of Human Societies (Norton, 1999)

Chapter 1: The Footprint
Leakey, Richard and Lewin, Roger, Origins Reconsidered: In Search of What Makes Us Human (Doubleday, 1992)
Steele, James and Shennan, Stephen (eds), The Archaeology of Human Ancestry (Routledge, 1996)

Chapter 2: The Ritual
Corballis, Michael C., From Hand to Mouth: The Origins of Language (Princeton University Press, 2003)
Deacon, Terence W., The Symbolic Species: the Co-evolution of Language and the Brain (Norton, 1997)
Durkheim, Émile, The Elementary Forms of Religious Life, [1912], trans. Karen E. Fields (Free Press, 1995)
Hinde, R.A. (ed.), Nonverbal Communication (Cambridge University Press, 1972)
Rappaport, Roy A., Ritual and Religion in the Making of Humanity (Cambridge University Press, 1999)

Chapter 3: Better Tools
Christiansen, Morton H. and Kirby, Simon (eds), Language Evolution (Oxford University Press, 2003)
Knecht, Heidi (ed.), Projectile Technology (Springer, 1997)
Mithen, Stephen, The Singing Neanderthals: The Origins of Music, Language, Mind and Body (Weidenfeld and Nicolson, 2005)
Pinker, Stephen, The Language Instinct: How the Mind Creates Language (Penguin, 1994)
Sampson, Geoffrey, Educating Eve: The 'Language Instinct' Debate (Cassell, 1997)

Chapter 4: Art
Bahn, Paul G. and Vertut, Jean, Journey Through the Ice Age (University of California Press, 1997)
Guthrie, R. Dale, The Nature of Palaeolithic Art (University of Chicago Press, 2005)
Lewis-Williams, David, The Mind in the Cave: Consciousness and the Origins of Art (Thames & Hudson, 2002)
White, Randall, Prehistoric Art: The Symbolic Journey of Humankind (Abrams, 2003)

Chapter 5: The Boat
Cunliffe, Barry, Facing the Ocean: The Atlantic and Its Peoples 8000 BC – AD 1500 (Oxford University Press, 2001)
Casson, Lionel, Ships and Seamanship in the Ancient World, revised edition (Johns Hopkins University Press, 1995)
Hourani, George Fadlo, Arab Seafaring in the Indian Ocean in Ancient and Early Medieval Times (Princeton University Press, 1951)
Needham, Joseph, Science and Civilisation in China, Vol. IV, Part 3 (Cambridge University Press, 1971)

Chapter 6: The Dog and Other Animals
Anthony, David W., The Horse, the Wheel, and Language: How Bronze-Age Riders from the Eurasian Steppes Shaped the Modern World (Princeton University Press, 2007)
Clutton-Brock, Juliet, A Natural History of Domesticated Mammals, 2nd edition (Cambridge University Press, 1999)
Serpell, James, In the Company of Animals: A Study of Human-Animal Relationships (Cambridge University Press, 1996)

Chapter 7: The Grindstone
Brody, Hugh, The Other Side of Eden: Hunter-gatherers, Farmers and the Shaping of the World, new edition (Faber and Faber, 2002)
Harlan, Jack R., Crops and Man, 2nd edition (American Society of Agronomy, 1992)
Vavilov, N.I., Origin and Geography of Cultivated Plants, [1926], trans. D. Löve (Cambridge University Press, 1992)

Zohary, Daniel and Hopf, Maria, Domestication of Plants in the Old World : The Origin and Spread of Cultivated Plants in West Asia, Europe, and the Nile Valley, 3rd edition (Oxford University Press, 2000)
Kiple, Kenneth F. and Ornelas, Kriemhild Coneè (eds), The Cambridge World History of Food, Vol. 1 (Cambridge University Press, 2000)

Chapter 8: Pottery
Habu, Junko, Ancient Jomon of Japan (Cambridge University Press, 2004)
Hodder, Ian, The Leopard's Tale: Revealing the Mysteries of Çatalhöyük (Thames and Hudson, 2006)

Chapter 9: The Public Works Programme
Adams, Robert McC., The Evolution of Urban Society: Early Mesopotamia and Prehistoric Mexico (Aldine, 1966)
Childe, Gordon V., 'The Urban Revolution', in Town Planning Review (Vol. 21, No. 1, 1950)
Wilson, Peter J., The Domestication of the Human Species (Yale University Press, 1988)
Wittfogel, K.A., Oriental Despotism, a Study of Total Power (Oxford University Press, 1957)

Chapter 10: The King
Fried, Morton H., The Evolution of Political Society: An Essay in Political Anthropology (McGraw-Hill, 1967)
Gat, Azar, War in Human Civilization (Oxford University Press, 2006)
Jacobsen, Thorkild, 'Primitive Democracy in Ancient Mesopotamia', in Toward the Image of Tammuz – see below)
Olsen, Mancur, Power and Prosperity: Outgrowing Communist and Capitalist Dictatorships (Oxford University Press, 2000)

Chapter 11: Metal
Craddock, Paul T., Early Metal Mining and Production (Smithsonian Institution Press, 1995)
Finley, M.I., The World of Odysseus, revised edition (The Viking Press, 1965)
Mauss, Marcel, The Gift: Forms and Function of Exchange in Archaic Societies, [1925], trans. Ian Cunnison (Norton, 1990)
Pollock, Susan, Ancient Mesopotamia: The Eden That Never Was (Cambridge University Press, 1999)
Wagner, Donald B., Iron and Steel in Ancient China (Brill, 1993)

Williams, Jonathan (ed.), Money: A History (Macmillan, 1998)

Chapter 12: The Ideology of the State
Cohen, Andrew C., Death Rituals, Ideology, and the Development of Early Mesopotamian Kingship (Brill, Netherlands, 2005)
Frazer, James G., The Golden Bough: A Study in Magic and Religion, revised edition, [1922] (Wordsworth, 1993)
Jacobsen, Thorkild, Toward the Image of Tammuz and Other Essays on Mesopotamian History and Culture, ed. William L. Moran (Harvard University Press, 1970)
Kemp, Barry J., Ancient Egypt: Anatomy of a Civilization, new edition (Routledge, 1991)

Chapter 13: Writing
Goody, Jack, The Logic of Writing and the Organization of Society (Cambridge University Press, 1987)
Kramer, Samuel Noah, History Begins at Sumer: Thirty-Nine Firsts in Recorded History (London, 1958)
Lord, Alfred B., The Singer of Tales (Harvard University Press, 1960)
Martin, Henri-Jean, The History and Power of Writing, trans. Lydia G. Cochrane (University of Chicago Press, 1994)
Ong, Walter J., Orality and Literacy: The Technologizing of the Word (Routledge, 1982)
Schmandt-Besserat, Denise, How Writing Came About, abridged edition (University of Texas Press, 1997)

Chapter 14: The Universal Questions
Cornford, Francis M., Before and After Socrates (Cambridge University Press, 1932)
Dodds, E.R., The Greeks and the Irrational (University of California Press, London 1951)
Eisenstadt, S.N. (ed.), The Origins and Diversity of Axial Age Civilizations (State University of New York Press, Albany, 1986)
Jaspers, Karl, The Origin and Goal of History (Yale University Press, 1953)
Smart, Ninian, World Philosophies (Routledge, 1999)

Chapter 15: The Zero
Hogben, Lancelot, Mathematics for the Million (Allen and Unwin, 1936)
Ifrah, Georges, From One to Zero: A Universal History of Numbers, trans. Lowell Bair (Penguin, 1987)
Kaplan, Robert, The Nothing That Is: A Natural History of Zero (Oxford University Press, 1999)

PART 2: INTO THE MODERN WORLD

For general background and history
Fernandez-Armesto, F., Civilizations (Macmillan, 2000)
Porter, R., The Greatest Benefit to Mankind: A Medical History of Humanity from Antiquity to the Present (HarperCollins, 1997)
Roberts, J.M., The New Penguin History of the World (Penguin, 2002)

Chapter 16: The Great Pestilence
Cohen Jr, S.K., The Black Death Transformed: Disease and Culture in Early Renaissance Europe (Hodder Arnold, 2003)
Landy, D. (ed.), Culture, Disease, and Healing: Studies in Medical Anthropology (Macmillan, 1977)
Roberts, J.M., A History of Europe (Helicon, 1996)
Spruyt, H.,The Sovereign State and Its Competitors (Princeton University Press, 1994)

Chapter 17: The Military Revolution
Bobbitt, P., The Shield of Achilles: War, Peace and the Course of History (Penguin, 2003)
Ferguson, N., The Cash Nexus: Money and Power in the Modern World 1700–2000 (Penguin, 2001)
Howard, M., War in European History (Oxford University Press, 1976)
Tilly, C., Coercion, Capital, and European States AD 990–1992 (Blackwell, 1992)

Chapter 18: The Scientific Revolution
Hall, A.R., The Revolution in Science 1500–1750 (Longman, 1983)
Oster, M. (ed.), Science in Europe, 1500–1800: A Secondary Sources Reader (Palgrave, 2002)
Shapin, S., The Scientific Revolution (University of Chicago Press, 1996)

Chapter 19: The Revolutionary Ideal
Furet, F., Revolutionary France 1770–1880 (Blackwell, 1995)
Hobsbawm, E.J., The Age of Revolution 1789–1848 (Little, Brown, 1962)
Mansel, P., The Court of France 1789–1830 (Cambridge University Press, 1988)

Chapter 20: The Industrialization of War
Hirst, P., War and Power in the Twenty First Century: The State, Military Conflict and the International System 1500–2100 (unpublished, 2001)
Townshend, C., The Oxford History of Modern War (Oxford University Press, 2005)

Chapter 21: The Medical Revolution
Landy, D. (ed.), Culture, Disease, and Healing: Studies in Medical Anthropology (Macmillan, 1977)
Strathern, P., A Brief History of Medicine from Hippocrates to Gene Therapy (Constable and Robinson, 2005)

Chapter 22: The Origins of Man
Bunch, B. and Hellemans, A., The Timetables of Technology: A Chronology of the Most Important People and Events in the History of Technology (Touchstone, 1994)
Lloyd, G., The Man of Reason (Methuen, 1984)
Rowbotham, S., Women in Movement (Routledge, 1992)
Thomson, H., This Thing of Darkness (Hodder Headline, 2005)
Truth, Sojourner, The Narrative of Sojourner Truth: A Northern Slave (Dover, 1987)

Chapter 23: The Museum's Gaze
Bennett, T., The Birth of the Museum: History, Theory, Politics (Routledge, 1995)
Karp, I., Kratz, C.A., Szwaja L., Ybarra-Frausto (eds), Museum Frictions: Public Cultures/Global Transformations (Duke University Press, 2006)
Message, K., New Museums and the Making of Culture (Berg, 2006)

Chapter 24: Setting the Earth on Fire
Gore, A., An Inconvenient Truth (Bloomsbury, 2006)

Chapter 25: A Theory of Everything
Berners-Lee, T. with Fischetti, M., Weaving the Web (Harpers, San Francisco, 1997)
Lederman, L.M. and Teresi, D., The God Particle: If the Universe is the Answer, What is the Question? (Dell Publishing, 2006)

Index